HOMEGROWN

Celebrating the Canadian Foods We Grow, Raise and Produce

HOMEGROWN

Celebrating the Canadian Foods We Grow, Raise and Produce

by Mairlyn Smith, PHEc

With recipes from the Ontario Home Economics Association

whitecap | www.whitecap.ca

Whitecap Books is known for its expertise in the cookbook market, and has produced some of the most innovative and familiar titles found in kitchens across North America. Visit our website at www.whitecap.ca.

editor: Patrick Geraghty
design: Kerry Designs
food photography: Mike McColl
food styling: Joan Ttooulias, PHEc
proofreader: Penny Hozy
book concept: Mairlyn Smith, PHEc

Printed in Canada

The recipes listed on page 407 have been used in other publications and have been used with permission.

Library and Archives Canada Cataloguing in Publication
Homegrown : celebrating Canadian food / Ontario Home Economics Association ; edited by Mairlyn Smith.

Includes index. ISBN 978-1-77050-232-1 (pbk.)

1. Cooking, Canadian. 2. Local foods--Canada. 3. Cookbooks I. Smith, Mairlyn, editor II. Ontario Home Economics Association, author

TX715.6.H646 2015 641.5971 C2014-908055-7

We acknowledge the financial support of the Government of Canada, the Province of British Columbia through the Book Publishing Tax Credit.

We acknowledge the financial support of the Government of Canada.
Nous reconnaissons l'appui financier du gouvernement du Canada.

15 16 17 18 5 4 3 2 1

*To my parents, Jack and Roberta, who suggested that I
become a home economist after visiting my
Grade 8 Home Ec teacher. Who knew that meeting
would lead me on this amazing food journey.*

CONTENTS

Quickbreads and Not-So-Quick Breads

10 Canadian Grains Make Fabulous Flours

14 Pancake Primer

16 Five Canadian Whole Grain Pancakes

16 Whole Grain Whole Wheat Pancake Batter

17 Cornmeal Pancake Batter

18 Buckwheat Buttermilk Pancake Batter

19 Oatmeal Buttermilk Pancake Batter

20 Basic Barley Pancake Batter with Variations

22 Red Lentil Waffles

24 Our Liquid Gold

27 West Coast Blackberry Syrup

28 Pear Sauce

30 Pantry Makeover

32 Pumpkin Oatmeal Muffins

34 Zucchini & Carrot Breakfast Muffins

38 Double Bran Muffins

40 Gluten-Free Toasted Walnut Pear Muffins

42 Apple Sage Cheddar Bread

43 Caramelized Onion and Cheddar Scones

44 Whole Wheat Seed Bread

48 Autumn Pumpkin Seed Bread (for a Bread Machine)

Eggs: Mother Nature's Little Vitamin Pill

53 One Healthy Egg

56 Upgrade Your Eggs: Four Basic Ways

56 It's Called Hard-Cooked, Not Hard-Boiled

58 Scrambled Eggs—It's Back to the Basics

59 Poaching Made Easy

60 Omelettes are Quick and Easy Works of Edible Art

61 Make-Ahead Morning French Toast Casserole

62 Crustless Kohlrabi Quiche

64 Quiche with Potato Crust

65 Quick Eggs Florentine

Bring on the Cheese, Please

69 Entertaining with Cheese

72 Great Canadian Cheese Fondue (Microwave Method)

73 Apple Maple Cheddar Spread

76 Blue Cheese and Pear Phyllo Tarts

80 Savoury Cheddar Shortbread Diamonds

82 Salute to the Grilled Cheese Sandwich

86 Shaved Asparagus Pizza

90 Spinach and Goat Cheese Pizza

92 Mac and Cheese

94 Mushroom and Spinach Cannelloni with
Italian Cheese Blend Sauce

96 Baked Goat Cheese with Cranberry or Plum Compote

Grains, Make Them Whole

102 What is a Whole Grain?

104 Creamy Herbed Polenta

106 Barley 101

109 Easy Family-Friendly Barley Pilaf (Microwave Method)

110 Pearl Barley and Butternut Squash Risotto

112 Barley Stuffed Acorn Squash

115 Greek Barley Salad

116 Wild Rice and Vegetable Pilaf

118 Wheatberry and Lentil Salad

119 The World of Oats

121 Jambalaya

124 Overnight Blueberry Irish Oatmeal for Two

126 Toasted Oatmeal Cookies

127 Oat Barley Cookies

A Soup for Every Season

131 Soup for Your Good Health

132 Spiced Ambercup Squash Soup with Maple Syrup

135 Root Vegetable Potage

136 Canadian Aged Cheddar and Asparagus Soup

138 Curried Carrot Soup

139 Traditional French Onion Soup

140 Mushroom Soup

142 Corn Chowder

144 Silky Summer Corn Bisque

145 Maple Parsnip Soup

146 Quebec-Style Pea Soup

147 Red Lentil and Kale Soup

148 Spicy Red Lentil Soup

150 Roasted Red Pepper, Pear, Corn and Carrot Soup

152 Shamrock Soup

154 Borscht

Vegetables—Make Room on Your Plate

161 What Does a Serving Size Look Like?

162 Roasted Brussels Sprouts with Cranberries

165 Baked Tomato Spinach Spaghetti Squash

166 Stir Fried Baby Bok Choy

167 Ratatouille

168 Not Your Regular Mashed Potatoes

170 Roasted Sweet Potatoes and Cranberries

172 Easy Rutabaga (or Turnip) and Sweet Potato Casserole

175 Grilled Corn

178 Asian-Style Eggplant

180 Gourmet Poutine, Eh!?

183 New Potatoes with Shallots and Mint

Salads—Salute to the Leafy Green

188 Waste Less and Enjoy More Fresh Produce

190 Beet Apple Coleslaw

192 Festive Fruit and Nut Coleslaw

193 Winter Pea Salad

194 Maple Brussels Sprout Slaw

196 Bohemian-Style Cucumber Salad

198 Apple Hemp Heart Salad

200 Lentil and Roasted Sweet Potato Salad

201 Shaved Zucchini and Summer Squash Salad

202 Sweet and Red Potato Salad

204 Kale Tossed Salad with Roasted Garlic Dressing

207 Grilled Vegetable, Barley & Feta Salad

208 Four Fabulous Dressings

208 Birch Syrup Salad Dressing

210 Ice Syrup Salad Dressing

211 Honey Mustard Salad Dressing

211 Fresh Ginger Maple Syrup Dressing

212 Tips for Farmers' Marketing

Legumes—The Big Bang from the Prairies

218 Beans, Legumes, Pulses: Who's Who and What's What

221 Cooking from Scratch

224 Falafel Patties with Tahini Sauce and Pickled Onions

228 French-Inspired Vegetarian Shepherd's Pie

230 Slow Cooker Baked Beans

232 Chickpea Burgers

234 Chipotle Black Bean Chili

237 Chickpea and Cauliflower Curry

238 Hummus, Canadian Style

240 Asian-Style Edamame and Corn Salad

Pork and Lamb—The Other Guys

245 A Crash Course in Cooking Pork

248 Herb-Stuffed Pork Loin Roast

251 Maple Pulled Pork

252 Pork Tenderloin with Wild Rice Stuffing

254 Canadian Cassoulet

256 Lettuce Cups

258 Food Safety in the Home

261 Curried Lamb Stew with Fall Vegetables

263 Lamb Chops

Fish and Seafood from Coast to Coast to Coast

267 Crab Cakes with Garlic Aioli

268 Mussels in Spicy Tomato Sauce

271 Spring Trout Cakes

272 Hot Smoked Salmon and Seaweed Salad
on Asian-Style Spoons

274 Seafood Chowder

276 Bouillabaisse

278 Bruschetta Grilled Pickerel

280 Crispy Oven Baked Pickerel with Greek
Yogurt Tartar Sauce

282 Cod Cakes with Asian-Style Coleslaw

284 Canadian Canned Salmon Cakes with Tartar Sauce

286 Fish Tacos with Red Pepper and Corn Salsa

288 Fresh Shrimp Pasta Salad

341 Beef and Mushroom Stew

340 Shepherd's Pie with Beef and Mushrooms

338 Gluten-Free PEI Potato Lasagna

337 Slow Cooker Bistro Beef and Beer Simmering Steak

336 Slow Cooker Beef and Barley Stew

334 Grilled Flank Steak on Roasted Kale Salad

332 Steak Grilling Chart

331 Beef Steak and Lentil Salad

328 "Kick-Ass" Barbecued Burgers

325 Beef Nutrition 101

Ode to Canadian Beef

318 Braised Goose in Dark Beer

316 Duck Pilaf with Kamut and Wild Rice

314 Grilled Turkey Scallopini Sandwich with
Pickled Vegetable Mayo

312 Turkey Tourtière

310 Chicken Cacciatore with Hot House Peppers

309 Stuffed Chicken Burgers

306 West Indian-Style Curry Chicken

305 Poultry Cooking Chart

302 Harvest Apple and Thyme Roasted Chicken
(with Planned Leftovers)

301 Grilled Jerk Chicken Thighs

Canadian Poultry

297 Asian-Style Nova Scotia Scallops with Miso Glaze

295 Lobster with Pasta and Cherry Tomatoes

294 Tandoori Crusted Cod

293 Salmon Teriyaki

292 Aquaculture in Canada

290 Salmon with Peach Salsa

342 Cracked Pepper and Horseradish–Crusted Oven

Roast with Easy Pan Gravy

344 Roasting Guide

345 Yorkshire Pudding

346 Bison Meat Loaf

Fruity Treats and Fresh-Picked Indulgences

351 Treats—A Cautionary Tale

352 Four Classic Canadian Crisps

352 Ginger Rhubarb Crisp

353 Blueberry Pear and Hazelnut Crisp

354 Cranberry Apple Crisp

355 Saskatoon Berry Crisp

356 Apple and Dried Cherry Bread Pudding

357 Saskatoon Maple Bread Pudding

358 Cranberry Maple Butter Tarts

360 Garden Carrot Cake

362 Beautiful Beetday Cake

364 Apple Fruitcake with Whisky Glaze

366 Saskatoon Cheesecake Swirl

368 Apple Blackberry Crumble Pie

371 Sour Cherry Pie Filling (or Topping)

372 Pumpkin Pie

374 Grilled Peaches

376 Yogurt Berry Pops

378 Double Cranberry Blondies

379 Pumpkin Muffin-Top Cookies

My mom and dad had a huge vegetable garden in our backyard in Vancouver, BC. They grew tomatoes, lettuce, beets, green beans, carrots, raspberries, cucumbers and corn. One year my dad even dabbled in Brussels sprouts—we ate them that Thanksgiving and everyone got three teeny tiny sprouts the size of a small green pea. They may have been Lilliputian but they were home grown and they were delicious.

When your parents grow vegetables, you learn to appreciate where your food comes from and the hard work it takes to grow, nurture and harvest produce, even on a very small scale. So it was a natural progression for me, as a lover of all fresh backyard produce, to become a lover of all local foods from coast to coast to coast.

This book is a celebration of what our Canadian farmers grow, make and produce, from vegetables and fruits to livestock, pulses, seeds, grains, eggs, dairy and nuts. It's also a tribute to the people who turn those commodities into products and ingredients like cheese, yogurt, flour, cereals and oil. If you have a choice at your grocery store, choose a Canadian food over its foreign twin. You can visit farms to learn where your food comes from and, of course, frequent farmers' markets if you can.

I eat local foods all year long. I plan my menus around what's available in Canada, switching from fresh peas in the summer to frozen Canadian peas in the winter and fresh BC blueberries in August and September to the frozen ones in the dead of winter. I choose Winter squash, beets, parsnips in the winter and never in the summer months. You get the drill.

I buy Canadian cheeses and local artisan crackers; I drink VQA wines and Canadian beers both craft and commercial; I always pick domestic apples over imports; and I even prefer my Canadian alternative to rice—hulless oats! Don't get me wrong, I'm never giving up citrus, tropical fruit or (Heaven forbid) chocolate, even though it means stepping outside our home and native land, but I choose local ingredients whenever possible because I am proud of what we grow in Canada.

This is a cookbook that demonstrates how we really can create recipes for any occasion strictly using Canadian foods and products. I didn't say no to condiments and ingredients like soy sauce or capers, because without those little extras this cookbook would have ended up as a pioneer cookbook full of bannock and beef jerky. But this book is a testament to the fantastic meals that can be created when Canada is featured firmly on the plate, and a chance to support and celebrate the people who produce our foods.

One hundred years ago, over half of our population were farmers. Today that number has dwindled down to only 2 percent of the population. So here's to the dairy farmers, the beef producers, the chicken farmers, the egg producers, the pork, lamb, goat and bison meat producers, the yogurt and cheese makers, the goat farmers, the produce growers, the bee keepers, the maple and birch syrup tappers, the fisherman, and the pulse, grain and seed growers in Canada.

Food connects us to our roots. It helps define who we are and where we've come from. My background is English, Irish and Scottish. My cooking roots and experiences have influenced who I am and who I have become as a cookbook author and as a person: sitting around the dinner table and using the good china and crystal connects me to my dearly departed Gran and her Sunday night dinners; Saturday night was Hockey Night in Canada and my dad's World Famous Burgers; picnics remind me of my mom and eating salmon sandwiches on the sea wall in Stanley Park.

Each one of the contributors to this collaborative cookbook is a professional home economist (PHEc) or PHEc in training, and each and every one of them brings their own unique background and stories to this cookbook.

Here are our stories showcasing Canadian foods—now go out and hug a farmer.

Peace, love and fibre,

Mairlyn

P.S. For the real deal on farming, check out www.realdirtonfarming.ca.

With heartfelt thanks I would like to acknowledge Mairlyn for all her hard work with the recipe revisions and testings that took place over three weekends in January 2014, utilizing the assistance of volunteers, OHEA members and students, who were given a wonderful opportunity to see professional home economists at work. Mairlyn spent months working on the manuscript, knocking it into shape, using all the correct culinary terminology and imbuing the book with her expertise and characteristic charm. She teaches and reveals to us all these delicious, decidedly healthy and truly Canadian recipes.

A better mentor I could not wish to work with.

Joan Ttooulias, PHEc
President, Ontario Home Economics Association
September 2014

Quickbreads and Not-So-Quick Breads

10 Canadian Grains Make Fabulous Flours

14 Pancake Primer

16 Five Canadian Whole Grain Pancakes

16 Whole Grain Whole Wheat Pancake Batter

17 Cornmeal Pancake Batter

18 Buckwheat Buttermilk Pancake Batter

19 Oatmeal Buttermilk Pancake Batter

20 Basic Barley Pancake Batter with Variations

22 Red Lentil Waffles

24 Our Liquid Gold

27 West Coast Blackberry Syrup

28 Pear Sauce

30 Pantry Makeover

32 Pumpkin Oatmeal Muffins

34 Zucchini & Carrot Breakfast Muffins

38 Double Bran Muffins

40 Gluten-Free Toasted Walnut Pear Muffins

42 Apple Sage Cheddar Bread

43 Caramelized Onion and Cheddar Scones

44 Whole Wheat Seed Bread

48 Autumn Pumpkin Seed Bread (for a Bread Machine)

QUICKBREADS

The Canadian Prairies are a treasure trove of grains that we mill into flour, providing the primary ingredient to all of your baking needs.

Savoury or sweet, warm from the pan or the oven, quickbreads are the answer to the person who loves the smell of baking goodness without the time it takes to create a yeast bread. They are the closest thing to instant gratification in the bread baking world as you can get. Divided into pancakes and muffins and loaves, we have a quickbread for any occasion. Want to host a Waffle Party? We've got you covered. How about bake a decadent scone or a gluten-free muffin. We've got your back.

Turning to yeast breads, we have two recipes to tantalize your taste buds—a nutrient-dense seed bread and a classic bread recipe for your bread machine.

CANADIAN GRAINS MAKE FABULOUS FLOURS

Take a whole grain, any whole grain, mill it and you end up with flour. Whether it is or isn't a 100% whole grain flour is another matter.

WHOLE WHEAT FLOUR

Buyer beware—whole wheat flour isn't 100% whole-grain unless the package says "Stone Milled Whole Wheat Flour." Regular whole wheat flour in Canada is a combination of the endosperm and the bran without the germ, which has been removed to increase the shelf life of the flour. (For more info on whole grains see "What is a Whole Grain?" on page 102.) The problem when you remove the most nutrient dense part of the grain, the germ, is that you're losing most of a grain's health benefits. How to avert this? Either buy stone milled whole wheat or add 1 to 2 Tbsp (15 to 30 mL) natural wheat germ for every 1 cup (250 mL) of whole wheat flour.

RED FIFE FLOUR

Back in 1842 Dave Fife from Peterbough, Ontario, began growing red wheat. The *Wheat Name Game* back in the 1800's was a combination of the wheat's colour plus the name of the farmer who grew it—hence Red Fife. (I'm planning on calling the arugula I grow this year in my garden *Green Smith*.) Red Fife is renowned for its baking quality, not only because it is stone milled and therefore a whole grain, but it produces light and tender breads. Although none of the pancakes in this chapter use Red Fife, feel free to use it instead of whole wheat. Want to use a recipe that calls for Red Fife? Check out the Caramelized Onion and Cheddar Scones on page 43; you'll thank me.

BARLEY FLOUR

Barley is a Canadian super food and its flour is no exception. The flour is made from whole grains and contains both cholesterol-lowering soluble fibre and GI tract–moving insoluble fibre. The milling process doesn't change the quality of the soluble flour, which means it's still a great source of powerful beta-glucans, which aid in lowering cholesterol. In 2013 barley received a Health Claim from Health Canada that allows barley products to promote the following:

- "Barley fibre helps reduce/lower cholesterol"
- "High cholesterol is a risk factor for heart disease"
- "Barley fibre helps reduce/lower cholesterol, (which is) a risk factor for heart disease"

You can buy barley flour in Western Canada at most grocery stores, including Co-op, Safeway and Sobey's. In Eastern Canada your best bet is at a Bulk Barn, a farmers' market or a health food store.

OAT FLOUR

Oat flour contains soluble fibre, similar to barley, which helps reduce your "bad" cholesterol (also known as low-density lipoprotein or "LDL" cholesterol). You can substitute up to 30 percent oat flour for all-purpose flour without affecting the end result texture.

You can make your own whole grain oat flour by grinding large flake oats in a food processor or you can buy it in a bulk store. Oats are grown in Alberta, British Columbia, Manitoba and Saskatchewan.

BUCKWHEAT FLOUR

Buckwheat really needs a PR campaign plus a new *handle* because it isn't actually wheat; it's a fruit seed related to rhubarb. This is a blessing for people living a gluten-free lifestyle, since buckwheat is actually gluten free (Tip: check the label of your buckwheat flour to ensure that it was milled in a gluten-free facility). High in rutin, which is in the flavonoid family, this substance has potent anticlotting powers that could help reduce heart attack and stroke. Buckwheat flour has a fairly strong flavour note so use accordingly. Try Canadian-grown Nunweiler's. Their buckwheat flour is grown in Saskatchewan and milled in their own facility in Alsask, SK.

SPELT FLOUR

Spelt is an ancient grain similar to wheat but with a tougher outer hull. Spelt has a nutty flavour and is slightly higher in protein than wheat flour. It can easily be substituted for whole wheat flour in any of the pancake recipes.

CORNMEAL

Cornmeal isn't considered flour, but it can be used in baking. For nutrition's sake, make sure you are buying stone-ground medium-grind cornmeal, which contains both the bran and the germ, making it a whole grain. Oak Manor, out of Ontario, is one of the last remaining cornmeal manufacturers. Their brand is available in most health food stores or in the organic section in Loblaws in Ontario.

1. For the perfect pancake, choose one of our five pancake recipes (page 16-20), mix the batter together and follow these four easy steps. Voila— its pancake time.

2. Heat a large non-stick skillet or griddle over medium heat. Use a pastry brush to lightly coat with oil.

3. Pour 1/4 cup (60 mL) of the batter into the hot pan to form a 4-inch (10 cm) pancake. You will probably fit 3 pancakes per pan.

4. Pancakes will be ready to flip when the underside is golden brown and there are bubbles on the top side of the pancake. Pancakes should only be flipped once.

5. Flip and cook the pancakes for additional 2 to 3 minutes or until underside is golden and the center springs back when pressed. If desired, keep all of the pancakes in a warm oven 200°F (95°C) until all of the batter is cooked.

PANCAKE PRIMER

Here are some PHEc (professional home economist) tips to ensure that every pancake and waffle is picture perfect.

- Measure all of the dry ingredients using a dry measuring cup.
- Measure liquid ingredients using a glass or wet measuring cup.
- No buttermilk? Make your own—use the same amount of milk, make sure it is 1% MF and add 1 Tbsp (15 mL) apple cider vinegar.
- Don't overstir pancake batter, it should be slightly lumpy.
- Preheat oven—if you want everyone eating their pancakes at the same time, including you, place cooked pancakes on an oven-proof pan, keep them in the oven as you cook the entire recipe and serve all at once.
- We like to use nonstick pans, which are best heated over medium heat.
- If you are using an electric griddle, heat to 375°F (190°C).
- To avoid adding extra fat calories, use a pastry brush to lightly coat the pan with oil.
- Flip only once, after the top side has bubbles showing.
- Use maple syrup sparingly. Yes, it's Canadian, yes, it tastes delicious and yes, it contains sugar. A little goes a long way.
- For an extra special treat, warm the syrup before serving.
- Leftover pancakes can be wrapped and frozen for a quick weekday breakfast. Stack between sheets of waxed paper or parchment paper and freeze in either a resealable freezer bag or a container. Frozen pancakes can be quickly reheated in toaster oven, or in microwave.

INGREDIENTS

1 cup (250 mL) whole wheat flour
   or spelt flour

1/4 cup (60 mL) natural wheat
   germ

1/4 cup (60 mL) ground flaxseed

1 Tbsp (15 mL) baking
   powder

1 tsp (5 mL) cinnamon

1 omega-3 egg

1 1/2 cups (375 mL) skim or 1%
   milk

FIVE CANADIAN WHOLE GRAIN PANCAKES:

OHEA members have created five excellent pancake batters using a variety of Canadian grains and flours—just mix the batter and follow the Pancake Primer method on page 14 to make a perfect Canadian pancake. Once the pancakes are dished out, drizzle with 100% maple syrup, Pear Sauce (see p. 28) or West Coast Blackberry Syrup (see p. 27).

Whole Grain Whole Wheat Batter Mairlyn Smith, PHEc

*"These light and fluffy pancakes are totally kid approved and
my go-to. I've been making a variation of them since my son
was in primary school, and I would always get the kids to make them
with me on Shrove Tuesday. The added wheat germ and
flaxseed send regular whole wheat flour into the nutrient
superstar zone."* —Mairlyn

METHOD

In a large bowl, whisk together the flour, wheat germ, ground flaxseed, baking powder and cinnamon. In a separate bowl, beat together the egg and milk. Add to the dry ingredients and mix just until lumpy (it will make sense when you see it).

Makes 12 pancakes. One serving = 4 pancakes
Per serving: 313 calories, 8 g Fat, 1 g Sat. Fat, 0 g Trans Fat, 381 mg Sodium,
44 g Carbohydrates, 8 g Fibre, 7 g Sugars, 0 g Added Sugars, 17 g Protein
Carbohydrate Choices: 2 1/2

Cornmeal Pancake Batter Michele McAdoo, PHEc and Mairlyn Smith, PHEc

"Sometimes two heads really are better than one—Michele McAdoo and I are both pancake fans, and we came up with this recipe during one of the testing weekends. It's a one bowl recipe, which means less dishes, and yes ... you're welcome!"—Mairlyn

METHOD

In a large bowl, whisk together milk, sugar, eggs and oil. Stir in flour, cornmeal, wheat germ and baking powder, until well combined. Before adding to the pan, stir batter once more to ensure the cornmeal hasn't sunk to the bottom of the bowl. If desired, add blueberries (see picture avec blueberries and sans blueberries on page 15).

Makes 18 pancakes. One serving = 3 pancakes
Per serving: 363 calories, 11 g total fat, 1.4 g Sat. Fat, 0.2 g Trans Fat, 487 mg Sodium, 57 g Carbohydrates, 5 g Fibre, 10 g Sugars, 9.4 g Added Sugars, 10 g Protein
Carbohydrate Choices: 3 1/2

INGREDIENTS

2 cups (500 mL) skim milk
1/4 cup (60 mL) packed dark brown sugar
2 omega-3 eggs
3 Tbsp (45 mL) canola oil
1 1/2 cups (375 mL) whole wheat or spelt flour
1 1/2 cups (375 mL) whole grain medium grind cornmeal (see note)
1 Tbsp (15 mL) natural wheat germ
3 Tbsp (45 mL) baking powder
1 1/2 cups (375 mL) blueberries (optional)

INGREDIENTS

1/2 cup (125 mL) buckwheat flour
1/2 cup (125 mL) whole wheat
1 Tbsp (15 mL) natural wheat
   germ
1 Tbsp (15 mL) granulated sugar
1 Tbsp (15 mL) baking powder
1 1/2 cups (375 mL) buttermilk
1 omega-3 egg
3 Tbsp (45 mL) canola oil

Buckwheat Buttermilk Pancake Batter Michele McAdoo, PHEc

"My Great Uncle Archie raised guinea hens that would wander around his yard. Their loud call drove me crazy because it sounded like they were saying "Buckwheat." The memory is so ingrained in my mind that whenever I eat buckwheat pancakes I always think of my uncle and his crazy guinea hens." —Michele

METHOD

In a large bowl, whisk together the flours, wheat germ, sugar and baking powder. In a separate bowl, beat together egg, buttermilk and oil. Add to the dry ingredients and mix just until lumpy (it will make sense when you see it).

Makes 10 pancakes. One serving = 2 pancakes
Per serving: 226 calories, 11 g Fat, 1.5 g Sat. Fat, 0.2 g Trans Fat, 277 mg Sodium, 25 g Carbohydrates, 2 g Fibre, 7 g Sugars, 2.5 g Added Sugars, 8 g Protein
Carbohydrate Choices: 1 1/2

Oatmeal Buttermilk Pancake Batter Olga Kaminskyj, PHEc

*"I love oatmeal and enjoy exploring new ways of using oats.
Many years ago, while my daughter was attending University of Guelph, one
of her classes was involved in making a functional foods calendar.
As a volunteer, I assisted the students with recipe editing and food styling,
and one of the recipes was for oatmeal pancakes. I loved the recipe, and
over the years I have developed many new variations of it. Then recently, a
good friend/colleague shared another oatmeal pancake recipe she
picked up from one of her quilting guild members. This Oatmeal
Buttermilk recipe combines the best of both recipes."* —Olga

METHOD

Combine buttermilk and oats in large glass mixing bowl. Microwave on
high for 1 minute; stir, cover and let stand for 1 hour to soften oats. In a
separate bowl, whisk together eggs, oil and vanilla extract; stir into oat
mixture. In a small bowl, combine flour, sugar, flaxseed, baking powder
and baking soda. Gently stir into oat mixture until just combined. If the
batter is running or very wet looking add 2 Tbsp (30 mL) whole wheat
flour and stir well.

Makes 12 pancakes. One Serving = 3 pancakes
Per serving: 439 calories, 16 g total fat, 2.9 g Sat. Fat, 0.3 g Trans Fat, 566 mg Sodium,
54 g Carbohydrates, 6.4 g Fibre, 13 g Sugars, 6.3 g Added Sugars, 16 g Protein
Carbohydrate Choices: 3

INGREDIENTS

2 cups (500 mL) buttermilk or
    plain kefir
2 cups (500 mL) large flake oats
2 omega-3 eggs
2 Tbsp (30 mL) canola oil
1 tsp (5 mL) pure vanilla extract
1/2 cup (125 mL) whole wheat
    flour or spelt flour
2 Tbsp (30 mL) granulated sugar
1 Tbsp (15 mL) ground flaxseed
1 tsp (5 mL) baking powder
1 tsp (5 mL) baking soda

Tip: You need to start the
    pancakes an hour before
    breakfast time.

INGREDIENTS

1 1/2 cups (375 mL) barley flour
2 tsp (10 mL) baking powder
2 omega-3 eggs
2 Tbsp (30 mL) liquid honey
1 cup (250 mL) skim or 1% milk

PHEC TIPS:

• To make apple barley pancakes, add 1 tsp (5 mL) ground cinnamon to the flour mixture. Replace 1/2 cup (125 mL) milk with 1/2 cup (125 mL) unsweetened apple sauce. Stir 1 cup (250 mL) diced apple into dry ingredients before adding liquid ingredients.

• To make blueberry barley pancakes, replace 1/2 cup (125 mL) milk with 1/2 cup (125 mL) blueberry yogurt. Gently stir 1 cup (250 mL) fresh blueberries into dry ingredients before adding liquid ingredients. Frozen blueberries can be used, but to prevent batter from turning a grey colour, instead of combining berries with batter, spoon batter onto pan, then sprinkle uncooked top of each pancake with approx. 1 1/2 Tbsp (22 mL) blueberries.

Basic Barley Pancake Batter Wendi Hiebert, PHEc

"As a freelance Professional Home Economist, I create recipes for clients who wish to promote their products on their websites, or through recipe booklets and cookbooks. A recipe development assignment with Alberta Barley introduced me to the versatility of barley flour. Although I had used pot and pearl barley, I hadn't cooked or baked with nutritious Canadian barley flour. Now I'm hooked and use it often to make muffins, cookies, loaves and these pancakes."—Wendi

METHOD

In a large bowl, whisk together the flour and baking powder. In a separate bowl, beat eggs and beat in honey and mik. Add to the dry ingredients and mix just until lumpy (it will make sense when you see it).

Makes 10 Pancakes. One serving = 2 Pancakes
Per serving: 236 calories, 7 g total fat, 0.8 g Sat. Fat, 0 g Trans Fat, 170 mg Sodium, 45 g Carbohydrates, 5 g Fibre, 7.6 g Sugars, 7.1 g Added Sugars, 9 g Protein
Carbohydrate Choices: 3

INGREDIENTS

1/3 cup (75 mL) dried red lentils

1 cup (250 mL) water

1 cup (250 mL) all-purpose flour

1 cup (250 mL) whole wheat flour

2 Tbsp (30 mL) natural wheat germ

1 Tbsp (15 mL) baking powder

1/4 cup (60 mL) unsweetened applesauce

1 1/2 cups (375 mL) skim milk

2 omega-3 eggs

1 tsp (5 mL) pure vanilla extract

Makes 12 waffles
One serving = 2 waffles (without toppings)
Per serving: 256 calories, 3.5 g Fat, 0.8 g Sat. Fat, 0 g Trans Fat, 201 mg Sodium, 42 g Carbohydrates, 4 g Fibre, 5 g Sugars, 0 g Added Sugars, 13 g Protein

Carbohydrate Choices: 2 1/2

Red Lentil Waffles Multi-seasonal Trevor Arsenault PHEc

"As a child, waking up to the smell of waffles on Saturday mornings and seeing a kitchen counter spread with toppings was always a great way to start the weekend. Even though I've moved away from home, I still enjoy the opportunity to keep up this family tradition. My favourite part is finding new combinations of toppings to keep this meal interesting." —Trevor

Red lentils in waffles? Seriously? Seriously. These light and delicious waffles are fabulous as a brunch loaded with fresh seasonal fruits and berries, or use them as the base for a main-course plate of chicken, vegetables or baked beans.

METHOD

1. Add lentils and water to a to a small sauce pan; cover, bring to the boil and stir. Reduce to simmer and cook uncovered for about 15 to 20 minutes, until lentils are very soft. Use a wire sieve to drain any remaining liquid. Set aside and cool to room temperature.
2. In a large bowl, combine flours, wheat germ and baking powder.
3. When the lentils are cooled, take a separate, medium bowl and whisk together the applesauce, milk, eggs, vanilla and lentils.
4. Add liquid ingredients to the dry ingredients. Whisk together until combined. Batter should be thick with small lumps.
5. Preheat oven to 250°F (120°C). Place a cooling rack on top of a large rimmed baking sheet.
6. Let batter rest while waffle iron preheats.
7. Once waffle iron is hot, lightly brush both sides with canola oil.
8. Add 1/3 cup (75 mL) batter to each side of the waffle iron, close the lid and cook until waffles are golden brown, about 5 minutes.
9. Transfer waffles to wire cooling rack, cover with foil, place in the oven to keep warm and continue cooking remaining batter.

PHEC TIPS:

- To create a waffle bar, provide a selection of sliced fresh fruit, warmed maple syrup, nut butters, applesauce and low-fat yogurt so everyone can personalize their plate.

- Cook more lentils than you will need for this recipe and either store the leftovers in the fridge or freeze in 1-cup (250 mL) portions. Cooked red lentils can easily be added to foods such as tomato sauce, soups, cooked rice, cooked ground beef, muffins and biscuits to increase fibre, protein and mineral content.

OUR LIQUID GOLD

Pancakes are really just an edible platform to showcase one of our greatest exports: 100% pure maple syrup. La Belle Province, Quebec is the world's biggest producer of Mother Nature's Elixir, with Ontario coming in third right behind the state of Vermont.

Every year, the temperature has to be just right for the sap to start running and maple syrup season to begin. Temperatures need to fluctuate below zero overnight and above zero during the day before the maple trees can be tapped for their sap. This miracle of nature usually occurs somewhere in March or April, and it is typically a very small window of opportunity that lasts for only 12 to 20 days.

HOW DO YOU MAKE MAPLE SYRUP?

First of all you need lots of maple trees—what we like to call a "sugar bush." The trees that can be sapped have to be at least 8 inches (20 cm) in diameter.

Sap is collected using either buckets or a line, then the liquid gold is transported to a sugar shack and boiled down until the sugar content reaches about 66 to 67.5 percent. The sap coming directly from the tree contains about two percent sugar content, so there is a fair amount of boiling down that takes place, so much boiling down that it takes approx. 10 1/2 gallons (40 L) of maple sap to make 4 cups (1 L) of maple syrup.

Each province that produces maple syrup has their own maple syrup regulations ensuring quality and cleanliness of all maple syrup production.

GRADES OF MAPLE SYRUP

Maple syrup is categorized and graded according to colour, clarity, density and strength of maple flavour. In Canada we have three grades and five colour classifications of maple syrup:

- Canada #1, which is divided into three colours: Extra Light, Light and Amber.
- Canada #2 has one colour: Amber
- Canada #3 has a variety of different colours ranging from Dark to Light, but mostly Dark

STORING MAPLE SYRUP

Maple syrup is perishable unless you store it correctly. Store any unopened containers in a cool, dry place. The Ontario Maple Syrup Producers Association suggests you store syrup in the fridge or freezer. Once you open that bottle of maple gold, close tightly and store in the refrigerator or in the freezer. Discard if it becomes mouldy.

MAPLE SYRUP FESTIVALS

You know you've made if someone throws a festival to honour you, and maple syrup is *king of the hill* in March and April when Quebec, Ontario, New Brunswick and Nova Scotia each celebrate the new maple syrup runs. For a festival near you, google search "maple syrup festivals."

West Coast Blackberry Syrup Summer/Early Fall

Susanne Stark, PHEc

"This syrup keeps in the fridge for two weeks, or you can process it in a hot water bath and give as a gift. It can be kept in the pantry for one year once processed." —Susanne

METHOD

1. In a medium-sized pot, place juice, sugar and syrup. Stir to combine. Bring to a boil and boil for 2 minutes

2. Serve warm or chill in the fridge, covered, for up to 2 weeks.

Makes 2 cups (500 mL) One serving = 2 Tbsp (30 mL)
Per serving: 60 Calories, 0 g Total Fat, 0 g Saturated Fat, 0 g Trans Fat, 8 mg Sodium, 15 g Carbohydrate, 0 g Fibre, 10 g Sugars, 8.8 g Added Sugars, 0 g Protein
Carbohydrate Choices: 1

INGREDIENTS

1 cup (250 mL) pure blackberry juice (see note)
1/2 cup (125 mL) granulated sugar
1/2 cup (125 mL) white corn syrup

INGREDIENT NOTES:
Blackberry Juice—To make berry juice, place fresh picked blackberries in a food processor or blender. Blend well and strain through a sieve to remove seeds and make juice. It takes approx. 4 cups (1 L) of berries to make 1 cup (250 mL) of juice.

INGREDIENTS

6 cups (1.5 L) unpeeled pears,
   washed and roughly diced
   (approx. 7 medium-sized
   pears)
1 cup (250 mL) water
1 Tbsp (15 mL) apple cider
   vinegar
1 tsp (5 mL) cinnamon
1/2 tsp (2 mL) ground ginger

Pear Sauce Summer/Fall

Joyce Ho, PHEc

This pear sauce makes a great change-up to maple syrup in the fall and
winter months, plus it's a great way to use up any overripe pears. Serve
as a dessert or sauce over yogurt or pancakes.

METHOD

1. In a medium saucepan over medium-high heat, place pears, water,
    vinegar, cinnamon and ginger.
2. Bring to the boil, stirring occasionally. Reduce heat to low, cover
    and simmer for 15 to 20 minutes.
3. Remove the lid, stir well and continue simmering for 15 to 20
    minutes or until the sauce begins to thicken. Depending on how
    ripe the pears are this may take longer. Rule of thumb: the riper the
    pear the longer the simmer.
4. Use an immersion blender to slowly break down the pears until you
    reach your preferred pear sauce consistency. Want it chunkier? Skip
    the immersion blender and use a potato masher instead.
5. Cool before serving or refrigerate for up to 1 week.

Makes 3 cups (750 mL) One serving = 1/2 cup (125 mL)
Per serving: 103 calories, 0.2 g Fat, 0 g Sat. Fat, 0 g Trans Fat, 0 mg Sodium,
27 g Carbohydrates, 5.4 g Fibre, 17 g Sugars, 0 g Added Sugars, 0.7 g Protein
Carbohydrate Choices: 1 1/2

PEARS

Unlike other fruits, pears don't ripen well on the tree; commercial pears are picked when they are mature and then allowed to ripen in a controlled environment. Buy unripe pears and store half in the fridge to slowly ripen while allowing the other half to ripen at room temperature. Ripening at room temperature takes between 2 to 4 days. Store ripened pears for up to 1 to 2 days in the fridge.

Pears contain soluble fibre which can help lower your chances of developing heart disease. One medium pear contains 100 calories, and is a source of potassium and Vitamin C.

The most commonly grown pear varieties in BC are Anjou, Bartlett and Bosc. In Ontario they are Bartlett, Clapp's Favourite, Bosc and Flemish Beauty. Bartlett pears are the most popular pear in Canada with its mild sweet flavour.

SHELF LIFE OF BASIC DRIED GOODS

SPICES:

Ground spices: 4–6 months

Whole spices (allspice, cinnamon sticks, nutmeg): 1–2 years

General note: If you bought your spices 3 years ago they must go! Their flavour has diminished.

PANTRY MAKEOVER

Those brave pioneers who helped build this country knew that if there was nothing in their larder, there was nothing on the table come the cold winter months.

Although we don't have to stock up in order to make it through the winter, a well-stocked pantry helps for those *flying by the seat of your pants* kind of dinner nights.

You should be able to open your pantry and make something for dinner. Think of it as the Magic Cupboard where ingredients live to make your life easier. If your pantry is just full of flour, cereal and canned soup, dinner could be a sad state of affairs (unless you have a Food Network star in your household).

Your pantry needs to be well thought out and accessible, and well stocked with foods that can be turned into a dinner. If it's cluttered with cans you can't even get to, that's not helpful. Make your pantry work for you.

- Location, location, location! For optimal shelf life, staples need to be stored in a cool dark place. That means far away from your stove, dishwasher or fridge, which all give off heat when in use. When in doubt, place your hand on the wall of the pantry to feel for warm spots. Feels warm? Relocate your pantry for maximum shelf life of your pantry items.
- Organize: keep all of the canned goods in a line with the new canned goods moving to the back of each row.

- For the *best quality* in canned goods, manufacturers recommend that you store most products no longer than one year and should be used before 2 years or before the expiration code date on the can.
- Canned fish can be stored for up to 5 years.
- Label canned goods with the month and year before storing.
- Never use a canned good that is: bulging, leaking or badly dented. This applies to glass jars that are cracked or have loose or bulging lids. Or a canned good that spurts liquid when you open it. These are all signs of botulism. No taste testing—botulism is deadly. Discard the entire can or jar and wash hands thoroughly. Lightly bleach surrounding area in pantry and allow to air dry.
- Know the shelf life of what you buy. Don't buy a huge bag of flour if you won't use up the entire bag within 6 to 8 months. For a more complete list see below.
- Store dry goods in see-through plastic containers to deter bugs and allow you to see what you have.
- If you are buying in bulk and have a large pantry, a great idea is to mark the date of purchase on the package, saving you from guessing how long it's been sitting on your shelf later.

SHELF LIFE OF BASIC DRIED GOODS

BAKING SUPPLIES:

Opened extracts used in baking: 1 year

Baking powder: 18 months

Baking soda: 2 years

Corn starch: 18 months

Brown sugar (in an airtight container): 4 months

White sugar (covered tightly): 2 years

White flour (air tight container): 6–8 months

Whole wheat flour (air tight container in the fridge or freezer): 6–8 months

Unsweetened cocoa powder: indefinitely

Chocolate: 18 months

Honey: 1 year

Dry cereal (unopened): 6–12 months

INGREDIENTS

TOPPING

1/4 cup (60 mL) large flake rolled oats

1/4 cup (60 mL) packed dark brown sugar

DRY INGREDIENTS

2 cups (500 mL) whole wheat flour

1 cup (250 mL) large rolled oat flakes

1/3 cup (75 mL) granulated sugar

2 Tbsp (30 mL) natural wheat germ

2 tsp (10 mL) baking powder

1/2 tsp (2 mL) baking soda

1 tsp (5 mL) cinnamon

1/2 tsp (2 mL) dried ginger

1/4 tsp (1 mL) ground cloves

1/4 tsp (1 mL) freshly ground nutmeg

WET INGREDIENTS

1 cup (250 mL) buttermilk

3/4 cup (180 mL) 100% pure pumpkin puree (see note)

1/4 cup (60 mL) pure maple syrup

1/3 cup (75 mL) canola oil

1 omega-3 egg

2 tsp (10 mL) pure vanilla extract

Pumpkin Oatmeal Muffins Multi-Seasonal

Amy Oliver, OHEA student member

"When the OHEA came up with a Canadian ingredients cookbook, I was thrilled. I love to see recipes using locally grown Canadian foods, so I started thinking about recipes that would include some of my favourite Canadian foods and was inspired to create this recipe because I love maple syrup and I seeing the pumpkin fields in the fall."—Amy

METHOD

1. Preheat oven 400°F (200°C). Line a muffin tin with 12 large paper muffin liners.
2. In a small bowl, mix together the topping ingredients and set aside.
3. In a large bowl, whisk together all of the dry ingredients. In a medium bowl, whisk together all of the wet ingredients. Add wet ingredients to dry ingredients and stir just until combined. Do not over mix.
4. Using a large ice cream scoop, scoop the mixture equally into the 12 muffin liners.
5. Sprinkle 2 tsp (10 mL) of topping mixture over each muffin.
6. Bake for 15 to 22 minutes or until a cake tester inserted into the centre of a muffin comes out clean.
7. Allow pan to cool slightly on a cooling rack for 5 minutes. Remove muffins from the pan and continue cooling before storing.
8. Muffins can be stored in a covered container for 2 to 3 days or frozen for up to 3 months.

Makes 12 muffins One serving = 1 muffin

Per serving: 258 Calories, 8 g Total Fat, 1 g Saturated Fat, 0.2 g Trans Fat, 135 mg Sodium, 40.2 g Carbohydrate, 3.8 g Fibre, 16 g Sugars, 13.9 g Added Sugars, 6.4 g Protein

Carbohydrate Choices: 2 1/2

PUMPKINS

Come October pumpkin patches, roadside stands, farmers markets and grocery stores are a sea of orange thanks to the growing popularity of this member of the squash family. Due to the growing popularity during Thanksgiving and Halloween, pumpkin sales have grown over the past twenty years right across Canada. Pumpkin festivals, haunted pumpkin patches, corn mazes, hayrides and pick-your-own have all contributed to the evergrowing popularity of this orange gourd.

Ontario grows more than half of all the pumpkins in Canada, with two-thirds of pumpkins used for fresh pumpkin products and the other third for processing into cans. New Brunswick and Quebec are the only other provinces that grow pumpkins for processing. Because of the longer growing seasons, very few pumpkins are grown in the prairies. (source: Stats Canada)

INGREDIENT NOTE:

Pumpkin Puree—Freeze leftover pumpkin puree in 3/4 cup (180 mL) portions for the next time you want to make these muffins.

PHEC TIPS:

• For photo-perfect muffins use a large ice cream scoop with a release handle.

• For an easier cleanup, line the muffin tin with paper muffin liners.

• Freeze muffins individually on a cookie sheet. Once frozen, put the entire batch into freezer bags or a container and store in the freezer for up to three months.

• Want to encourage culinary skills at home? Invite your kids into the kitchen and teach them how to cook. Start with a batch of muffins. Bonus if you have boys—they'll tell you *stuff* while they're cooking you wouldn't be able to drag out of them any other time.

DRY INGREDIENTS

2 cups (500 mL) whole wheat
    flour
3/4 cup (175 mL) packed dark
    brown sugar
1/2 cup (125 mL) large flake oats
1/4 cup (60 mL) ground flaxseed
    or ground flaxseed meal (see
    page 37)
1/4 cup (60 mL) unsalted raw
    pumpkin seeds
1/4 cup (60 mL) currents
    (optional)
2 Tbsp (30 mL) natural wheat
    germ
2 tsp (10 mL) baking powder
2 tsp (10 mL) cinnamon

WET INGREDIENTS

1 cup (250 mL) skim milk
1/2 cup (125 mL) canola oil
2 omega-3 eggs
1 cup (250 mL) finely grated
    zucchini (see note)
1 cup (250 mL) finely grated
    carrot (see note)
1/2 cup (125 mL) finely chopped
    apple, peel on

Zucchini & Carrot Breakfast Muffins Multi-seasonal

Joan Ttooulias, PHEc

"I know what you're going to say '14 ingredients for a muffin! That's way too many ingredients and too much effort.' Please try this recipe once and I know you'll be delighted with the results. You can always double up the recipe and freeze half the batch, or just measure and mix the dry ingredients and keep in a resealable bag or container in the fridge (labelled of course) to mix with the wet ingredients when the inclination strikes." —Joan

METHOD

1. Preheat oven to 375°F (180°C). Line a muffin tin with 12 large paper muffin liners.
2. In a large bowl, whisk together all of the dry ingredients.
3. In a medium bowl, whisk together all of the wet ingredients.
4. Pour wet ingredients into the dry ingredients and stir just to combine.
5. Using a large ice cream scoop, scoop the mixture equally into the muffin liners.
6. Bake for 25 to 30 minutes or until a cake tester inserted into centre of a muffin comes out clean.
7. Allow pan to cool slightly on a cooling rack for 5 minutes. Remove muffins from the pan and continue cooling before storing.
8. Can be stored in a covered container for 2 to 3 days or frozen for up to 3 months.

Makes 12 muffins One serving = 1 muffin
Per serving: 297 Calories, 14 g Total Fat, 1.5 g Saturated Fat, 0.2 g Trans Fat, 83 mg Sodium, 36.4 g Carbohydrate, 4 g Fibre, 16.3 g Sugars, 13.5 g Added Sugars, 7.4 g Protein
Carbohydrate Choices: 2

INGREDIENT NOTE:

Grated Vegetables—When grating the zucchini and carrot, you need to choose the finest grate on your hand-held grater or food processor.

FLAXSEED 101

- Flaxseed comes whole, ground or as a meal.
- For economy, buy flaxseeds whole and then grind them up in a coffee bean mill.
- Don't become overzealous and grind them into flour. Just keep pulsing until it looks like coarse sand.
- Once flaxseed has been ground, store in a covered container in the fridge. It will stay fresh for up to three months.
- You can buy flaxseed already ground, located in the refrigerated section of your grocery store. That's the big tip-off—you need to store it your fridge as well.
- Flaxseed meal and ground flaxseed are not standardized. Depending on the company you purchase your ground flaxseed from there can be varying amounts of fat in their ground flaxseed. The fat is a heart healthy fat and you don't want too little, so for heart health choose ground flaxseed or, better yet, grind your own.
- Whole flaxseeds are difficult to digest and act as a laxative. Grind them up and your body will absorb the omega-3 fatty acids and the plant lignins.

HEALTH BITE

Ground flaxseed can help lower your cholesterol, which can help reduce your chances of developing heart disease. We recommend 1 to 2 Tbsp (15 to 30 mL) ground flaxseed per day.

Sound the celebratory bells: flaxseed received a Health Claim from Health Canada in 2014 because of its ability to lower cholesterol.

FLAXSEED

Flaxseed is grown in Alberta, Manitoba, New Brunswick, Nova Scotia, Prince Edward Island and Saskatchewan which is the leader, producing 82% of all flaxseed grown in Canada.

DRY INGREDIENTS

1 cup (250 mL) whole wheat flour

1/2 cup (125 mL) wheat bran

3/4 cup (175 mL) ground flaxseed

2 Tbsp (30 mL) natural wheat germ

1/2 cup (125 mL) chopped dried apple (see note)

1 Tbsp (15 mL) cinnamon

1 1/2 tsp (7 mL) baking powder

1 tsp (5 mL) baking soda

WET INGREDIENTS

1/2 cup (125 mL) oat bran (see note)

1 1/4 cups (300 mL) 1% milk

1 Tbsp (15 mL) apple cider vinegar

1 omega-3 egg

One 4.5 oz (128 mL) jar strained prunes baby food (see note)

1/2 cup (125 mL) packed dark brown sugar

1/4 cup (60 mL) pure maple syrup

Double Bran Muffins Multi-seasonal

Mairlyn Smith, PHEc

"A coffee bean mill is the only kitchen tool that grinds up flaxseeds enough. Trust me, I have tried blenders, food processors, an old-fashioned coffee bean grinder and a hammer. The coffee bean mill works the best." —Mairlyn

METHOD

1. Preheat oven to 400°F (200°C). Line a muffin tin with 12 large paper muffin liners.
2. In a large bowl, whisk together all of the dry ingredients.
3. In a medium bowl, whisk together all of the wet ingredients.
4. Pour the wet ingredients into the dry ingredients and mix till just combined.
5. Using a large ice cream scoop, scoop the mixture equally into the prepared pan.
6. Bake for 20 to 25 minutes or until cake tester inserted into centre of a muffin comes out clean.
7. Allow to cool on a wire rack for 5 minutes, remove from the pan and continue cooling before storing. Can be stored in a covered container for 2 to 3 days or freeze for up to 3 months.

Makes 12 muffins One serving = 1 muffin
Per serving: 188 Calories, 4.5 g Total Fat, 0.6 g Saturated Fat, 0 g Trans Fat, 171 mg Sodium, 35 g Carbohydrate, 5.6 g Fibre, 18.5 g Sugars, 13.5 g Added Sugars, 6 g Protein
Carbohydrate Choices: 2

HEALTH BITE

- Who needs more fibre? Almost everyone, says the Canadian Foundation for Digestive Health (and they know a thing or two about your GI tract). With fibre coming from the whole wheat flour, wheat and oat brans, flaxseed, wheat germ, apple and prunes, one of these muffin babies will add 5.6 g of fibre to your daily quotient.
- When you increase your fibre you need to increase the amount of liquids you are drinking or you will become constipated; sort of a weird reverse double whammy.

INGREDIENT NOTES:

Apple—Chopped dried apples are available in packages or at a bulk store.

Oat Bran—Yes, oat bran is "technically a dry ingredient," but it is listed with the wet ingredients because it needs time to absorb the liquid.

Baby Food Prunes—You can find baby food prunes in the baby food section. Pick a brand with no added sugars or starches.

INGREDIENTS

1 1/4 cups (300 mL) sorghum
  flour
2/3 cup (150 mL) amaranth flour
1/4 cup (50 mL) tapioca starch
1 1/2 tsp (7 mL) xanthan gum
1 Tbsp (15 mL) gluten-free baking
  powder
1/2 tsp (2 mL) iodized salt
2 omega-3 eggs
2 Tbsp (25 mL) walnut oil
3/4 cup (175 mL) water
1/4 cup (50 mL) pure maple syrup
1 cup (250 mL) toasted chopped
  walnuts
1/3 cup (75 mL) diced ripe fresh
  pears (see note)

Gluten-Free Toasted Walnut Pear Muffins Summer/Fall

Donna Washburn, PHEc and Heather Butt, PHEc (with permission from *Complete Gluten-Free Cookbook* [Robert Rose 2007])

"We both love pears and often purchase baskets of them. We then wait patiently, checking daily for ripeness. When they're ready we immediately pull out the muffin tins, roast the walnuts and whip up these delights. We've worked hard to showcase the delicate pear flavour, accomplished by sweetening the muffins with pure Canadian maple syrup we purchase from a local farmer."—Donna and Heather

METHOD

1. In a large bowl or plastic bag, combine the sorghum flour, amaranth flour, tapioca starch, xanthan gum, baking powder and salt. Mix well and set aside.
2. In a separate bowl, use an electric mixer to beat eggs, walnut oil, water and syrup until combined. Add dry ingredients and mix just until combined. Stir in walnuts and pears. Spoon batter evenly into each cup of the prepared muffin tin. Let stand for 30 minutes.
3. Preheat oven to 350°F (180°C) and bake muffins for 20 to 23 minutes or until firm to the touch. Remove from pan immediately and let cool completely on a rack.

Makes 12 muffins One serving = 1 muffin
Per serving: 203 Calories, 10.8 g Total Fat, 1.2 g Saturated Fat, 0 g Trans Fat, 393 mg Sodium, 23.8 g Carbohydrate, 3 g Fibre, 4.8 g Sugars, 4.1 g Added Sugars, 5 g Protein
Carbohydrate Choices: 1 1/2

WALNUTS

We grow walnuts mostly in Ontario and hazelnuts mostly in BC. The black walnut is the most successfully grown nut tree in Ontario. The Eastern Chapter of the Society of Ontario Nut Growers (ECSONG) encourages people to plant walnut trees on unused properties.

INGREDIENT NOTE:

Pears—No ripe pears? You can use a 5 oz (142 mL) can of diced pears, drained.

PHEC TIP:

To make this recipe egg-free, omit eggs from recipe and combine 1/4 cup (60 mL) flax flour or ground flaxseed with 1/2 cup (125 mL) warm water. Let the mixture stand for 5 minutes, then add to the liquid ingredients. Increase baking time by 2 to 3 minutes.

1 cup (250 mL) whole wheat flour

1 cup (250 mL) sifted all-purpose flour

1 Tbsp (15 mL) natural wheat germ

2 tsp (10 mL) baking powder

1/2 tsp (2 mL) ground sage

1/2 cup (125 mL) shredded old white cheddar cheese

2 large apples, scrubbed, peel left on, coarsely grated using the large holes on a box grater

3 Tbsp (45 mL) fresh chopped sage

1/4 cup (60 mL) unsalted butter

2 Tbsp (30 mL) canola oil

1/4 cup (60 mL) packed dark brown sugar

2 omega-3 eggs

Apple Sage Cheddar Bread Multi-seasonal

Amy Oliver, OHEA Student Member

"My Grandma always said,"You can never have a slice of apple pie unless you have a piece of sharp cheddar cheese." Inspired by my Grandma's saying I decided to combine the flavours of apple, cheddar cheese and sage." —Amy

METHOD

1. Preheat oven to 350°F (180°C). Lightly oil a 9- × 5-inch (2 L) loaf pan.
2. In a large bowl, whisk together both flours, wheat germ, baking powder and ground sage. Toss in cheddar cheese, chopped apples and fresh sage.
3. In a medium bowl, beat the butter, oil and sugar together until fluffy. Slowly add eggs until combined. Adding the eggs slowly will prevent the butter, sugar and eggs from splitting.
4. Fold egg mixture into the flour mixture until well blended.
5. Spoon into the prepared pan, smooth top and bake for 45 to 50 minutes or until a cake tester inserted into centre of the bread comes out clean.
6. Cool pan on a wire cooling rack for 10 minutes, remove bread and cool completely. Store bread, covered or wrapped, for 2 days at room temperature or frozen for up to 3 months.

Makes 12 slices One serving = 1 slice
Per serving: 206 Calories, 10 g Total Fat, 4.4 g Saturated Fat, 0.3 g Trans Fat, 266 mg Sodium, 23.8 g Carbohydrate, 2 g Fibre, 7.3 g Sugars, 4.7 g Added Sugars, 5.7 g Protein
Carbohydrate Choices: 1 1/2

Caramelized Onion and Cheddar Scones Multi-seasonal
Joan Ttooulias, PHEc

These deliciously decadent savoury scones are perfection all on their own—trust me, they were gone in a flash during recipe tasting—however, Joan assures us that they are equally fabulous with soup or stew. Before you scarf down more than one of these, check out the grams of fat … just warning you.

METHOD

1. In a large skillet over medium-low heat, add oil and onions and sauté for 20 to 25 minutes or until onions are lightly browned. Remove from heat and cool. Reserve for Step 3.
2. Preheat oven to 425°F (220°C). Line a 10- × 15-inch (25 × 38 cm) rimmed baking sheet with parchment paper.
3. In a large bowl, mix together the flours, cheese, butter, baking powder and salt. Add onions and combine.
4. In a glass measuring cup, whisk together the buttermilk, mustard and egg. Make a well in the flour mixture, pour buttermilk mixture in and stir gently to form a soft dough.
5. Using *damp hands* pat dough into a 9-inch (23 cm) square on a lightly floured surface. Cut into 16 equal squares and place on prepared pan.
6. Bake for 25 to 30 minutes until risen and lightly browned. Serve warm. Leftover scones can be frozen.

Makes 24 scones One serving = 1 scone
Per serving: 207 Calories, 12.8 g Total Fat, 7.4 g Saturated Fat, 0.6 g Trans Fat, 212 mg Sodium, 17.4 g Carbohydrate, 2.6 g Fibre, 1.6 g Sugars, 0 g Added Sugars, 6.2 g Protein
Carbohydrate Choices: 1

INGREDIENTS

1 Tbsp (15 mL) canola oil
3 onions, finely chopped
2 cups (500 mL) red fife flour
2 cups (500 mL) whole wheat flour
1 1/2 cups (375 mL) shredded extra-strong Canadian Cheddar cheese
1 cup (250 mL) frozen unsalted butter, grated (see note)
1 Tbsp (15 mL) baking powder
1 tsp (5 mL) iodized salt
1 1/4 cups (310 mL) buttermilk
3 Tbsp (45 mL) honey mustard
1 omega-3 egg

INGREDIENT NOTE:
Butter—Freeze butter for 15 minutes, then grate using the coarse side of a grater; grated butter incorporates easily with flour mixture.

PHEC TIP:
Place a frozen scone in a lunch bag; it'll thaw just before lunch time for you to enjoy with a bowl of soup.

INGREDIENTS

3 cups (750 L) lukewarm water
(approx. 100°F/38°C)
2 Tbsp (30 mL) traditional active
yeast
2 tsp (10 mL) granulated sugar
1/3 cup (75 mL) liquid honey
1/4 cup (60 mL) canola oil
1 cup (250 mL) natural bran or
wheat germ (see note)
1 cup (250 mL) quick oats
3/4 cup (175 mL) sunflower seeds
1 Tbsp (15 mL) iodized salt (see
note)
6 cups (1.5 L) whole wheat flour
(approx.)
Additional oats or seeds to pat
onto surface

Whole Wheat Seed Bread Multi-seasonal
Jan Main, PHEc

Want to make yeast breads but feel slightly intimidated by the cycle of kneading, waiting for the yeast to rise, and then kneading again? Batter breads to the rescue! Batter breads only rise once and don't require a lot of kneading, but they still provide the same great yeast bread taste.

"This wholesome loaf is a perfect accompaniment to soups and salads, not to mention freshly made preserves in the summer." —Jan

METHOD
1. Lightly oil two 9- × 5-inch (2 L) loaf pans or line with wet parchment paper, well wrung out (see p. 388). Set aside.
2. Rinse a very large mixing bowl with hot water to warm it up, then add the lukewarm water.
3. Sprinkle yeast and sugar over the water. Let stand about 10 minutes or until yeast becomes frothy.
4. Whisk in honey, oil, bran (or wheat germ), oats, sunflower seeds and salt (do not omit!). Using a wooden spoon, beat in flour 1 cup (250 mL) at a time, making sure you beat until the batter is smooth before adding more flour. When all the flour has been added, beat vigorously until well blended. Dough will be heavy and moist.
5. Divide dough in half and pat into the prepared pans. Sprinkle unbaked loaves with additional quick oats and sunflower seeds, pressing into the surface of each loaf. Cover loaves with a clean tea towel and let stand in a warm place for about 45 minutes or until risen. Note: this is a heavy bread so it won't rise as high as a regular yeast bread.

INGREDIENT NOTE:

Iodized Salt—Salt has an important function in yeast development, so don't omit it!

Natural Bran/Wheat Germ—To make this a whole grain bread use 1/2 cup (125 mL) wheat germ and 1/2 cup (125 mL) natural bran.

PHEC TIPS:

Bread may be served warm from the oven but needs to be cut into thick slices. It slices more easily if cooled.

6. About 5 minutes before the dough has risen, preheat oven to 375°F (190°C). Bake loaves for 40 to 45 minutes or until a deep golden brown. Loaves should produce a hollow sound when tapped.
7. Cool loaves on racks for 10 minutes before removing from pans. Cool completely before storing.

Makes two 9-inch (2 L) loaves, 16 slices per loaf
One serving = 1 slice
Per serving: 147 Calories, 3.4 g Total Fat, 0.6 g Saturated Fat, 0 g Trans Fat, 297 mg Sodium, 24 g Carbohydrate, 3.4 g Fibre, 6.8 g Sugars, 6 g Added Sugars, 7.4 g Protein
Carbohydrate Choices: 1 1/2

ARE YOU EATING YOUR IODINE?

Iodine is an important trace mineral whose main function is to help the thyroid gland make thyroid hormones. Thyroid hormones are secreted into the blood and then carried to every tissue in the body. They help the body use energy, stay warm and they keep the brain, heart, muscles and other organs working on an even keel. The average Canadian adult requires 150 mcg per day.

Without enough iodine you can develop a goiter, an enlargement of the thyroid gland that was common in Canada until the 1920's when iodine was added to regular table salt. The best sources of iodine are

found naturally in seafood and seaweed, as well as in dairy products. Smaller amounts are found in beans, eggs and whole grains. It is uncommon to develop an iodine deficiency if you are eating seafood on a regular basis, or if you regularly ingest seaweed, beans, dairy products, whole grains or eggs. In my experience, however, I have noticed that a large percentage of Canadians do not eat seafood on a regular basis (two to three times a week). Factor in diets that limit dairy products or people who avoid eating whole grains, beans and eggs, and I believe we have the makings of a *perfect iodine deficiency storm*.

The recipes in this book are low to very low in sodium, but at least they aren't low in iodine. Your taste buds may tell you that recipes need more salt, but before you start waving a salt shaker around like a fairy wand, bear in mind that 1/4 tsp (1 mL) iodized salt has 428 mg of sodium and 95 mcg of iodine.

Note: To make sure that you are getting enough iodine, eat a well-balanced diet. Do not take an iodine supplement as it can interfere with other medications, and too much iodine is just as bad as too little. Check with your doctor is you think you might have an iodine deficiency.

INGREDIENTS

1/3 cup (75 mL) water

2/3 cup (150 mL) canned 100% pumpkin puree (see note)

1 omega-3 egg

1/4 cup (60 mL) skim milk powder

1 tsp (5 mL) iodized salt

1/4 cup (60 mL) packed brown sugar

2 Tbsp (30 mL) canola oil

1 3/4 cups (425 mL) whole wheat flour

2/3 cup (150 mL) all-purpose flour or bread flour

2 Tbsp (30 mL) natural wheat germ

1/3 cup (75 mL) pumpkin seeds, toasted (see note)

1/2 tsp (2 mL) ground allspice

1/4 tsp (1 mL) ground ginger

1/4 tsp (1 mL) ground nutmeg

1 3/4 tsp (8 mL) bread machine yeast

Autumn Pumpkin Seed Bread (for a Bread Machine)
Multi-seasonal

Donna Washburn, PHEc & Heather Butt, PHEc (with permission from *300 Best Canadian Bread Machine Recipes* [Robert Rose 2010])

"Autumn is my favourite season, with the colorful maples and the bountiful harvest. I grew up carving pumpkins and roasting the seeds. It seemed only natural for me to think of a yeast bread combining the two along with my favorite spices." —**Donna**

This bread machine loaf is a celebration of the colours, textures and flavours of autumn. Along with the pumpkin puree, it has toasted pumpkin seeds for crunch.

METHOD

1. Measure all ingredients into the bread machine baking pan in the order recommended by the manufacturer. Insert pan into the oven chamber.

2. Select the whole wheat cycle. When baking finishes, stop the machine and remove the pan. Immediately remove the loaf and place on a cooling rack.

Makes 12 slices One serving = 1 slice
Per serving: 179 Calories, 5.6 g Total Fat, 0.8 g Saturated Fat, 0.1 g Trans Fat, 221 mg Sodium, 26 g Carbohydrate, 2.8 g Fibre, 6.8 g Sugars, 4.7 g Added Sugars, 6.7 g Protein
Carbohydrate Choices: 1 1/2

INGREDIENT NOTE:

Pumpkin Puree—Canned pumpkin puree must be warmed to room temperature or the loaf will be short and heavy. Do not substitute with pumpkin pie filling.

Pumpkin Seeds—To toast seeds, place in a small skillet over medium heat and gently toast until they start to pop. Remove from heat and cool.

Eggs: Mother Nature's Little Vitamin Pill

53 One Healthy Egg

56 Upgrade Your Eggs: Four Basic Ways

56 It's Called Hard-Cooked, Not Hard-Boiled

58 Scrambled Eggs—It's Back to the Basics

59 Poaching Made Easy

60 Omelettes are Quick and Easy Works of Edible Art

61 Make-Ahead Morning French Toast Casserole

62 Crustless Kohlrabi Quiche

64 Quiche with Potato Crust

65 Quick Eggs Florentine

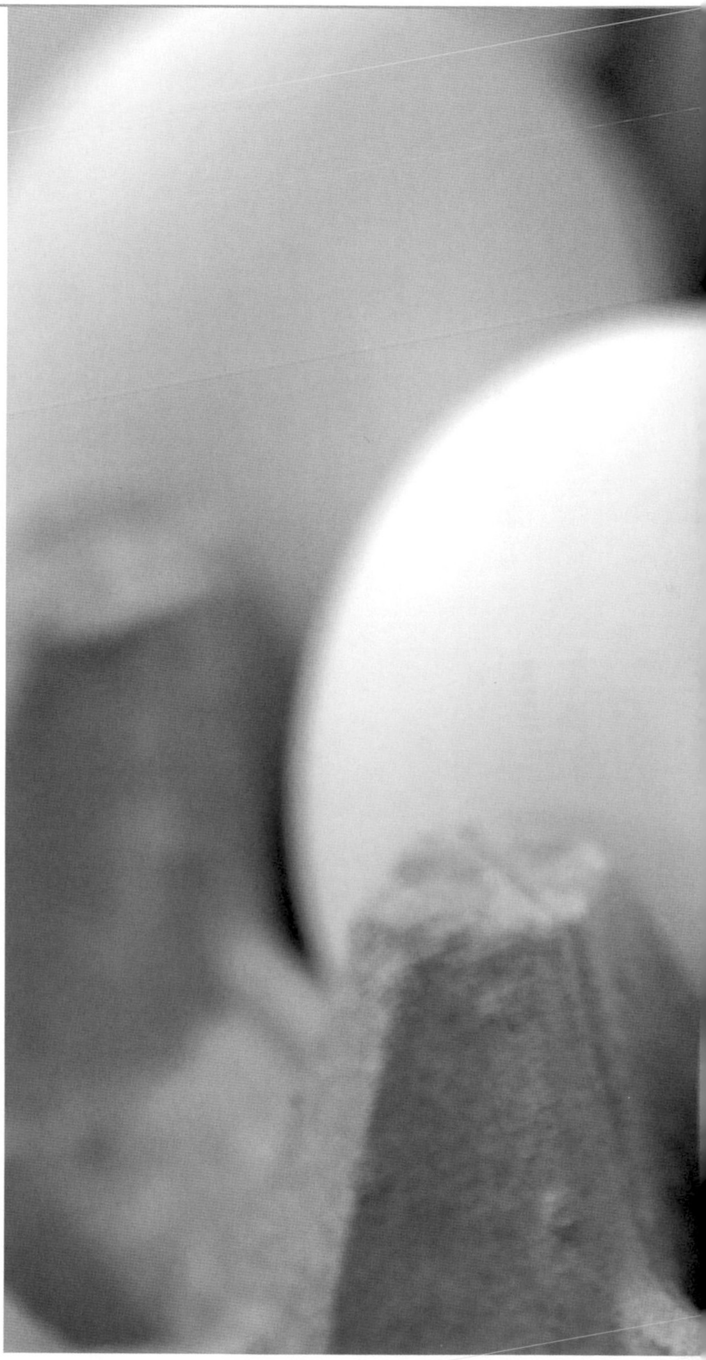

E G G S

There are more than 1,000 egg farmers and farm families in Canada who produce fresh high-quality local eggs for their fellow Canucks.

Egg farmers across Canada follow strict feed regulations set up by the Canadian Food Inspection Agency (CFIA), so all egg-laying hens are fed a balanced diet that is steroid and hormone free to ensure high-quality eggs.

ONE HEALTHY EGG

Eggs are nutrient-dense gifts from Mother Nature. Your average egg weighs in at 70 calories and has 6 grams of high quality protein along with a whole lot of vitamins and minerals.

Eggs are rich in antioxidants, specifically lutein and zeaxanthin, both of which are vital for reducing your chances of developing macular degeneration (adult onset blindness). Eggs also contain choline, a micronutrient needed in brain development and general function.

Healthy Canadians can enjoy eggs; the latest research shows that a healthy adult can enjoy one egg every day without increasing their risk of heart disease. It isn't the cholesterol in food that raises your cholesterol, it's the saturated fat, and good news, eggs are low in saturated fat. If you are a person living with diabetes, check with your doctor or registered dietician to see how many eggs you can eat a week.

Brown and white-shelled eggs are all the same as far as their nutrient profiles go, and the same goes for flavour and overall quality. The only actual difference between them is the breed of hen who laid them.

OMEGA-3 EGGS

I am a fan of omega-3 fatty acids. Omega-3 fatty acids are considered heart and brain healthy, two of my favourite organs to take care of. The problem is that your body can't produce its own omega-3s, it needs to get this essential fatty acid from food sources like fish (specifically fatty fishes like salmon and rainbow trout), flaxseed, walnuts, hemp hearts, canola oil and omega-3 eggs.

Hens that are fed a diet of flaxseed produce omega-3 eggs. These eggs contain the same omega-3 fatty acids found in fish, which your body can absorb with greater efficiency than foods containing the plant version of omega-3 fatty acids. Basically, unless you're eating two servings of fatty fish per week, only using canola oil, eating walnuts

EGG STORAGE QUIZ

Where is the best place to store your eggs? If you said in their original carton in the main body of the fridge, you might want to consider becoming a *Professional Home Economist*, because you are correct. Yes, I know those *cute little egg containers* on the door of your fridge are indeed cute, but the door is not the coldest storage place in your fridge to store them. Plus the original carton prevents your eggs from absorbing any odours you may have lurking about in the nether regions of your fridge. Keep your eggs in their carton and store in main body of the fridge.

every day and sprinkling ground flaxseed or hemp hearts onto your food you probably aren't getting enough omega-3s in your diet. Cue the omega-3 egg. I have suggested you eat this type of egg throughout the book, but that's my personal decision. Bottom line: eggs are Mother Nature's little vitamin pill. All eggs are great, but if you want an extra hit of omega-3s choose an omega-3 egg.

EGG WHITES

Due to strict agricultural guidelines and the ethics and practices used by the Egg Farmers of Canada, fresh Canadian eggs are edible raw, including the whites. Egg Farmers of Canada advise using only Grade A eggs that have been (properly) stored in the fridge (see Egg Storage Quiz on page 53). The shell needs to be clean and free of any cracks. Follow food safety rules and wash hands before and after handling the eggs. Eat the dish right away or store in the fridge right away and eat within the same day of preparation, discarding any leftovers.

Pasteurized egg whites are egg whites that have been heated to a temperature high enough to kill any bacteria before packaging in cartons. They are sold where you buy your eggs and can be used in recipes where raw egg whites are eaten, such as eggnog or meringue.

UPGRADE YOUR EGGS: FOUR BASIC WAYS

IT'S CALLED HARD-COOKED, NOT HARD-BOILED

One of my food pet peeves is when people boil the living daylights out of an egg, turning a tender cooked egg into a rubbery cooked egg.

To clarify the Hard Cooking Rules, here are some tips from the pros who know everything there is to know about eggs, the Egg Farmers of Canada:

- Place eggs in a single layer on the bottom of pot and cover with cold water. The water should be about an inch (2.5 cm) or so higher than the eggs. Cover the pot with a lid.
- Over high heat, bring your eggs to a rolling boil.
- Remove from heat and let stand in water for 18 to 23 minutes depending on the size: 18 minutes for medium sized eggs, 20 minutes for large eggs and 23 minutes for extra large eggs.
- Drain water and immediately run cold water over eggs until cooled. Rapid cooling helps prevent a green ring from forming around the yolks.

SERVING SUGGESTION:

To make your hard cooked eggs into devilled eggs, cut 12 hard cooked eggs in half lengthwise. Remove yolks and place in a medium bowl; set egg whites on a large plate. Mash yolks with a fork. Stir in 1/4 cup (60 mL) low fat mayonnaise or salad dressing, 2 tsp (10 mL) mustard, 2 tsp (10 mL) vinegar or pickle juice and 2 diced shallots. If necessary, add a little more mayonnaise for a creamier texture. Season with pepper. Spoon or pipe yolk mixture into egg white halves. Sprinkle paprika over top. Serve immediately or store, covered, in the refrigerator. Serve within two days. (Wendy Hebert, PHEc)

PHEC TIPS:

Want to glam up your Devilled Eggs? Teresa Makarewicz, PHEc suggests the following toppings:
- Chopped cooked bacon with chives
- Smoked salmon with fresh dill sprigs
- Slivered red onion, capers and fresh dill sprigs
- Cooked thin asparagus spears with crab or baby shrimp
- Diced cucumber and tomatoes with chopped fresh flat-leaf parsley
- Thinly sliced olives with roasted red pepper slices

SCRAMBLED EGGS—IT'S BACK TO THE BASICS

In a hurry? Scrambled eggs are a *go-to* dinner solution.

Two eggs scrambled is dinner for one.

- In a small bowl, whisk 2 eggs, 2 Tbsp (30 mL) water or milk until frothy.
- Over medium heat, heat small skillet, add a tiny amount of oil or unsalted butter.
- Pour in beaten eggs and reduce heat to medium-low. Gently stir eggs until large soft pieces (curds) form.
- Cook until eggs are thickened and no longer runny or raw looking.
- Season with iodized salt and pepper if desired, add grated cheese, chopped cherry tomatoes, chopped green onions or hot sauce. Be creative.

SERVING SUGGESTION:

Stuff a warm whole-wheat tortilla with scrambled eggs, shredded old cheddar, diced red onion and top with salsa. To warm the tortillas, microwave for 10 to 15 seconds; this will prevent them from breaking when you roll them up. (Maria McLellan PHEc)

POACHING MADE EASY

Master poaching and before you know it you will be hosting an eggs benedict brunch.

- Fill a small saucepan with approx. 3 inches (8 cm) of water.
- Heat over medium heat until water gently simmers. Reduce heat to low.
- Break a cold fresh egg into small dish or saucer. Holding the dish just above simmering water, gently slip egg into water. Repeat with remaining eggs.
- Cook in barely simmering water until white is set and yolk is cooked as desired, 3 to 4 minutes for a soft semi-runny yolk, 5 to 7 for a harder yolk.
- Remove eggs with slotted spoon and drain well. Place on a plate lined with paper towels.

SERVING SUGGESTIONS:

For traditional eggs benedict, Emily Kichler (OHEA student member) suggests topping toasted whole wheat English muffins with one of the following three suggested toppings:

- Shredded old Canadian Cheddar with cooked peameal bacon and arugula.
- Crumbled goat cheese and Canadian smoked salmon with thin slices of red onion and chopped fresh dill.
- Sliced tomatoes, fresh basil leaves and sliced mozzarella.

OMELETTES ARE QUICK AND EASY WORKS OF EDIBLE ART

Use your imagination when it comes to filling your omelette.

- In a small bowl, whisk together 2 eggs, 2 Tbsp (30 mL) water and salt and pepper to taste, until very frothy.
- Heat a small non-stick skillet over medium-high heat. Add a small amount of oil or unsalted butter. Pour in egg mixture and gently tip the pan so the egg mixture goes right to the edges. As eggs start to set around the edge, take a heat-resistant spatula and gently lift up an edge, tipping the pan so the raw egg flows underneath. Continue around the pan, lifting the cooked egg and letting any raw egg flow underneath.
- When eggs are almost set on the surface but still look moist, cover half of the omelette with a filling of your choice (see below). Slip spatula under the unfilled side; fold over onto filled half.
- Cook for a minute, then slide omelette onto a plate.

SERVING SUGGESTION:

Beat 2 eggs until frothy and prepare 1/4 cup (60 mL) of each: sliced mushrooms, diced onion and finely chopped broccoli. Heat a small skillet over medium heat, add 2 tsp (10 mL) canola oil, pour in eggs and sprinkle the vegetables over top. Reduce heat to low, cook on one side until set, flip like a pancake and cook until egg is set. Serve. (Debbie Lui, PHEc)

Make-Ahead Morning French Toast Casserole

Multi-seasonal Linda Reasbeck, PHEc

This recipe is great for a special breakfast like Christmas or Easter morning or when you have overnight guests. Prepare this the night before and bake it in the morning.

METHOD

1. Line a 9- × 13-inch (3.5 L) glass baking pan with wet parchment paper (see page 388).
2. Cut slices of raisin bread into quarters horizontally and then vertically, then stand the forty quarters up in the prepared pan. (Who knew you'd need geometry skills for a make-ahead breakfast recipe?)
3. Slice sausages into 3/4-inch (2 mm) pieces and tuck between slices of bread, sprinkling the extras on top.
4. In a large bowl, beat together eggs, milk, vanilla, cinnamon and nutmeg.
5. Pour mixture over the prepared bread and sausage. The liquid will be absorbed into the bread overnight.
6. Cover with plastic wrap (avoid plastic wrap touching the food) and refrigerate for 8 hours or overnight.
7. For the topping, mix together the brown sugar, walnuts and butter in a medium bowl. Cover and set aside until the next morning.
8. Preheat oven to 350°F (180°C). Remove bread mixture from the fridge and remove wrap. When the oven is hot, spoon the butter topping overtop.
9. Bake uncovered for 40 to 50 minutes or until knife inserted in the centre comes out clean. Let stand 5 to 10 minutes before serving.

Makes 10 cups (2.5 L) One serving = 1 1/4 cups (310 mL)
Per serving: 540 Calories, 27.7 g Total Fat, 8.2 g Saturated Fat, 0.4 g Trans Fat, 407 mg Sodium, 58.2 g Carbohydrate, 3 g Fibre, 36 g Sugars, 28.2 g Added Sugars, 17.3 g Protein
Carbohydrate Choices: 4

INGREDIENTS

FRENCH TOAST
10 slices of raisin bread
5 oz (150 g) fully cooked skinless sausages (see note)
6 omega-3 eggs
3 cups (750 mL) 1% milk
1 tsp (5 mL) pure vanilla extract
1/2 tsp (2 mL) cinnamon
1/4 tsp (1 mL) freshly ground nutmeg (see note)

TOPPING
1 cup (250 mL) packed dark brown sugar
1 cup (250 mL) coarsely chopped walnuts
1/4 cup (60 mL) melted unsalted butter

INGREDIENT NOTES:
Sausages—Maple Leaf Fully Cooked Sausages come in one 10 oz (300 g) package with two separate packages containing 5 oz (150 g) each. Use one of the packages for this recipe and freeze the rest for next time.
Nutmeg—Freshly ground nutmeg tastes so much better than pre-ground nutmeg and is easy to make. Use a whole nutmeg and either a small, regular grater or a nutmeg grater.

Crustless Kohlrabi Quiche Spring/Summer

Diana Rodel, PHEc

"Kohlrabi 'bulbs' are not actually bulbs but swollen stems that grow above ground. When purchasing fresh kohlrabi, choose a bunch with greens that are deep green in colour (yellowed leaves reveal that they are not fresh). To store fresh kohlrabi in the refrigerator prior to use, break off the leaves from the bulbs. Wash leaves in cold water, pat dry and wrap in paper towels or tea towel. Place in a container or resealable bag and then refrigerate. Should stay fresh for up to five days." —Diana

METHOD

1. Preheat oven to 350°F (175°C). Using a pastry brush coat a 9-inch (23 cm) pie plate with the oil.

2. To prepare the kohlrabi, take 1 kohlrabi and trim the stems and leaves. Scrub the bulb well and pat dry; grate the bulb and set aside. Rinse leaves and chop. You should end up with 1 1/2 cups (375 mL) grated kohlrabi and approximately 1 cup (250 mL) chopped leaves.

3. Heat a large non-stick frying pan over medium heat. Add the butter (or non-hydrogenated margarine), leek and red pepper and sauté for 2 to 4 minutes or until the leek is soft.

4. Add grated kohlrabi and sauté for 1 to 2 minutes.

5. Add chopped kohlrabi leaves and water. Cover and cook for 10 minutes.

6. In a large bowl beat together the eggs, cheese and black pepper. Add kohlrabi mixture and stir well. Pour into the prepared pan.

7. Bake loosely covered with aluminium foil for 25 minutes, then uncovered for 15 minutes or until set.

8. Remove from oven and let stand for 5 minutes before serving.

Makes one 9-inch (23 cm) quiche One serving = 1/4 quiche
Per serving: 236 Calories, 14.2 g Total Fat, 6.3 g Saturated Fat, 0 g Trans Fat, 370 mg Sodium,
9 g Carbohydrate, 2.6 g Fibre, 3.7 g Sugars, 0 g Added Sugars, 18.4 g Protein
Carbohydrate Choices: 1/2

INGREDIENT NOTE

Leeks—You've seen them in the produce aisle—those great big onion-looking things—and yes indeed leeks are part of the heart-healthy onion family. They have a milder flavour than a regular onion and add a mild sweetness that is less sweet than a sweet onion. Leeks are grown in sand and need a shower (aka a really good rinse) under running tap water before you start cooking with them. Cut them in half lengthwise, but not all the way through, fan open under running water.

KOHLRABI

Next time you want to play "Name the mystery vegetable," pick kohlrabi. It's in the family of healthy vegetables called Brassicas (other members include the more commonly eaten broccoli, cabbage, cauliflower and kale) and its flavour is similar to broccoli stems. It prefers to grow in colder climates, which is why it loves growing in Canada. You can find kohlrabi in larger grocery stores, Asian grocery stores and farmers markets. Choose smaller bulbs as they are more tender than the larger ones.

INGREDIENTS

5 omega-3 eggs

3/4 cup (175 mL) skim milk

1 large potato, scrubbed, peel left on and thinly sliced

2 slices of cooked ham, chicken or turkey, cubed (see note)

1/4 cup (60 mL) shredded old white cheddar cheese

10 grape or cherry tomatoes, cut in half

PHEC TIP:

This recipe is a great way to use leftover cooked ham, chicken or turkey. We like to call them repurposed or re-invented ingredients, not leftovers!

Quiche with Potato Crust Multi-seasonal Debbie Lui, PHEc

"I learned how to make quiche volunteering for a lunch program in London, Ontario. When I didn't have the right ingredients in my pantry to make a crust, I came up with the idea to use potatoes. I used potato slices to make a shell, and it turned out great." —**Debbie**

METHOD

1. Preheat oven to 350°F (180°C). Lightly oil a 9-inch (23 cm) glass pie plate and set aside.
2. In a medium bowl, whisk together eggs and milk.
3. Thinly slice potato and line the pie plate with layered potato slices, making sure there aren't any holes for the egg mixture to seep through.
4. Evenly sprinkle the ham (or chicken or turkey) evenly on top.
5. Pour egg mixture in pie shell. Sprinkle cheese on top.
6. Gently place sliced tomatoes on the surface.
7. Bake for 30 to 35 minutes or until a toothpick inserted comes out clean. Serve hot.

Makes one 9-inch (23 cm) quiche One serving = 1/8 quiche
Per serving: 129 Calories, 5.8 g Total Fat, 2.3 g Saturated Fat, 0 g Trans Fat, 176 mg Sodium, 10.3 g Carbohydrate, 1 g Fibre, 2.5 g Sugars, 0 g Added Sugars, 9 g Protein
Carbohydrate Choices: 1/2

Quick Eggs Florentine Spring/Summer Mary Johnston, PHEc

"Growing up on a farm, my mother would serve this in the spring and summer when there was lots of baby spinach in the garden and she needed a quick dinner because we were busy bringing in the hay. It was my job to pick and wash the spinach and drain it so that it was ready for use." —Mary

METHOD

1. Wash and spin-dry spinach. Cook for approximately 2 minutes in the microwave. Let cool slightly, drain and chop coarsely; set aside.
2. In a medium saucepan over medium-high heat, cook bacon until crisp. Remove from pan, set on a paper towel, discard fat and wipe out pan with a paper towel.
3. Add 2 tsp (10 mL) oil and mushrooms, sauté for 4 to 5 minutes, remove from pan and set aside. Add onion to the pan and sauté for 2 minutes.
4. Add the remaining oil and stir in the flour and dry mustard. Stir until the mixture is slightly golden in colour and bubbling.
5. Reduce heat and stir in the milk, stirring until thickened. If necessary add a bit more milk to make a sauce.
6. Add the spinach, salt and pepper and stir in. Turn the heat to medium-low.
7. Make 4 equally sized wells in the spinach mixture and crack an egg directly into each of the wells.
8. Top with the sautéed mushrooms. Cover with a lid and cook until the eggs reach the desired level of doneness. Crumble bacon over top and serve.

Makes 2 servings One serving = 1/2 recipe
Per serving: 391 Calories, 28.3 g Total Fat, 7.6 g Saturated Fat, 0.2 g Trans Fat, 607 mg Sodium, 14.4 g Carbohydrate, 3 g Fibre, 6 g Sugars, 0 g Added Sugars, 21.4 g Protein
Carbohydrate Choices: 1

INGREDIENTS

4 cups (1 L) loosely packed baby spinach
2 slices lower sodium bacon
1 Tbsp (15 mL) canola oil, divided
1/2 onion, finely chopped
1 Tbsp (15 mL) all-purpose flour
1/2 tsp (2 mL) dry mustard
1/4 cup (60 mL) skim milk
10 medium cremini mushrooms, sliced
1/4 tsp (1 mL) iodized salt
1/4 tsp (1 mL) freshly ground black pepper
4 omega-3 eggs

Bring on the Cheese, Please

69 Entertaining with Cheese

72 Great Canadian Cheese Fondue (Microwave Method)

73 Apple Maple Cheddar Spread

76 Blue Cheese and Pear Phyllo Tarts

80 Savoury Cheddar Shortbread Diamonds

82 Salute to the Grilled Cheese Sandwich

86 Shaved Asparagus Pizza

90 Spinach and Goat Cheese Pizza

92 Mac and Cheese

94 Mushroom and Spinach Cannelloni with

Italian Cheese Blend Sauce

96 Baked Goat Cheese with Cranberry or Plum Compote

CHEESE

CANADIANS LOVE THEIR CHEESE, PURE AND SIMPLE.

Every province produces its own distinctive cheeses, from Salt Spring Island Cheese Company in British Columbia to Glasgow Glen Farm in PEI. With big name cheese companies like Maple Dale from Ontario, Kraft Canada Inc. and Agropur (a Canadian Agricultural cooperative headquartered in Longueuil, Quebec), Canada's got a cheese for you.

And it might even be a winning cheese at that. In 2013 a Canadian aged Lankaaster took home the Top Prize at the Global Cheese Awards in Somerset, England (the birthplace of cheddar), earning the designation "Supreme Global Champion." This winning cheese was made by Glengarry Cheesemaking, from Lancaster, Ontario.

For a full list of Canadian cheese makers go to cheese-fromage.agr.gc.ca or check out cheeseloverca.wordpress.com

"I've never met a cheese I didn't like." —The Reluctant Gourmet, food blogger

"Cheese is milk's leap toward immortality." —Cliff Fadiman, American intellectual, author, editor, radio and television personality

ENTERTAINING WITH CHEESE

Cheese platters are and will forever be a great way to entertain (especially when served alongside Canadian VQA wines [see page 71]), and assembling one is easier than you might think. All you need is a plate or tray—generally wood, glass or marble, though in a pinch a regular plate will do just fine—and a variety of your favourite cheeses. Then its *party time*.

For a Wine and Cheese Party, the Dairy Farmers of Canada recommend serving approx. 1/2 lb (250 g) of cheese for each guest. For a pre-dinner nibble it's 1 to 1 1/2 oz (25 to 30 g) per person.

Arrange your cheese platter and then cover it with a damp cloth and refrigerate. Bring the platter out 45 minutes before serving to let the cheeses come to the perfect temperature for tasting.

Serve along with crackers, assorted bread, fruit, pickles and/or nuts.

But which cheeses do you pick from? Match your personality with your favourite cheeses. Here's a handy quiz to help you along the way.

CHEESE PLATTER QUIZ:

Circle the one which most applies to you:

You are late coming home from work.

A. Always

B. Sometimes

C. Never

D. I quit my job because I won *Lotto 649*

You love planning parties.

A. Always

B. Sometimes

C. Never

D. I would rather go over Niagara Falls in a barrel

Does decant mean:

A. Gradually pouring one liquid from one container into another container

B. Something to do with alcohol

C. Counting backwards while standing on one foot

D. Opening any type of VQA wine that you have in your wine cellar

Scoring:

If you circled all A's choose Cheese Platter #1

If you circled all B's choose Cheese Platter #2

If you circled all C's choose Cheese Platter #3

If you circled all D's do whatever you want

PLATTER #1

This isn't your first cheese rodeo. You are a lover of all great cheeses, especially ones made in Canada. Choose exciting original Canadian cheeses like: Bleu Bénédictin, Fox Hill Parmesan, Comtomme, Okanagan Double Cream Camembert, Silani Friulano, and Saint-Paulin.

PLATTER #2

You are a cheese lover and willing to try new and different cheeses, just so long as you can sort of pronounce most of them. Try these: Balderson 3- or 5-year-old White Cheddar, Bothwell Monteray Jack, Sir Laurier d'Arthabaska, Comox Brie, and Fox Hill Smoked Gouda.

PLATTER #3

You are a *fly by the seat of your pants* kind of person who loves having friends over, but in a *"I have a bottle of wine and some cheese so let's be merry"* kind of way. Always have in your fridge your favourite Canadian aged white Cheddar, Havarti, and a Gouda. You never know when a wine and cheese party will hit you.

PLATTER #4

Go to your favourite upscale restaurant and order a Canadian artisanal cheese platter and a great glass of VQA wine; text me, I'll join you.

For more ideas check out www.dairygoodness.ca/cheese/cheese-and-wine-planner/our-combinations.

VQA WINES

VQA stands for Vintners Quality Alliance. When a bottle of wine is labelled VQA you are assured that the wine was made from grapes grown in Canada and that the wine was created and cellared in Canada. In other words, you are buying 100% Canadian wine. The two provinces that use VQA as a designation are Ontario and British Columbia; these wines are tasted by a qualified panel for quality characteristics prior to being able to use the VQA symbol on their wine.

Wines of Distinction is a category given to BC wines that are made with 100% BC grapes but did not undergo the BC VQA certification process. *Wines of Nova Scotia* is the designation given to bottles of wine made from grapes grown and produced in Nova Scotia.

Cellared in Canada is a category of wines that are made up of either all foreign grapes or a combination of foreign and domestic grapes, then cellared in Canada.

INGREDIENTS

2 cups (500 mL) shredded Classic
  Oka cheese, rind removed
3 cups (750 mL) shredded extra
  old white Canadian cheddar
  (we used 5-year-old)
1/2 garlic clove, peeled
2 Tbsp (30 mL) cornstarch
One 13 oz (370 mL) can
  evaporated skim milk
1/8 tsp (0.5 mL) freshly ground
  pepper
1 pinch freshly grated nutmeg
Assorted bread, apples, blanched
  vegetables

PHEC TIP:

No party? No problem! You can
make this fondue and use it like
a cheese sauce: drizzle it over
steamed vegetables or combine
with your favourite whole grain
or high fibre pasta. All you need
is cheese . . .

Great Canadian Cheese Fondue (Microwave Method) Fall/Winter
Emily Dobrich, SHEA student member

Oka cheese was first created in 1893 by Trappist monks in Quebec. World famous, Oka is still crafted in those very same cellars of the Cistercian Abbey. It has a unique flavour that takes an ordinary cheese fondue to a whole new cheese level. The method used in this recipe is slightly non-conventional, but it is easy and, best of all, it works every time.

METHOD

1. In a large bowl, toss the Oka and cheddar cheeses together.
2. Rub garlic clove on the inside of a large microwave-safe bowl. Discard clove.
3. Add cornstarch and then whisk in 1/4 cup (60 mL) milk until smooth. Whisk in remaining milk.
4. Microwave mixture on high for 3 minutes. Stir until smooth and then add cheese, stirring to combine.
5. Microwave on high for one minute intervals for an additional 5 minutes, until cheese is melted and fondue has thickened. Stir before serving. Can be stored in the fridge for up to 2 days. Reheat in a sauce pot over medium-low heat on the stove.

Makes 4 cups (1 L) One serving = 1/2 cup (125 mL)
Per serving: 294 Calories, 21.3 g Total Fat, 13 g Saturated Fat, 0.5 g Trans Fat, 489 mg Sodium, 8 g Carbohydrate, 0 g Fibre, 6.2 g Sugars, 0 g Added Sugars, 19 g Protein
Carbohydrate Choices: 1/2

Apple Maple Cheddar Spread Fall/Winter

Emily Richards, PHEc (with permission from Dairy Farmers of Canada)

Many professional home economists work in the food industry—you are probably familiar with some of them via their recipes, you just don't know their names. Case in point: two fabulous recipe developers, Emily Richards and Jennifer MacKenzie, have both worked on and created recipes for the Dairy Farmers of Canada (DFC). Here is one of several recipes they created for the DFC's online recipe vault, which also appeared in the Dairy Farmers' annual Milk Calendar.

METHOD

1. Using the large holes of a box cheese grater, grate the apple and squeeze out juice; set grated apple aside.
2. In a medium bowl, using a hand mixer, beat cream cheese and cream until smooth. Stir in grated apple, cheese, maple syrup, chives, Dijon mustard and garlic until combined.
3. Cover and refrigerate for at least 1 hour to blend flavours or for up to 2 days. (Spread will thicken upon standing.)
4. Transfer to serving container and garnish with chives and/or apple slices (if using). Serve with crackers, flatbreads and/or celery sticks.

Makes 1 cup (250 mL) One serving = 3 Tbsp (45 mL)
Per serving: 137 Calories, 9 g Total Fat, 5.4 g Saturated Fat, 0 g Trans Fat, 211 mg Sodium, 9 g Carbohydrate, 0.6 g Fibre, 7 g Sugars, 2.2 g Added Sugars, 6.2 g Protein
Carbohydrate Choices: 1/2

INGREDIENTS

1 red apple, scrubbed well, peel left on, cored
1/2 cup (125 mL) light cream cheese, softened
1/3 cup (80 mL) 5 % MF cream
1/2 cup (125 mL) shredded white Canadian extra sharp cheddar cheese (see note)
1 Tbsp (15 mL) pure maple syrup
1 Tbsp (15 mL) fresh chives or green onions, chopped
1/2 tsp (2 mL) Dijon mustard
1 small garlic clove, minced and set aside
Chives or thin apple slices (optional)
Crackers, flatbreads and/or celery sticks (for serving)

INGREDIENT NOTE:

Cheddar Cheese—For true cheddar lovers, use a Canadian sharp cheddar cheese aged three years for this recipe. The contrast of its sharp bite will go perfectly with a sweet crisp local red-skinned apple.

CHEDDAR CHEESE

Cheddar may have originated in England, but thanks to our forefathers (who brought the knowledge of cheddar making to Canada with them), Canada has become a world leader in all things cheddar.

Terroir (the combination of the land, sun, rain, wind and its effect on food) affects the type of pasture and feed that dairy cows consume. Factor in the breed of dairy cow (is it Holstein, Jersey, Ayrshire, Brown Swiss or a Guernsey) and the fact that Canada has one of the highest standards for safety and quality in milk production in the world, and this all translates into one thing: Canada produces high quality milk, which leads to exceptionally high quality Canadian cheeses.

In general we produce smoother and creamier style cheddars than other countries. Ontario is Canada's largest cheddar producer, with Balderson and Black River Cheese (just to name a few) leading the way.

What type of cheddar should you use? It really depends on your personal taste, but the rule of thumb is:
- mild and medium are great in sandwiches and omelettes
- old for shredding, slicing, snacking or wine pairings
- extra old for shredding, baking, snacking or wine pairings

As far as colour, cheddar's natural colour is a creamy white, but many companies add a tasteless food colour to their cheddars to give it that orange colour.

Most Canadians consume cheese made with cow's milk, but goat and sheep milk cheeses are becoming more popular in Canada.

INGREDIENTS

1 firm Bartlett pear

2 tsp (10 mL) unsalted butter

1 onion, diced

1/2 tsp (2 mL) iodized salt, divided

3 omega-3 eggs

3/4 cup (185 mL) 35% MF whipping cream

3/4 cup (185 mL) 0% MF plain Greek style yogurt

1/4 tsp (1 mL) fresh ground black pepper

8 sheets of Phyllo pastry, thawed (see note)

3 Tbsp (45 mL) melted unsalted butter

3/4 cup (175 mL) crumbled Canadian blue cheese

INGREDIENT NOTES:

Phyllo Pastry—Working with phyllo can be a tad tricky. To keep it from drying out while you're working with it, place a clean tea towel over top of it.

Joan Ttooulias PHEc and Cathy Ireland PHEc making the tarts together

Blue Cheese and Pear Phyllo Tarts Fall/Winter

Emily Richards, PHEc (with permission from Dairy Farmers of Canada)

These show-stopping first course tarts are worth the time and effort they take to make. We tweaked this recipe from Emily after Joan Ttooulias suggested that we borrow a phyllo technique from Jamie Oliver (you know, that cute, smart, enthusiastic English chef . . .).

METHOD

1. Preheat oven to 425°F (220°C). Line a rimmed baking sheet with parchment paper.
2. Cut pear in half lengthwise; scoop out core and stem with a small spoon. Place cut sides down and cut lengthwise into 1/4-inch (0.5 cm) thick slices. Place on prepared baking sheet and roast for about 18 minutes, flipping over halfway, until golden and tender. Transfer to a cutting board and let cool completely. Reduce oven temperature to 375°F (190°C).
3. Meanwhile, in a medium skillet, heat butter over medium heat. Add onion and 1/4 tsp (1 mL) salt. Cook, stirring occasionally, for 5 to 10 minutes, or until onion is tender and slightly golden. Set aside to cool.
4. In a large bowl, preferably with a pouring spout, whisk together eggs, cream and yogurt. Whisk in remaining salt.
5. Chop pear slices into 1/4- to 1/2-inch (0.5 to 1 cm) pieces; set aside.
6. You will need two 12-cup muffin pans.
7. Place 2 sheets of phyllo on top of a clean dry counter. Very lightly brush with half of the melted butter. Place two more sheets on top. Carefully transfer to the muffin pan. Very, very gently press the phyllo into each of the muffin cups. Set aside and cover with a clean tea towel. Repeat the process with the remaining phyllo and the second pan.

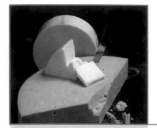

8. Equally spoon onions into the bottom of the 24 muffin tins, divide blue cheese and pears over top, making sure each tart is getting the same amount. Pour cream mixture over top.

9. Carefully place muffin pans into oven and bake for 25 to 30 minutes or until the tart filling has set and the pastry is golden brown, checking at the 10- to 15-minute mark for excess browning, cover loosely with foil.

10. Allow to cool a little before serving (tarts will deflate as they cool). Using either a knife or kitchen scissors, separate the 12 tarts from the pan. See picture.

11. Serve immediately to raves; pat yourself on the back for a job well done!

Makes 24 tarts One serving = 1 tart
Per serving: 94 Calories, 6.6 g Total Fat, 3.8 g Saturated Fat, 0 g Trans Fat, 153 mg Sodium, 5.8 g Carbohydrate, 0.5 g Fibre, 1.08 g Sugars, 0 g Added Sugars, 3 g Protein
Carbohydrate Choices: 1/2

WHAT DOES THE "MF" STAND FOR ON THE LABELS OF DAIRY PRODUCTS?
MF stands for milk fat. O% MF would mean there is zero fat from milk in the product. 5% would mean there is five percent fat from milk in the product.

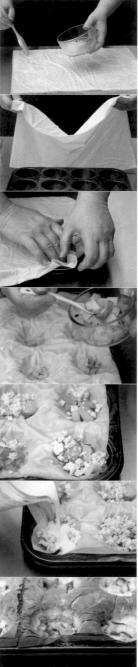

INGREDIENTS

1/2 sweet red pepper, coarsely
  chopped

1 1/2 cups (375 mL) shredded
  Canadian old white cheddar
  cheese

1/2 cup (125 mL) cold unsalted
  butter, cubed

2 cups (500 mL) all-purpose flour

2 tsp (10 mL) granulated sugar

1 tsp (5 mL) ancho chili powder
  (see note)

1/4 tsp (1 mL) iodized salt

2–3 Tbsp (30–45 mL) water
  (approx.)

1 egg white, beaten

1 tsp (5 mL) coarse sea salt
  (approx.)

Savoury Cheddar Shortbread Diamonds Multi-seasonal

Jennifer MacKenzie, PHEc (with permission from Dairy Farmers of Canada)

Savoury shortbread is a glamorous nibble to enjoy with a glass of VQA red or sparkling white wine.

METHOD

1. In large food processor, pulse red pepper until finely chopped. Add cheese, butter, flour, sugar, chili powder and salt. Pulse until dough starts to hold together, adding the water a little at a time.

2. Turn out dough into a bowl and knead lightly until smooth. Shape into a flat square. On a sheet of parchment paper with a floured rolling pin, roll out to a 9- × 13-inch (23 × 33 cm) rectangle, approx. 1/4-inch (5 mm) thick. Slide onto a baking sheet and refrigerate for at least 20 minutes or until cold.

3. When dough is chilled, preheat oven to 300°F (150°C).

4. Using a pizza cutter or a knife, cut the dough lengthwise into 8 equal strips. On a diagonal, make 7 cuts along each strip, approx.

1 inch (2.5 cm) apart, so you have 56 diamonds. (There will be triangles at the ends of the strips—either press together into diamonds or bake as is.)

5. Lightly brush tops with egg white and lightly sprinkle with coarse sea salt. Separate shortbread pieces on the parchment so they are at least 1/2 inch (1 cm) apart. Use a second parchment-lined baking sheet to accommodate the rest of the diamonds.

6. Bake, one sheet at a time, for about 27 minutes or until firm and just starting to turn golden around the edges. Let cool in pan on a wire rack for 3 minutes then transfer to cooling rack. Serve warm or let cool. (Shortbread can be stored in a cookie tin at room temperature for up to 5 days. Warm in a 350°F/180°C oven for about 5 minutes before serving.)

Makes about 56 shortbread diamonds One serving = 3 shortbread diamonds
Per serving: 150 Calories, 9.7 g Total Fat, 6 g Saturated Fat, 0.4 g Trans Fat, 140 mg Sodium, 11 g Carbohydrate, 0.5 g Fibre, 0.7 g Sugars, 0.5 g Added Sugars, 5 g Protein
Carbohydrate Choices: 1

INGREDIENT NOTE:

Ancho Chili Powder—Unlike regular chili powder, ancho is a pure chili powder rather than a blend. It is typically used for chili and has a moderate amount of heat. It can be found in larger grocery stores and specialty spice or bulk stores, but if you can't find it you can use 1/2 tsp (2 mL) regular chili powder + 1/2 tsp (2 mL) paprika as a substitute. (Source: Dairy Farmers of Canada)

SALUTE TO THE GRILLED CHEESE SANDWICH

Grilled cheese sandwiches are about as Canadian as you can get and without a doubt one of our favourite comfort foods. Here are 10 ingenious spins by the members of OHEA, all made with Canadian cheeses:

- Old cheddar with a Branston pickle on homemade multigrain bread. (Susan Donaldson, PHEc)
- Applewood smoked cheddar, maple mustard and thinly sliced red onion on sourdough bread. (Heather Howe, PHEc)
- Mild white cheddar, Granny Smith apple slices and crisply cooked bacon on sourdough bread, served with homemade sweet tomato relish. (Evelyn Hullah, PHEc)
- Sliced Havarti—plain or Jalapeno—with crispy bacon and lots of thin slices of ripe pear, on the Good Bread Company's Walnut Whole Wheat bread (made in Vittoria, Ontario) and served with spiced red wine jelly. (Mary Etta McGraw, PHEc)
- Extra old cheddar, sliced homegrown tomatoes and sliced dill pickles on caraway/rye bread. (Margaret Murray, PHEc)
- Brie, sliced pear and peach chutney on pumpernickel bread. (Linda M. Reasbeck, PHEc)
- Brie, sliced Granny Smith apple, a few dried cranberries and a slice of roasted turkey on multigrain bread. (Jennifer Rennie, PHEc)
- Mozzarella, sliced tomato and fresh basil leaves on pumpernickel bread. (Stephanie Varriano, RD, PHEc)
- Swiss with kosher dills on pumpernickel. (Susan Wheatley, PHEc)
- Thinly sliced Niagara Gold with sliced red onions and spinach leaves on homemade Sour Cream bread. (Nicoline Williams, PHEc)

DAIRY FARMERS OF CANADA

Dairy Farmers of Canada (DFC) is the national policy, lobbying and promotional organization representing the farmers of 12,529 Canadian dairy farms. DFC strives to create stable conditions for the Canadian dairy industry, today and in the future. It works to maintain policies that foster the viability of Canadian dairy farmers and to promote dairy products and their health benefits.

Dairy farmers fund its operations, including promotional activities. (Source: Dairy Farmers of Canada)

INGREDIENTS

TOPPING

1 large bulb of garlic

2 tsp (10 mL) canola oil, divided

2 cups (500 mL) **thick stalk**
 asparagus (approx. 1 bunch)

1/4 tsp (1 mL) iodized salt

1/4–1/2 tsp (1–2 mL) fresh
 ground black pepper

3/4 cup (185 mL) light Canadian
 ricotta cheese

1/2 cup (125 mL) grated
 Canadian Parmesan cheese

3 Tbsp (45 mL) finely chopped
 basil

3 Tbsp (45 mL) finely chopped
 chives

1/2 tsp (1 mL) red pepper flakes
 (optional)

DOUGH

3/4 cup (180 mL) whole wheat
 flour, divided

3/4 cup (180 mL) all-purpose
 flour, divided

1/4 cup (60 mL) natural wheat
 bran

2 Tbsp (30 mL) ground flaxseed

One 1/4 oz (8 g) envelope pizza
 yeast (see note)

1 1/2 tsp (7 mL) granulated sugar

3/4 tsp (4 mL) iodized salt

2/3 cup (150 mL) very warm
 water (120–130°F/48–54°C)

2 Tbsp (30 mL) canola oil

Shaved Asparagus Pizza Spring/Early Summer

Erin MacGregor, PHEc, RD

*"Pizza is a year round winner, but this version has major spring flair.
Shaving the asparagus gives it a light feel and is visually stunning. Look for
stalks thick enough to shave with a vegetable peeler. If the stalks are too thin,
slice them thinly on the diagonal."*—Erin

METHOD

1. Preheat oven to 425°F (220°C).

2. Remove outer layers of loose skin from garlic bulb. Cut 1/2 inch (1 cm) off the top of the bulb (the pointed end), exposing the inside of the individual cloves. Place cut side up on a piece of aluminum foil, drizzle with 1 tsp (5 mL) oil and wrap bulb tightly in foil. Roast for 30 to 40 minutes in an oven-safe dish. When cool enough to handle, turn bulb upside down and squeeze out the softened brown cloves. Start the pizza once the garlic has cooled.

3. To make the toppings, start by holding the asparagus stalks by their thick woody ends and use a vegetable peeler to shave each spear into thin ribbons. Transfer shavings into a large bowl and toss with oil, salt and pepper. Set aside.

4. In a separate bowl, combine ricotta, parmesan, roasted garlic, basil, chives and red pepper flakes (if using). Set aside.

5. To make the dough, mix together 1/4 cup (60 mL) whole wheat flour and 1/4 cup (60 mL) all-purpose flour in a small bowl and set aside.

6. In a large bowl, combine the rest of the whole wheat and all-purpose flours, wheat bran, flaxseed, pizza yeast, sugar and salt. Add water and oil and mix until well blended. Add the reserved flour as needed to make a smooth dough.

7. Turn dough and any loose pieces out on to a well-floured surface.

INGREDIENT NOTE:

Pizza Yeast—Homemade pizza right out of the oven is hard to beat and the good news for lovers of homemade pizza is, it just got easier. Fleischmann's has come up with an easy to use yeast formulated especially for pizza making—applicably sold as "Pizza Yeast." All you do is add the yeast to your dry ingredients, add the liquid ingredients, mix and knead, skipping the rising process. If you can't find pizza yeast, use quick rise yeast and follow the directions on the package using the ingredients in this recipe.

PHEC TIP:

Change up the pizza by adding grilled onions, mushrooms or another seasonal vegetable on top.

8. Knead until dough is smooth and elastic, approximately 3 minutes.
9. Press or roll dough out to fill a pizza pan. Set aside.
10. Spread ricotta mixture over uncooked crust leaving a 1/2-inch (1 cm) border. Top evenly with shaved asparagus.
11. Bake for 12 to 15 minutes until crust is brown and asparagus begins to char. Cool for 2 to 3 minutes before slicing. Serve.

Makes one 12-inch (30 cm) pizza crust One serving = 1/6 pizza
Per serving: 307 Calories, 12.3 g Total Fat, 3 g Saturated Fat, 0 g Trans Fat, 574 mg Sodium, 35.7 g Carbohydrate, 5.3 g Fibre, 6.5 g Sugars, 3.2 g Added Sugars, 14 g Protein
Carbohydrate Choices: 2

WHO KNEW YOU COULD BBQ A PIZZA?

1. Preheat barbecue on high. Divide dough into four equal balls. Place 4 pieces of parchment paper on your counter. Roll or press dough in to 4 circles. Lightly brush both sides with 1 Tbsp (15 mL) canola oil.
2. Place pizza dough on the grill and peel off parchment paper. Close lid, reduce heat to medium-high for 1 minute. Rotate pizza 1/4 turn and continue to grill for 1 minute.
3. Remove from grill and flip the grilled side up. Spread ricotta mixture over uncooked crust leaving a 1/2-inch (1 cm) border. Top evenly with shaved asparagus.
4. Turn off one side of the grill and place pizzas on that side. Close lid and bake for 6 to 8 minutes or until the asparagus has wilted. Serve.

INGREDIENTS

DOUGH

1 Tbsp (15 mL) granulated sugar

1 cup (250 mL) warm water
(100–110°F/38–43°C)

1 tsp (5 mL) traditional yeast

2 Tbsp (30 mL) natural wheat
germ

1 tsp (5 mL) iodized salt

2 cups (500 mL) whole wheat
flour

1/2 tsp (2 mL) canola oil

TOPPINGS

1 tsp (5 mL) dried basil

1/2 tsp (2 mL) dried oregano

1/2 tsp (1 mL) dried thyme

2 tsp (10 mL) water

1/2 tsp (2 mL) canola oil

2 cloves garlic, minced

One 5 oz (140 g) pkg low fat
goat cheese

3/4 cup (180 mL) loosely packed
spinach, roughly chopped

2.6 oz (75 g) cooked chicken
breast, shredded (see note)

3/4 cup (185 mL) cherry
tomatoes, halved

1 cup (250 mL) shredded low-fat
mozzarella cheese

Spinach and Goat Cheese Pizza Summer/Fall

Corinne Kamphuis, PHEc

*"My family grows spinach, cherry tomatoes and fresh herbs
in the summer, so I'm always looking for ways to use my homegrown
ingredients. Flatbreads and pizzas are family favourites so this recipe
makes for a happy family. I used to make this pizza using a cream
cheese and pesto base, however I switched to goat cheese and an
herb spread to lower the fat content and increase some of
the nutrients."* —Corrine

METHOD

For the yeast purists in the pizza-making crowd, here's one for you. It's
also a great way to re-invent leftover chicken.

1. To make the dough, combine sugar and water in a large bowl.
   Sprinkle yeast overtop and let sit for 10 minutes (until the yeast is
   foaming on top). Add wheat germ, salt (do not omit!) and flour. Mix
   until a soft dough is formed.
2. Move dough onto a lightly floured surface, and knead for
   approximately 15 minutes.
3. Lightly oil a large bowl. Place dough in the bowl, cover and let sit
   in a warm place until dough has doubled in bulk (approximately 1
   hour).
4. Roll dough into a 12-inch (30 cm) round disc. Place in a preheated
   400°F (200°C) oven for 8 to 10 minutes. Remove crust from the
   oven and let cool on a wire rack.

5. In a small bowl mix together basil, oregano, thyme and water. Let sit for 3 minutes.
6. Remove goat cheese from its package and place in a medium bowl.
7. Heat oil in a frying pan. Add herb mix and garlic and cook over low to medium heat for 3 to 4 minutes, until garlic is softened. Add the herb and garlic mixture to the goat cheese. Mix thoroughly and spread evenly over crust.
8. Top with spinach, chicken and cherry tomatoes. Sprinkle Mozzarella cheese over top.
9. Bake for 10 minutes then broil until cheese is golden brown, approximately 2 minutes. Cool for 2 to 3 minutes before slicing. Serve.

Makes one 12-inch (30 cm) pizza crust One serving = 1/6 pizza
Per serving: 295 Calories, 8.4 g Total Fat, 3.7 g Saturated Fat, 0 g Trans Fat, 614 mg Sodium, 35.5 g Carbohydrate, 4.8 g Fibre, 3.3 g Sugars, 1.2 g Added Sugars, 19.3 g Protein
Carbohydrate Choices: 2

INGREDIENT NOTE:
Shredded Chicken—To shred a cooked chicken breast into small shreds you will need two forks. Use one fork to hold the chicken breast steady. Place the chicken breast on a clean plate or clean cutting board and use the other fork to drag or scrape across the meat, forming small shreds.

SPINACH

Spinach loves cooler weather and a sandy soil—two plusses for many parts of Canada. These green nutrient-dense leaves are available fresh from March to September, depending on where you are living. If you are living in BC give a shout out to your growing season—your local spinach arrives at market in March. The people living in Ontario and Quebec have to wait until May, with the Prairies and the Maritimes having the longest wait. Their local spinach isn't available until June.

INGREDIENTS

2 Tbsp (30 mL) canola oil

3 Tbsp (45 mL) whole wheat flour

1 shallot, diced

1 tsp (5 mL) dry mustard

1/8 tsp (0.5 mL) nutmeg

2 cups (250 mL) skim milk

1 1/2 cups (375 mL) macaroni
pasta

1 1/2 cups (375 mL) shredded old
white cheddar

1/2 cup (125 mL) shredded
Gruyere

1 Tbsp (15 mL) grated Canadian
Parmesan cheese

1/4 cup (60 mL) whole wheat
bread or Panko crumbs (see
note)

Mac and Cheese Multi-seasonal Michele McAdoo, PHEc

Al dente pasta (Italian for "to the tooth," or—food translation—it isn't mush, and it's slightly firm when you chew it) has a lower glycemic index than overcooked pasta, which means that good old regular pasta can be a healthy choice for you, so long as you cook it correctly.

When making a pasta dish that needs to be baked, undercook the pasta even further. The pasta will cook to the correct mouthfeel in the oven and won't become a mushy high glycemic index mess.

METHOD

1. Preheat oven to 350°F (180°C). Line a 9-inch (2.5 L) casserole pan with wet parchment paper (see page 388).
2. Put a large pot of water on high heat and bring to the boil.
3. Meanwhile, heat oil in a medium saucepan and whisk in flour.
4. Whisk in mustard and nutmeg. Slowly pour in milk, whisking the entire time. Bring to a low boil and let simmer for 2 to 3 minutes or until thickened, whisking occasionally.
5. Meanwhile, add pasta to the boiling water and cook for 5 minutes; it should be firm but not crunchy. Drain.
6. While the pasta is draining, add cheddar and Gruyere cheeses to the white sauce. Stir until melted.

7. Add drained pasta to the cheese sauce; stir to evenly coat. Spoon mixture into the prepared casserole pan.
8. In a small bowl, mix together bread crumbs and Parmesan cheese, sprinkle over pasta. Bake for 20 minutes or until bubbly and the pasta is al dente. Serve.

Makes 4 cups (1 L) mac and cheese One serving = 1 cup (250 mL)
Per serving: 550 Calories, 28 g Total Fat, 13.2 g Saturated Fat, 0.2 g Trans Fat, 414 mg Sodium, 46.5 g Carbohydrate, 2.4 g Fibre, 8.2 g Sugars, 0 g Added Sugars, 27.5 g Protein
Carbohydrate Choices: 3

AND THE WINNER IS...

We have amazing and versatile cheese makers in Canada. Not only are we famous for our cheddars, but Canadian cheese makers are making Ricotta, Gouda, Blue, Swiss, Parmesan, Smoked, Flavoured, Mozzarella, Brine Ripened and a variety of soft and semi soft cheeses.

The Grand Champion Cheese honoured at the annual Canadian Cheese Grand Prix for 2015 was a Cream-enriched Soft Cheese with bloomy rind from Laliberté, Fromagerie du Presbytère, QC.

INGREDIENT NOTE

Panko Crumbs—Panko Bread Crumbs are made fresh from specially baked, crustless bread. They tend to be crisper and lighter than regular bread crumbs. For testing these recipes, we used the whole wheat version made by Kikkoman, which is available in Canada. You can use regular whole wheat bread crumbs instead of whole wheat panko, but the topping won't be as crispy. Shas Sha Co. also makes crispy spelt breadcrumbs, which are available across Canada and another substitute for panko.

PHEC TIP:

To bump up the nutrient score of this recipe, add 1 cup (250 mL) of one or more of the following: steamed pieces of cut-up broccoli, green beans or peas. Add vegetables to the pasta and sauce mixture before spooning into the casserole pan.

1 Tbsp (15 mL) canola oil

One 8 oz (227 g) pkg sliced fresh
  cremini mushrooms, chopped

2 small fresh Portobello
  mushrooms, chopped

1/2 onion, diced

1 clove garlic, minced

3 cups (750 mL) baby spinach

1/4 cup (60 mL) unsalted butter

1/4 cup (60 mL) all-purpose flour

4 1/2 cups (1.12 L) skim milk

1/4 tsp (1 mL) ground nutmeg

1/4 tsp (1 mL) iodized salt

1/4 tsp (1 mL) fresh ground black
  pepper

2 cups (500 mL) shredded Italian
  cheese blend, divided (see
  note)

1 omega-3 egg

One 16 oz (475 g) container light
  Canadian ricotta cheese

20 oven ready cannelloni tubes

1 Tbsp (15 mL) chopped fresh
  parsley

INGREDIENT NOTE:

Italian Cheese Blend—Make
your own Italian cheese blend
using 1 cup (250 mL) grated
mozzarella, 1/2 cup (125 mL)
grated Swiss and 1/2 cup (125
mL) grated parmesan.

Mushroom and Spinach Cannelloni with Italian Cheese Blend Sauce Fall/Winter

Shirley Ann Holmes, PHEc (with permission from Mushrooms Canada)

Professional home economists work in the food industry creating recipes for marketing boards and food companies. In the early 1990s, then OHEA member Shirley Ann Holmes adapted this recipe from a Mushrooms Canada consumer contest; we gave it a 2014 makeover.

METHOD

1. Preheat oven to 350°F (180°C). Line 13- × 9-inch (33 × 23 cm) baking dish with wet parchment paper (see page 388).
2. Heat a large non-stick skillet over medium heat; add oil and mushrooms and sauté until mushrooms have browned, approximately 4 to 5 minutes.
3. Add onion and garlic and sauté for 2 minutes. Add spinach and stir just until wilted. Remove from heat, tip into a bowl and set aside to cool.
4. Wipe out the pan with a paper towel, return to heat and reduce to medium. Add butter and let melt, stir in flour until smooth and bubbling. Gradually whisk in milk; increase heat and, stirring constantly, bring to boil. Gently boil for about 2 minutes or until thickened and smooth. Add nutmeg, salt and pepper plus 1 cup (250 mL) of the shredded Italian cheese blend; stir just until melted and remove from heat. Spread 1 cup (250 mL) of sauce on bottom of the prepared pan.

5. In a food processor, pulse cooled mushroom mixture, egg and ricotta cheese and process until well mixed; pipe mushroom filling (see note) into cannelloni and arrange in single layer in the sauce.

6. Pour remaining sauce over top of pasta, taking care that each tube is well covered. Cover and bake for 45 minutes, then uncover and sprinkle with remaining 1 cup (250 mL) Italian cheese blend and bake for 10 minutes or until hot and bubbling. Broil to just brown the top. Allow to cool 5 minutes, top with parsley, cut into 10 equal servings.

Makes 10 servings One serving = 1/10 recipe
Per serving: 304 Calories, 14 g Total Fat, 7.6 g Saturated Fat, 0.5 g Trans Fat, 376 mg Sodium, 28 g Carbohydrate, 1.3 g Fibre, 10 g Sugars, 0 g Added Sugars, 16.8 g Protein
Carbohydrate Choices: 2

HEALTH BITE

Mushrooms may be little balls of fungus, but they pack a nutritional wallop. Four or five mushrooms contain a legion of B vitamins plus minerals—selenium, copper, potassium, iron and zinc. Those same four or five mushrooms, depending on the variety, even offer 1 to 2 g of fibre. Mushrooms are the only vegetable that contains vitamin D, and the winner in this category is the Shiitake mushroom. One serving supplies 48 percent of the recommended daily value for this important sunshine vitamin.

PHEC TIPS:
- No piping bag? No worries: use a large resealable plastic bag, fill with mushroom mixture, cut a 1-inch (2.5 cm) hole in the bottom corner of bag and pipe the filling into the shells. (Cathy Ireland, recipe taster)
- To make ahead, bake covered for 45 minutes. Cool, wrap and freeze for future use. Thaw in refrigerator overnight; bake covered in oven until hot; remove cover, sprinkle cheese on top and proceed as above.

INGREDIENTS

Cranberry Sauce (makes 2
    cups/500 mL)
1 cup (250 mL) granulated sugar
1 cup (250 mL) water
3 cups (750 mL) fresh or frozen
    cranberries

Plum Compote (makes 2
    cups/500 mL)
4 black plums, pitted and
    chopped
1 Tbsp (15 mL) unsalted butter
1 Tbsp (15 mL) packed brown
    sugar
1 Tbsp (15 mL) pure maple syrup

Baked Goat Cheese
10 oz (300 g) plain goat cheese
    (approx. 1 log), partially frozen
    (for easier slicing)
1/3 cup (80 mL) finely chopped
    walnuts
4 oz (120 g) prosciutto (approx.
    8 slices)

Baked Goat Cheese with Cranberry or Plum Compote
Multi-seasonal Joan Ttooulias, PHEc

This elegant appetizer starts off with warmed goat cheese and is
followed by a choice of either Cranberry Sauce or Plum Compote
spooned over top. Oh and then there's the fried prosciutto…and maybe
a glass of VQA wine…

Note: This is a high-end appetizer that comes with high-end
calories, grams of fat and sodium. Treat this appetizer as a treat; I
repeat, treat this as a treat.

METHOD

1. To make cranberry sauce: In medium saucepan dissolve sugar in
   water over medium heat. Add cranberries, bring to a boil, reduce
   heat and simmer for 10 minutes or until berries are cooked; cool.
   Serve sauce at room temperature. Store leftovers in a covered
   container in the fridge for up to 1 week.
2. To make plum compote, cook plums in a microwave at 50% power
   for 10 minutes. Stir in butter, brown sugar and maple syrup. Serve
   compote at room temperature. Store leftovers in a covered container
   in the fridge for up to 1 week.
3. Partially freeze the goat's cheese for 30 minutes to firm. Preheat
   oven to 425°F (220°C). Cut using a sharp knife into 8 equal
   portions.
4. Press both sides of goat cheese slices into the walnuts and place on
   a parchment lined baking sheet. Bake for 5 minutes.
5. In a large skillet over medium-high heat, fry the prosciutto for 30
   seconds each side just to warm. Place two goat's cheese slices on
   a serving plate. Drape a prosciutto slice over each piece of cheese.
   Add 2 Tbsp (30 mL) of compote or sauce. Serve immediately.

Makes 8 slices goat cheese One serving = 2 goat cheese slices with 2 Tbsp (30 mL) Plum Compote
Per serving: 362 Calories, 27 g Total Fat, 13.4 g Saturated Fat, 0 g Trans Fat, 876 mg Sodium,
5.3 g Carbohydrate, 0.9 g Fibre, 4 g Sugars, 1.5 g Added Sugars, 23.4 g Protein
Carbohydrate Choices: less than 1

One serving = 2 goat cheese slices with 2 Tbsp (30 mL) Cranberry Sauce
Per serving: 399 Calories, 26.4 g Total Fat, 13 g Saturated Fat, 0 g Trans Fat, 877 mg Sodium,
16.8 g Carbohydrate, 1.4 g Fibre, 14.3 g Sugars, 12.6 g Added Sugars, 23.4 g Protein
Carbohydrate Choices: 2 1/2

GOAT'S MILK

When it comes to the Canadian Dairy Goat Industry, Ontario and
Quebec are leading the way.

Woolwich Dairy, the largest goat cheese manufacturer in Canada is
based in Orangeville, Ontario. This family owned and operated dairy
has been in business for the past 30 years. They make over 50 goat's
milk cheeses as well as goat's milk ice cream, including my personal
favourite: chocolate.

The Dairy Sheep Industry is relatively small in comparison to the
Dairy Cow and Dairy Goat Industries. More of a niche product, local and
artisan sheep cheese producers sell sheep cheese at farmers' markets
and higher-end grocery stores. Monforte Dairy, out of Stratford, Ontario,
is one of the leaders of sheep cheese production in Canada.

GOT A GOAT?

The fat particles in goat's milk are much smaller than the fat particles in
cow milk. This makes it sometimes easier to tolerate by people who are
lactose intolerant. Goat's milk is similar to cow milk in the protein and
calcium departments, weighing in with nine grams of protein and 337
milligrams of calcium per cup, compared with eight grams of protein
and 276 milligrams of calcium in one cup of cow's milk.

Grains, Make Them Whole

102 What is a Whole Grain?

104 Creamy Herbed Polenta

106 Barley 101

109 Easy Family-Friendly Barley Pilaf (Microwave Method)

110 Pearl Barley and Butternut Squash Risotto

112 Barley Stuffed Acorn Squash

115 Greek Barley Salad

116 Wild Rice and Vegetable Pilaf

118 Wheatberry and Lentil Salad

119 The World of Oats

121 Jambalaya

124 Overnight Blueberry Irish Oatmeal for Two

126 Toasted Oatmeal Cookies

127 Oat Barley Cookies

Grains are grown in every province in Canada but have become an iconic symbol of *Life on the Prairies*. We grow a wide variety of grains from barley to wheat, but not all grains grown in Canada are designated official grains under the Canada Grain Act. Some of the most popular *official* grains are: barley, oats, rye, triticale, wheat, flaxseed, buckwheat and corn. The types of commodities not considered a grain are: canary seed, quinoa, kamut and spelt.

We've created recipes using the most popular grains—barley, oats, wheat, cornmeal—and we threw in wild rice as a salute to Manitoba.

WHAT IS A WHOLE GRAIN?

The family of grains can be confusing. Botanically speaking, true grains are members of the grass family, and the Canadian grown members include: wheat, oats, rye, millet, corn, triticale, spelt, kamut and barley. We also grow buckwheat and quinoa, which are *considered* grains in the food world, but technically aren't grains at all. We also grow wild rice which isn't actually a rice but a grass. For 140 recipes using quinoa, check out the OHEA's *The Vegetarians Complete Quinoa Cookbook* (Whitecap 2012) which won The People's Choice Award at Taste Canada's Food Writing Awards in 2013.

They may have different botanical names but what every grain, sometimes called a "kernel," has in common are these three parts: the bran, the endosperm and the germ. The healthiest way to eat a grain is when all three of these parts are included, hence the term "whole grain".

The **bran** is the outer layer of the grain/kernel and provides our bodies with B vitamins, minerals and much needed fibre.

The **germ** is where the *germination* takes place and although it is the smallest part of the grain/kernel it packs a whollop of nutrients. Its function is to provide food for the seed if it was planted, as in the word "germination." It provides both the seed and our bodies with B vitamins, vitamin E, minerals and healthy fats.

The **endosperm** is the inner layer of the seed. Its job is to supply energy through its carbohydrate and protein content. There is a small amount of vitamins, minerals and fibre.

Refine a grain and you lose the bran and the germ, plus it's bye-bye to most of the fibre and at least 80% of the disease-protecting antioxidants.

Some grains like oats and barley are covered in an inedible papery outer layer called a hull. In most cases the hull is mechanically removed to make the grain edible, but there are varieties of hulless oats and barley that are grown in Canada. See Hulless Oats on page 120.

HEALTH BITE

Whole grains are good for you. Unless you're a person living with celiac disease or have been diagnosed by a doctor with a gluten sensitivity, whole grains should be included in your diet.

Whole grains are full of fibre and loaded with vitamins, minerals and antioxidants that can help reduce the risk factors for many long-term diseases. The health rule of thumb is that the least amount of processing of a whole grain equals the highest amount of health benefits.

Every time you choose a whole grain *over* a refined grain you are also reducing your chances of developing heart disease, type 2 diabetes and certain cancers. Plus your GI (gastrointestinal) tract is begging for whole grains. Your gut needs food for the good bacteria that helps promote a healthy immune system. If you don't eat foods that feed these good bacteria, your gut will suffer and so will your long-term health.

INGREDIENTS

1 cup (250 mL) whole grain
    medium ground cornmeal
4 cups (1 L) 1% milk
1/2 tsp (2 mL) iodized salt
1 Tbsp (15 mL) finely chopped
    fresh basil
1 Tbsp (15 mL) finely chopped
    fresh parsley
3/4 cup (175 mL) finely shredded
    extra old white cheddar

Creamy Herbed Polenta Multi-seasonal

Erin MacGregor, PHEc, RD

Professional home economist and registered dietician Erin MacGregor came up with this great no-fuss technique for making soft polenta. This is super easy to make and great with stews or the Ratatouille on page 167 seen in the picture on the adjacent page.

METHOD

1. Preheat oven to 350°F (180°C).
2. Whisk together cornmeal, milk and salt in a 9-inch (1.5 L) ovenproof covered dish.
3. Bake for 40 minutes with cover on. Remove cover and bake for an additional 10 minutes.
4. Remove from oven, stir in herbs and cheese and let sit for 15 minutes to thicken. Serve.

Makes 5 cups (1.25 L) One serving = 1/2 cup (125 mL)
Per serving: 132 Calories, 5 g Total Fat, 2.6 g Saturated Fat, 0 g Trans Fat, 233 mg Sodium, 15 g Carbohydrate, 1 g Fibre, 5.5 g Sugars, 0 g Added Sugars, 7.1 g Protein
Carbohydrate Choices: 1

BARLEY 101

"It's always better to eat your barley than to drink your barley ...
just kidding!"
—John F. Smith (Mairlyn's dad)

Barley can be eaten as a hot or cold side dish, added to soups and salads, prepared as a morning cooked cereal or consumed in alcohol. My dad's right: the barley that's good for your heart is the type you eat, not the type you drink.

Barley may be one of the oldest cereal grains grown in the world (dating back 10,000 years) but in recent years it's become a newly discovered grain here in Canada, gaining popularity mainly because it is rich in beta-glucan, a type of soluble fibre that has been linked to reducing blood cholesterol. It also tastes great, with a nutty flavour, and can be used instead of rice in most dishes.

Eat 1/2 cup (125 m) cooked pearl or pot barley daily and you've reached 60 per cent of the daily amount of soluble fibre shown to help lower cholesterol. Add a medium apple, another source of soluble fibre, and you are in the *soluble fibre zone*.

In 2013 barley received a health claim from Health Canada, which is *no mean feat.* The process is long and complicated and takes years of scientific research. Thanks to the work by Agriculture and Agri-Food Canada scientist Dr. Nancy Ames and her team in Winnipeg, Manitoba, the health claim applies to foods that contain at least one gram of beta-glucan from barley grain products per serving. This includes dehulled or hulless barley, pearl (or pot) barley, barley flakes, grits, meal flour and bran as well as beta-glucan enriched milling fractions. These ingredients can be used in a wide variety of recipes for cooking or baking. To learn more about barley check out www.gobarley.com.

BASIC BARLEY PREPARATION

The ratio of barley to liquid is 1 cup (250 mL) pot barley to 3 cups (750 mL) of liquid (use lower or no sodium added chicken, vegetable, beef broth or plain water). Bring to a boil, cover, reduce the heat and simmer for 40 to 50 minutes or until cooked. It should be chewy but not rubbery or mushy. Stir once or twice to evenly distribute any remaining liquid, remove from heat and let sit covered for 5 to 10 minutes. You will get around 3 to 3 1/2 cups (750 to 875 mL) cooked barley. Serve. Leftovers can be stored in the fridge in a covered container for up to 4 days. Reheat as is, add to a soup or use in a salad.

TYPES OF BARLEY

- Whole grain barley, sometimes called hulled barley, is the whole grain form of barley. Only the inedible outer hull or husk has been removed.
- Pearled barley has gone through a pearling machine (which removes the tough outer hull and polishes the kernel) until the bran layer has been removed.
- Pot barley has gone through a pearling machine for less time than pearled barley, so most of the bran is intact.
- Soluble fibre remains present in the barley regardless of the pearling.

BARLEY

Canadians are constantly appearing in food research news. Case in point: there is a new type of barley developed in Canada called Quick Cooking Barley. Progressive Foods Inc., a food company out of Alberta, has created a precooked and dried hulless whole-grain barley that cooks up in 10 minutes. It's convenient and nutrient dense; I've tried it and I love it.

Barley is the third largest crop grown in Canada, just behind wheat and canola. Barley is grown throughout Canada, though Alberta takes Gold as the leader of the barley growing pack.

Easy Family-Friendly Barley Pilaf (Microwave Method)
Multi-seasonal Sue Soderman, PHEc

"This is a great side dish to replace the usual rice or potatoes. Best of all it's easy to make and cooks in a short time." —Sue

Barb Holland PHEc, our microwave expert, tested the recipe using a 1100-watt microwave oven.

METHOD
1. In an 8-cup (2 L) microwave-safe casserole dish with a lid, combine mushrooms, shallot and butter.
2. Cover and microwave on high for 1 minute.
3. Add broth and barley and microwave on high for 10 to 12 minutes or until the barley is almost tender and most of the liquid is absorbed, stirring once.
4. Add peas, cover and let stand for 10 to 15 minutes or until most of the liquid has been absorbed. Stir in salt, season with pepper and serve.

Makes 4 cups (1 L) One serving = 1/2 cup (125 mL)
Per serving: 127 Calories, 1.4 g Total Fat, 0.7 g Saturated Fat, 0 g Trans Fat, 109 mg Sodium, 25 g Carbohydrate, 5.2 g Fibre, 1.7 g Sugars, 0 g Added Sugars, 4.5 g Protein
Carbohydrate Choices: 1

INGREDIENTS

3 cremini mushrooms, sliced
1 large shallot, diced
2 tsp (10 mL) unsalted butter
2 cups (500 mL) no salt added chicken broth
1 cup (250 mL) pearl barley, rinsed using a wire strainer
1 cup (250 mL) frozen peas, no need to thaw
1/4 tsp (1 mL) iodized salt
Pepper to taste

PHEC TIP:
This recipe stores well and any leftovers can be reheated in the microwave the next day.

INGREDIENTS

1 very small butternut squash
(approx. 1 lb/450 g)

2 Tbsp (30 mL) canola oil, divided

1/8 tsp (0.5 mL) cracked black
pepper

5 cups (1.25 L) no salt added
chicken broth, divided

2 small shallots, finely diced

2 Tbsp (30 mL) fresh thyme,
picked from stems

1 cup (250 mL) pearl barley,
lightly rinsed using a wire
strainer (see note)

1/2 cup (125 mL) Canadian VQA
dry white wine

1/2 cup (125 mL) grated
Canadian parmesan cheese

1/2 tsp (2 mL) iodized salt

INGREDIENT NOTE:

Barley—In this recipe, don't
over rinse the barley—you need
the starch to help thicken the
risotto, so a light rise will do.

Pearl Barley and Butternut Squash Risotto Fall/Winter

Emily Kichler, SHEA Student Member

This risotto is decadent, delicious and a healthier spin on the usual risotto made with refined rice. It's creamy and flavourful, but also full of fibre, vitamins and nutrients.

METHOD

1. Preheat oven to 425°F (220°C). Line a rimmed baking sheet with parchment paper.

2. Peel butternut squash, cut in half, remove seeds with a spoon and dice into 1/2-inch (1 cm) cubes. You should have approx. 4 cups (1 L) of diced squash. Spread cubes onto a baking sheet, drizzle with 2 tsp (10 mL) oil and sprinkle with pepper. Bake for about 15 to 25 minutes, or until tender, tossing halfway through. When cooked through, remove from heat and cool.

3. While the squash is roasting, heat the chicken stock in another saucepan and let it simmer.

4. Meanwhile, in a medium saucepan over medium-low heat, heat remaining oil and add shallots. Sauté for about 10 to 15 minutes or until soft and translucent.

5. Stir in thyme and barley, stirring in well to coat each grain with the oil for about 4 minutes; do not allow mixture to brown.

6. Deglaze the saucepan by adding the wine and stirring to incorporate, scraping any flavoured bits sticking to the bottom of the pan. Wait until the wine has been fully absorbed, then add 1

cup (250 mL) of the hot chicken stock, stirring occasionally. The mixture should be cooking at a vigorous simmer over medium heat.

7. When most of the chicken stock has been absorbed and the barley starts to get thick and dry, add another 1/2 cup (125 mL) stock. Don't allow the barley to get too dry as the starch can burn on the bottom of the pot. Continue this process of adding the stock by 1/2 cup (125 mL) additions and stirring frequently until all the stock has been added and the barley is tender. Don't move, stay with your risotto—you need to tend to it. Bring a book, listen to music, but do not answer the phone; you need to focus. This should take about 35 to 40 minutes.

8. Remove the risotto from the heat and stir in the roasted squash, Parmesan cheese and salt. Serve immediately.

Makes 5 1/2 cups (1.3 L) One serving = 1 cup (250 mL)
Per serving: 307 Calories, 8.5 g Total Fat, 2.2 g Saturated Fat, 0 g Trans Fat, 433 mg Sodium, 45 g Carbohydrate, 7.8 g Fibre, 4 g Sugars, 0 g Added Sugars, 10.3 g Protein
Carbohydrate Choices: 2 1/2

SQUASH

Butternut squash is one of the most popular winter squash grown in Canada; following closely behind is Buttercup, Acorn and Spaghetti. This squash is a powerhouse of the disease-lowering antioxidant beta-carotene and the blood pressure-lowering mineral potassium; including any one of these squash to your diet is a boost to your health.

INGREDIENTS

1/3 cup (80 mL) pearl barley,
rinsed using a wire strainer

1 cup (250 mL) no salt added
chicken broth

2 medium-sized acorn squashes
(see note)

1 small onion, diced

1 clove garlic, minced

3/4 cup (185 mL) chopped button
mushrooms

1 roasted red pepper, chopped
(see note)

1/2 apple (Northern Spy, Russet
or a tart Canadian apple),
diced

1/2 cup (125 mL) chopped
walnuts

1/2 tsp (2 mL) crumbled dried
sage leaves

Salt and pepper (optional)

1/2 cup (125 mL) shredded old
cheddar cheese

PHEC TIP:

For show appeal we cut the squash sidewise to feature the detail of the edges (see pic). There is less of a cavity so you will have more stuffing than needed. Bake off extra stuffing in an oiled casserole dish.

Barley Stuffed Acorn Squash Fall/Winter

Rosemary Vanderhoeven, PHEc

"On the farm I grew up on we always had a large vegetable garden and squash was a vegetable that I looked forward to eating each fall. Mom prepared it simply; she roasted it and melted her homemade butter on top. This recipe adds a few more ingredients and dresses the squash up into a superb main dish while adding a modern twist to an old favourite." —**Rosemary**

METHOD

1. Place barley in a small saucepan with broth and bring to the boil; cover, reduce heat to simmer and cook until tender, about 25 to 35 minutes.

2. Preheat oven to 375°F (190°C). Line a 9- × 13-inch (23 × 33 cm) rimmed baking sheet with wet parchment paper (see page 388). Set aside.

3. Scrub squash well. Cut in half lengthwise and remove seeds, scooping out some squash to make a larger cavity. Place squash cut side down on the prepared pan.

4. Bake for 45 minutes or until flesh is tender when pierced with a sharp knife. Remove squash and increase oven temperature to 425°F (220°C). If the parchment paper is burnt, discard and reline pan with clean parchment paper.

INGREDIENT NOTES:

Squash—To prevent the squash halves from rolling around in the pan, cut a small slice off the rounded side of each squash half so they will sit flatly in the pan.

Roasted Red Pepper—For convenience, feel free to buy roasted peppers in a glass bottle. Freeze any leftovers, or see How To Roast Your Own Peppers on page 151.

5. In a 4-cup (1 L) microwave-safe container, cook onion and garlic in microwave on high for 1 minute. Stir. Add mushrooms and cook for 1 additional minute on high. Stir, add cooked barley, roasted red pepper, apple, walnuts and sage. Mix together and cook on high for 1 minute. Taste and season with salt and pepper if desired.

6. Place squash in prepared pan and spoon mixture into squash halves. Sprinkle cheese on top. Bake for 10 minutes or until cheese is bubbly and mixture is heated through.

Makes 4 servings One serving = 1/2 squash
Per serving: 353 Calories, 17 g Total Fat, 5 g Saturated Fat, 0.2 g Trans Fat, 207 mg Sodium, 44.4 g Carbohydrate, 8.5 g Fibre, 5 g Sugars, 0 g Added Sugars, 11.8 g Protein
Carbohydrate Choices: 2 1/2

Greek Barley Salad Spring/Summer Carol Frail, PHEc

A great spin on the traditional Greek salad.

METHOD

1. In a medium saucepan, combine barley and broth. Bring to a boil, cover, reduce heat to medium-low and simmer for approximately 25 to 35 minutes, or until barley is cooked and all of the broth has been absorbed. Remove from heat, fluff with a fork and cover. Let sit for 5 minutes. Spread out on a large baking sheet to cool.

2. Make the salad in a large bowl; toss together red pepper, cucumber, tomato, capers and onion. Set aside.

3. For the dressing, take a small bowl and whisk together the oil, vinegar, garlic, oregano, salt and pepper.

4. When the barley has cooled (about 30 minutes), add the barley to the vegetables and toss.

5. Just before serving, drizzle the dressing over the salad and toss until evenly coated. Crumble feta cheese and sprinkle over top. Serve immediately.

Makes 6 cups (1.5 L) One serving = 1 cup (250 mL)
Per serving: 244 Calories, 11.7 g Total Fat, 1.8 g Saturated Fat, 0.2 g Trans Fat, 296 mg Sodium, 29.4 g Carbohydrate, 6.7 g Fibre, 3.7 g Sugars, 0 g Added Sugars, 6.6 g Protein
Carbohydrate Choices: 1 1/2

INGREDIENTS

Salad
1 cup (250 mL) pot barley, rinsed using a wire strainer
3 cups (750 mL) no added salt chicken broth
1 red pepper, diced
1/2 English cucumber, diced
1 medium tomato, diced and drained
2 Tbsp (30 mL) capers, drained and minced
1/2 small red onion, peeled and thinly sliced

Dressing (makes approx. ½ cup/125 mL)
1/4 cup (60 mL) canola oil
3 Tbsp (45 mL) apple cider vinegar
1 large clove garlic, minced
1/2 tsp (2 mL) dried oregano
1/4 tsp (1 mL) iodized salt
Pepper to taste

1/4 cup (60 mL) feta cheese, crumbled

INGREDIENTS

1 cup (250 mL) wild rice

2 1/2 cups (625 mL) no salt
added chicken broth

1 Tbsp (15 mL) canola oil

1 medium carrot, scrubbed well
and diced

1 rib celery, thinly sliced

1 small onion, diced

1 small red sweet pepper, diced

2 cloves garlic, minced

1 cup (250 mL) thinly sliced
cremini mushrooms (approx. 3
large mushrooms)

2 tsp (10 mL) dried oregano
leaves

2 tsp (10 mL) dried thyme leaves

2 Tbsp (30 mL) chopped fresh
parsley

1/4 tsp (1 mL) salt

Freshly ground black pepper, to
taste

PHEC TIPS:

• We need a good variety of
vegetables in our diet every
day. This pilaf will help with
that! Other vegetables can be
substituted as desired. Try diced
zucchini or tomatoes, sliced leeks,
cauliflower or broccoli florets or
chopped kale. Instead of sautéing
the vegetables, another option is
to roast them in the oven while
the wild rice is cooking.

Wild Rice and Vegetable Pilaf Multi-seasonal Wendi Hiebert PHEc

*"I first tasted wild rice many years ago while living in the small northern
Manitoba community of Cranberry Portage. Some friends harvested wild rice
on their property just outside of town, and I quickly learned to love the chewy
texture and nutty flavour of this aquatic grain (it's not actually rice!) and
appreciate its versatility.
This pilaf was originally made with just celery and mushrooms, but over the
years I've added other vegetables to boost the colour of the dish, as well as to
incorporate more vegetables into my diet."* —Wendi

METHOD

1. Combine wild rice and broth in a medium saucepan and bring to a
    boil. Reduce heat, cover and simmer until rice is tender but slightly
    chewy and split open, about 40 to 45 minutes. Remove from heat
    and let stand, covered, for 5 minutes. Drain any remaining broth, or
    reuse later if desired (see PHEc Tip).

2. A few minutes before rice finishes cooking, heat oil in a large skillet
    over medium heat. Add carrot, celery, onion and sweet pepper.
    Cook, stirring frequently, for 5 minutes. Add garlic, mushrooms
    oregano and thyme. Continue to cook, stirring frequently until
    vegetables are tender, about 3 to 4 minutes.

3. Stir cooked rice and parsley into vegetables and season with salt
    and pepper.

Makes 3 cups One serving = 3/4 cup (185 mL)
Per serving: 219 calories, 4 g Fat, 0.4 g Sat. Fat, 0 g Trans Fat, 210 mg Sodium,
39 g Carbohydrates, 4.7 g Fibre, 5.9 g Sugars, 0 g Added Sugars, 8.2 g Protein

PHEC TIPS:

• Don't throw out the broth drained from the cooked rice. Save it and add it to homemade soup or stew. If
desired, water can be substituted for the broth in the recipe. Turn this dish into a salad by letting the cooked rice
and vegetables cool, then adding a few splashes of your favourite vinaigrette.

Dressing (makes 6 Tbsp/90 mL)

3 Tbsp (45 mL) canola oil

2 Tbsp (30 mL) white wine
vinegar

2 tsp (10 mL) liquid honey

1/4 tsp (1 mL) iodized salt

1 pinch freshly ground black
pepper

Salad

3/4 cup (185 mL) wheat berries,
rinsed and drained

1 cup (250 mL) cooked brown
lentils (see p. 221-222) *or*
use canned lentils, rinsed and
drained

1 cup (250 mL) toasted walnut
halves (see note)

3 thinly sliced green onions

1 large red-skinned apple,
scrubbed well, cored and
chopped

INGREDIENT NOTE:

Walnuts—To toast walnuts,
preheat oven to 350°F (180°C),
spread out on a baking sheet
and roast for 5 minutes. Remove
from oven and let cool; chop and
set aside.

Wheatberry and Lentil Salad Fall/Winter Erin MacGregor, PHEc, RD

*"Wheat berries are whole, unprocessed wheat kernels that contain
the bran, the germ and the endosperm. This recipe works well
as a side and is a great potluck contribution. Adding lentils,
a good source of protein, makes it a meal in itself."*—Erin

METHOD

1. In a small sauce pan, cover wheat berries with 1 1/2 to 2 inches (4
   to 5 cm) of water. Bring to a boil, reduce heat to medium-low and
   simmer uncovered for 45 minutes. Drain and cool.
2. Make the dressing in a small bowl; whisk together oil, vinegar,
   honey, salt and pepper.
3. In a large bowl, combine the wheat berries, lentils, walnuts, green
   onions and apple. Pour dressing over top and toss well. Serve.

Makes 5 1/2 cups (1.3 L) One serving = 3/4 cup (175 mL)
Per serving: 266 Calories, 16.2 g Total Fat, 1.4 g Saturated Fat, 0 g Trans Fat, 77 mg Sodium,
25.6 g Carbohydrate, 5 g Fibre, 5.3 g Sugars, 1.5 g Added Sugars, 7.7 g Protein
Carbohydrate Choices: 1 1/2

THE WORLD OF OATS

If you've been oat hunting at your local grocery store, you are well aware that oats come in many shapes and sizes. There are steel-cut and rolled oats. To add to the confusion steel-cut oats have multiple names, and rolled oats come in subcategories.

Steel-Cut Oats: These are the cleaned whole-grain oat that has been cut with steel cutters. But just to keep you on your toes, they're *sometimes* called Scotch or Irish oats. Used mostly for hot cereal, this cooked oat is chewy and has a nuttier flavour than rolled oats. It's the kind my Granny ate, and she lived to be 98 (which she always credited to her morning bowl of oats when she was growing up).

Large Flake or Old Fashioned Rolled Oats: These oats are the same as the cleaned whole grain oats used to make steel-cut. The difference lies in the processing. Rolled oats have been toasted, hulled, steamed and then flattened or rolled out with giant rollers, hence the name.

Quick Cooking Oats: These are similar to rolled oats, but they have been cut before being steamed and flattened. This helps them cook quicker.

Instant Oats: These convenient oats are mostly sold flavoured with added sugars and salt. They are cut, precooked, dried, steamed and then flattened, which is why all you need to do is add boiling water. They come as whole grain (which means the oat bran has been added back in) or regular. If convenience is important, choose the instant whole grain version.

Oat Bran: This is the outer husk of the whole oat, which contains most of the fibre and some of the fat. Keep it in a cool dry place; I store mine in the fridge or freezer. Look for plain oat bran, sometimes called oat

cereal or oat porridge. In Canada, Rogers and Quaker both sell plain oat bran.

HEALTH BITE

Oats, oat bran and oatmeal are very high in soluble fibre, and it's the same kind of soluble fibre that barley contains: beta-glucan. This type of soluble fibre dissolves in water and becomes a thick viscous gel that slowly travels through the intestine, slowing down the absorption of glucose (which helps to stabilize blood sugars, a definite bonus for people living with diabetes). Beta-glucans prevent the re-absorption of bile, which forces your liver to get its cholesterol from your blood. The beta-glucans in your blood in turn sop up the "bad" LDL (low-density lipoprotein) cholesterol. I like to envision it as a drain cleaner commercial—the foamy soluble fibre cleaners unplugging your arteries as they go. The oat fibre may also bind to any cholesterol in your intestine, soaking it up and escorting it out of your body.

HULLESS OATS

The All-Canadian substitute for rice is hulless oats. Oats have hairy fibres on the outside layer, and hulless (or "naked") oats, specifically the AC Gehl variety, were developed in Canada with the help of Agriculture and Agri-Food Canada (AAFC) scientists led by Dr. Vern Burrows, aka Dr Oats, in the mid 1990's.

HOW TO COOK HULLESS OATS

To properly cook a pot of hulless oats, bring 2 cups (500 mL) water to a vigorous boil and add 1 cup (250 mL) hulless oats. Reduce heat to a low boil for approximately 35 to 40 minutes. Doneness test: the oats will be plumper and the texture should be soft and chewy. Note: Some kernels will open, most will not, and all of the water will have been absorbed. Remove from heat, fluff with a fork and let sit for 5 to 10 minutes.

Jambalaya Fall/Winter

Mairlyn Smith, PHEc

(adapted with permission from *Healthy Starts Here!* [Whitecap 2011])

"This is my spin on a Jambalaya I once had in New Orleans. The hulless oats add a Canadiana spin as well as a chewy characteristic. I adapted this recipe from my cookbook Healthy Starts Here! *(Whitecap 2011)."*—Mairlyn

METHOD

1. Heat a large pot over medium heat. Once the pot is fully heated, push the sausage meat out of the casing and brown the meat. (It's sort of fun and sort of gross all at the same time.) Break it up with the back of a wooden spoon as you are browning it.

2. Add onion and sauté for about 5 minutes. Add garlic, both peppers and celery and sauté for 2 minutes.

3. Add thyme, cayenne, salt and hullless oats and stir until the oats are well coated and the spices smell fragrant.

4. Add tomatoes, making sure to scrape the bottom of the pot with a wooden spoon so the little browned bits are incorporated into the dish—this will add flavour and prevent the oats from sticking while they're cooking.

5. Bring to the boil, cover, reduce heat to simmer and cook for 45 to 50 minutes or until the oats are tender and cooked through, stirring occasionally. Once the oats are tender, remove from heat, stir, replace lid and let sit for 10 minutes. Serve. Store any leftovers in a resealable container in the fridge for up to four days.

Makes 7 cups (1.75 L) One serving = 1 1/4 cups (310 mL)
Per serving: 177 Calories, 5 g Total Fat, 1.3 g Saturated Fat, 0 g Trans Fat, 492 mg Sodium, 22 g Carbohydrate, 4.5 g Fibre, 6.6 g Sugars, 0 g Added Sugars, 12.8 g Protein
Carbohydrate Choices: 1

INGREDIENTS

2 spicy Italian turkey sausages (approx. 10 oz/280 g)
1 onion, diced
4 cloves garlic, minced
1 red pepper, coarsely chopped
1 green pepper, coarsely chopped
3 stalks celery, coarsely chopped
2 Tbsp (15 mL) ground thyme
1/4 tsp (1 mL) cayenne pepper
1/4 tsp (1 mL) iodized salt
1 cup (250 mL) hulless oats, rinsed and drained
One 28 fl oz (796 mL) can no salt added diced tomatoes

1 Tbsp (15 mL) hemp hearts

1–2 Tbsp (15–30 mL) ground
flaxseed

1/4 tsp (1 mL) cinnamon

1/2 cup (125 mL) fresh seasonal
(or frozen local) fruit or berries,
or 1/4 cup (60 mL) dried
berries or fruit

Grab a bowl of Canadian 100% whole grains for breakfast

Not to glorify the world's perception of Canadians and our cold winter months, but we really do embrace a bowl of hot porridge during the winter, eh? For heart health and the health of your GI tract, choose 100% whole grain cereal: steel-cut oats, oatmeal, Sunny Boy or Ancient Grains—they're all loaded with both soluble and insoluble fibre. Soluble fibre helps reduce your "bad" LDL cholesterol levels as well as ridding your body of toxins, whilst insoluble fibre keeps everything moving along your GI tract as it exits the building.

Follow the directions on the package, then bump up your nutrient score in every bowl by adding:

CHOOSE FROM:

- Sunny Boy originated in Camrose, Alberta and uses locally grown wheat, rye and flaxseed to create their hot cereal. See sunnyboyfoods.com/our-food/hot-cereal.
- Roger's 9 Grain includes wheat, oats, millet, flaxseed, rye, barley, triticale, sunflower seeds and corn meal. See www.rogersfoods. com/rogers-9-grain.
- Roger's Ancient Grains includes oat, rye, barley, spelt and khorasan flakes, oat bran, millet, flaxseed and quinoa flakes. See www. rogersfoods.com/porridge-oats-ancient-grains.
- Quaker's line includes steel-cut and large flake oats, as well as instant whole grain oats.

1 1/4 cups (310 mL) cold water

1/4 cup (60 mL) Scottish, Irish or
steel-cut oats

1/4 cup (60 mL) oat bran

1/4 cup (60 mL) dried
blueberries or any dried fruit

1/2 cup (125 mL) skim milk *or*
fortified organic soy beverage

Generous sprinkle of cinnamon

Sweetener to taste (optional)

Overnight Blueberry Irish Oatmeal for Two Fall/Winter

Mairlyn Smith, PHEc (with permission from *Healthy Starts Here!* [Whitecap 2011])

If you don't think that you have time to make oatmeal from scratch every morning, this is the answer for you: the nutty chewy goodness of cooked steel-cut oats in about 10 minutes. You can double, triple or quadruple this recipe, just get a bigger pot.

METHOD

1. A couple of hours before you get ready for bed, bring the water to the boil in a medium microwave-safe container. When the water has boiled, stir in oats, cover and let sit for 30 minutes. (If you don't have a microwave, just boil the water and add the oats.)

2. Put into the fridge. I wrote to Health Canada about the safety of leaving this out all night on the counter and the Coles notes of their response was, "ARE YOU OUT OF YOUR MIND? NO!"

3. As soon as you get up the next morning, take the oatmeal out of the fridge, stir and pour into a small pot on the stove. If it looks really thick add a little more water.

4. Heat over medium and bring back to the boil. Add oat bran and dried blueberries, stir well and let simmer for 5 minutes, stirring occasionally.

5. Remove from heat, stir, divide in half, add milk, sprinkle with cinnamon, and sweetener of choice if desired, and enjoy.

Makes approx. 1 1/2 cups (375 mL) One serving = 3/4 cup (175 mL) with skim milk
188 Calories, 2.4 g Total fat, 0.4 g Sat Fat, 0 g Trans Fat, 36 mg Sodium, 37.8 g Carbs, 5 g Fibre,
13.9 g Sugars, 2 g Added Sugars, 8 g Protein
Carbohydrate Choices: 2

BLUEBERRIES

Drive along a country road in the Fraser Valley, BC and you will see why Canada is the world's second-largest producer and exporter of these nutrient-dense little orbs. In British Columbia, Ontario, Quebec and the Atlantic provinces, workers handpick the sweetest fruits for the table market, while mechanical pickers scoop up the berries destined for freezing and processing.

Low bush and high bush blueberries are grown in different parts of the country. Low bush or wild blueberries are grown in Quebec, the Maritimes and in Ontario. British Columbia pretty much has cornered the market in high bush or cultivated blueberries, growing 93 percent of all high bush blueberries in Canada.

SOY BEVERAGES

You can only make milk from mammals, so any liquid "milk" made from beans, seeds, nuts or grains must be called a beverage. All soy beverages are fortified with vitamins and minerals. To make sure you're getting those benefits in every serving, shake the carton well before pouring. When it comes to soy beverages, choose one that has been made with a whole soybean. My recommendation is to avoid beverages using carrageenan, a thickener derived from seaweed, which may cause health problems.

INGREDIENTS

4 cups (1 L) old-fashioned rolled
oats

1 tsp (5 mL) baking powder

1 tsp (5 mL) ground cinnamon

3/4 cup (185 mL) unsalted butter,
softened

3/4 cup (185 mL) packed dark
brown sugar

1/2 cup (125 mL) granulated
sugar

1 Omega-3 egg

1 tsp (5 mL) pure vanilla extract

1 cup (250 mL) finely diced
red-skinned apple (choose a
sweet, firm apple such as an
Empire or Gala)

PHEC TIP:

Feel free to substitute 1 cup (250
mL) raisins for the apple.

Toasted Oatmeal Cookies (food processor) Multi-seasonal

Cathy Ireland, PHEc

"I remember my mom baking cookies every week, and I like carrying on that tradition with my kids. This recipe makes me feel like my kids are getting some nutrition, so I don't feel guilty if they have a couple on their way out the door in the morning!" —Cathy

METHOD

1. Position rack in the middle of the oven. Preheat oven to 350°F (175°C). Line a cookie sheet with parchment paper and set aside.
2. Spread oats on a separate rimmed baking sheet and bake until lightly toasted, about 20 minutes; stir after 10 minutes.
3. Grind oats in a food processor using the blade attachment until they're the consistency of whole wheat flour. Add baking soda and cinnamon.
4. Using a hand held mixer or a wooden spoon, beat butter and sugars in a large bowl, until blended. Add egg and vanilla and continue to beat until smooth. Add flour mixture and stir in the apple.
5. Drop dough onto the prepared pan in 1 tsp (5 mL) amounts, spacing each 2 inches (5 cm) apart. Flatten slightly with a fork.
6. Bake 10 to 12 minutes or until golden brown. Cool on baking sheets for 2 minutes, then remove and place on wire racks. Cool completely. Store in a covered container for up to 1 week or freeze for up to 3 months.

Makes 45 cookies One serving = 1 cookie
Per serving: 70 calories, 2 g Fat, 0.9 g Sat. Fat, 0 g Trans Fat, 6 mg Sodium,
12 g Carbohydrates, 0.85 g Fibre, 6 g Sugars, 5.8 g Added Sugars, 1.25 g Protein
Carbohydrate Choices: 1

Oat Barley Cookies Multi-seasonal

Katie Brunke, OHEA Student Member

Soluble fibre can help lower your cholesterol. Aside from apples, the pulse family and eggplant, good old Canadian oats and barley are loaded with it. For more info see page 39.

METHOD

1. Position rack in the middle of the oven. Preheat oven to 325°F (160°C). Line 2 large rimmed baking sheets with parchment paper.
2. In a large bowl, mix together rolled oats, barley flour, baking soda, baking powder and cinnamon; set aside.
3. In a separate large bowl, use electric beaters to beat together the butter, honey and maple syrup until smooth. Once fully combined, beat in the egg until mixture is thick.
4. Slowly beat the dried mixture into the wet mixture until fully combined.
5. Using a large spoon, mix in dried cranberries until well combined.
6. Using a cookie scoop (or your hands) make small dough balls, approx. 2 Tbsp (30 mL) each. Place dough balls on the prepared baking sheets, spacing each ball 1 inch (2.5 cm) apart. You will get 12 cookie balls per baking sheet.
7. Bake until lightly browned, about 15 to 18 minutes. Let cookies cool for 5 minutes, remove from pan and continue cooling on a wire rack for 10 minutes before serving. Cookies can be stored in a container with a tight fitting lid for up to 1 week.

Makes 24 cookies One Serving= 1 cookie
Per serving: 148 calories, 5 g Fat, 2.8 g Sat. Fat, 0.2 g Trans Fat, 101 mg Sodium, 24.3 g Carbohydrates, 2 g Fibre, 11 g Sugars, 10.1 g Added Sugars, 2.6 g Protein
Carbohydrate Choices: 1 1/2

INGREDIENTS

2 cups (500 mL) large flake rolled oats
1 cup (250 mL) barley flour
3/4 tsp (4 mL) baking soda
1/2 tsp (2 mL) baking powder
1/2 tsp (2 mL) cinnamon
1/2 cup (125 mL) unsalted butter, at room temperature
1/4 cup + 2 Tbsp (90 mL) liquid honey
1/4 cup + 2 Tbsp (90 mL) pure maple syrup
1 omega-3 egg
1 cup (250 mL) dried cranberries

A Soup for Every Season

131 Soup for Your Good Health

132 Spiced Ambercup Squash Soup with Maple Syrup

135 Root Vegetable Potage

136 Canadian Aged Cheddar and Asparagus Soup

138 Curried Carrot Soup

139 Traditional French Onion Soup

140 Mushroom Soup

142 Corn Chowder

144 Silky Summer Corn Bisque

145 Maple Parsnip Soup

146 Quebec-Style Pea Soup

147 Red Lentil and Kale Soup

148 Spicy Red Lentil Soup

150 Roasted Red Pepper, Pear, Corn and Carrot Soup

152 Shamrock Soup

154 Borscht

IS IT BROTH OR STOCK?
Broth is a clear liquid made by boiling water with meat, fish, poultry or vegetables. It generally comes sold in cans, Tetra Pak packaging or in a dried version as either a powder or a cube. Stock is a heartier liquid made from simmering a source of protein (meat, fish or poultry and/or fresh bones) with water, vegetables and seasoning. Usually homemade, stocks can be purchased at higher-end grocery stores or speciality food shops. We have used broth in all of the recipes because it's an easier and more accessible choice. If you have homemade stock, use it instead of the broth for a heartier flavour.

Soup is the ultimate chameleon. It can morph itself into a starter, a hot or cold entrée, a remedy for a cold or an aid in your weight loss program. If you've got a menu dilemma, soup can be part of the solution.

Using locally grown ingredients we have a soup for every season, 15 in total, so have a read through and choose one to make this week.

SOUP FOR YOUR GOOD HEALTH

All soups will make you feel full. Any guesses as to why? The vegetable content? The range of complex carbohydrates? Yes, to all of the above, but the main reason soups make you feel full is because they all have a high water content.

Want to lose weight? Choose a broth based or vegetable based soup to begin your meal. Studies have shown that people who eat one of these two types of soup as a first course end up consuming less calories for the entire meal. A serving of the traditional Asian miso soup is one solution, or for a quick and easy soup heat up some no-salt-added chicken broth, toss in diced carrots and celery and some minced garlic. Heat through until the vegetables are tender. Remove from heat and sprinkle with thinly sliced green onions and serve. Both of these soups are low in calories, plus both will help fill you up before the main course.

Want to arm your body with immune enhancing warriors? Choose a broth-based soup made with mushrooms, garlic, ginger and hot peppers. Although all mushrooms are powerful immune enhancers, shiitake mushrooms have long been heralded in Japan as super immune enhancers. Science has shown that mushrooms increase T-cell function, which in turn strengthens your immune system.

Want your family to eat more vegetables? Soups are great vehicles for sneaking them in. Try *Spiced Ambercup Squash Soup with Maple Syrup* on page 132 to get your beta carotene fix for the day, or try either of the two soups using red lentils on page 147-148 to up your legume intake. Legumes are heart healthy, rich in protein, low in fat and are loaded with disease lowering antioxidants, and soups are a great way to add them to your diet.

INGREDIENTS

One 3 lb (1.4 kg) ambercup
   squash (see note)

3 Tbsp (45 mL) canola oil, divided

1 large onion, chopped

3 cloves garlic, minced

3 cups (750 mL) no salt added
   vegetable broth

1 Empire apple, peeled, cored and
   chopped

1 tsp (5 mL) grated fresh ginger
   (see note)

1 tsp (5 mL) Madras curry powder

1/2 tsp (2 mL) cinnamon

1/4 tsp (1 mL) nutmeg, freshly
   grated

1/2 tsp (2 mL) iodized salt

1/4 tsp (1 mL) freshly ground
   black pepper

1–2 Tbsp (15–30 mL) amber or
   dark pure maple syrup

2 cups (500 mL) skim milk

1/8–1/4 tsp (0.5–1 mL) green
   Tabasco sauce

16 chives, for garnish (optional)

Spiced Ambercup Squash Soup with Maple Syrup

Fall/Winter Jennifer Goodwin, PHEc

"I was never a fan of squash but thanks to my Grandmother's encouragement I finally relented and began to grow a few varieties. I found that I actually liked the darker, denser and sweeter heritage-type squashes; enter turban, buttercup and ambercup. Then several years ago I tried a cup of butternut squash soup at a local restaurant and though it was delicious. I left thinking I could create something even better. After several experiments using ambercup squash, this soup was created, a fusion of spices and homegrown produce that has become a family favourite."—Jennifer

This deep orange coloured soup has the best of both flavour-note worlds; it's a little bit spicy and a little bit sweet. It was a huge hit the day we tested it, and the flavours are well worth the work it takes to hack open the squash.

METHOD

1. Preheat oven to 375°F (190°C). With a large sturdy knife, cut the squash in half and remove seeds and pulp. Peel and dice into 1-inch (2.5 cm) chunks; place into a large roasting pan. Drizzle with 1 1/2 Tbsp (22 mL) oil and toss to coat. Roast for 45 minutes or until the squash is soft and beginning to brown slightly. Toss occasionally throughout the roasting process to prevent burning.

2. When the squash is cooked, heat a large saucepan over medium heat. Add the rest of the oil plus the onion and garlic, sautéing until soft and slightly browned, about 5 to 7 minutes. Remove from heat and add the squash.

3. Place the empty roasting pan on a separate element over medium heat and pour in broth. Once the liquid begins to boil, reduce to

INGREDIENT NOTE:

Ambercup Squash—
Ambercup squash is a deep orange squash that looks like its cousin the buttercup squash. Its flesh is darker in colour and slightly sweeter in flavour. Can't find an Ambercup? Buttercup (or their more distant cousin Butternut) will also work for this recipe.

Ginger—Peel ginger using the bowl of a spoon, holding the stalk of the spoon and then dragging it down the sides of the ginger; wrap and store any leftover ginger in the freezer. Grate into recipes as needed.

PHEC TIP:
This soup may be quite thick depending on the type and age of the squash. Add more broth, water or milk until you reach desired thickness.

simmer, scrapping up any bits for added flavour. Pour into the large saucepan.

4. Add apple, ginger, curry, cinnamon, nutmeg, salt and pepper. Return to heat and bring to a gentle boil; reduce heat, cover and simmer until the apple is soft, about 15 minutes.

5. Add maple syrup, milk and Tabasco and stir in well. Remove from heat. Using a hand held immersion blender, puree the soup OR transfer to a blender or food processor and puree in smaller batches and return soup to saucepan. Garnish with whole chives if desired. See picture.

6. Reheat if necessary; serve or store in the fridge for up to two days. Freeze any leftovers up to three months.

Makes 8 cups (2 L) One serving = 1 cup (250 mL)
Per serving: 176 Calories, 5.7 g Total Fat, 0.5 g Saturated Fat, 0 g Trans Fat, 202 mg Sodium, 31 g Carbohydrate, 4 g Fibre, 13 g Sugars, 1.5 g Added Sugars, 4.3 g Protein
Carbohydrate Choices: 2

MADRAS CURRY POWDER

In traditional South Asian cuisine, a curry is a dish cooked in a sauce. To most Canadians however, a curry is a powder that you add to a dish to give it heat. Curry powders are created by blending many spices together, and blends of curry powders range from spicy to very spicy, depending on what area that curry blend was created. Sweating cools you down, so areas that are very hot tend to have curry blends that produce sweating. Madras is an area in India that is very hot, hence this blend is fairly spicy.

Root Vegetable Potage Fall/Winter

Emily Dobrich, SHEA Student Member

"Potage is a type of thick soup or stew of French origin. The vegetables are cooked until they are tender so that the flavours have had time to "mingle and meld." I think one of the greatest comforts during a true Canadian winter, especially after time spent outside in the cold, is the reward of a warm bowl of potage. This hearty and filling dish hits the spot perfectly."—Emily

METHOD

1. In a large Dutch oven or a large heavy bottomed pot, melt butter over medium heat. Add onions and sauté for 3 to 5 minutes. Add garlic and sauté for 1 minute. Add leeks, rosemary, thyme and sage and continue sautéing for approximately 3 minutes, or until the leeks have softened.
2. Add the rest of the vegetables and stir well.
3. Pour in the vegetable broth, add salt and bring to a boil. Cover, reduce to medium-low and simmer for 35 to 45 minutes or until vegetables are very soft and tender. Season with pepper and serve. Stores for up to 3 days covered in the fridge, or freeze any leftovers for up to 3 months.

Makes 16 cups (4 L) One serving = 2 cups (500 mL)
Per serving: 172 Calories, 3.3 g Total Fat, 2 g Saturated Fat, 0.2 g Trans Fat, 231 mg Sodium, 35.4 g Carbohydrate, 5.2 g Fibre, 12.8 g Sugars, 0 g Added Sugars, 3.3 g Protein
Carbohydrate Choices: 2

INGREDIENTS

2 Tbsp (30 mL) unsalted butter

2 large onions, diced

3 cloves garlic, minced

3 leeks, thinly sliced (see note p. 63)

1 tsp (5 mL) dried rosemary

1/2 tsp (2 mL) dried thyme leaves

1/2 tsp (2 mL) dried sage

2 carrots, scrubbed well, chopped into 1/2-inch (1 cm) cubes

1 small rutabaga, peeled and chopped into 1/2-inch (1 cm) cubes

2 parsnips, scrubbed well and chopped into 1/2-inch (1 cm) cubes

2 large sweet potatoes, scrubbed well and chopped into 1/2-inch (1 cm) cubes

3 large baking potatoes, scrubbed well and chopped into 1/2-inch (1 cm) cubes

8 cups (2 L) no salt added vegetable broth

1/2 tsp (2 mL) iodized salt

Pepper to taste

INGREDIENTS

1 1/2 lb (700 g) asparagus,
   trimmed and cut into 1-inch
   (2.5 cm) pieces (see note)
4 medium Yukon Gold potatoes,
   peeled and diced
1 onion, chopped
2 1/2 cups (625 mL) no salt
   added chicken broth
2/3 cup (160 mL) water
1/2 tsp (2 mL) dried thyme leaves
1 cup (250 mL) 1% or skim milk
1/2 tsp (2 mL) iodized salt
1/2 cup (125 mL) shredded
   white Canadian aged cheddar
   cheese, divided
Freshly ground pepper to taste
1 Tbsp (15 mL) chopped fresh
   chives

Canadian Aged Cheddar and Asparagus Soup Spring
Teresa Makarewicz, PHEc

Anyone you know an asparagus abstainer? This soup is a great way to re-introduce the unbelievably good-for-you asparagus to naysayers.

METHOD

1. In a large pot over high heat, combine asparagus, potatoes, onion, broth, water and thyme.
2. Bring to a boil, reduce heat to medium-low, cover and simmer for 10 to 15 minutes or until vegetables are tender.
3. Remove from heat. Using a hand held immersion blender, puree the soup OR transfer to a blender or food processor and puree in smaller batches and return soup to saucepan.
4. Stir in milk, salt and 1/4 cup (60 mL) of the cheese. Heat over medium heat, stirring often, for about 5 minutes or until hot and the cheese has melted; season with pepper to taste.
5. Ladle into warm bowls; top bowls evenly with remaining cheese and chives. Serve.

Makes 6 cups (1.5 L) One serving = 1 1/4 cups (310 mL)
Per serving: 245 Calories, 5 g Total Fat, 3.1 g Saturated Fat, 0.1 g Trans Fat, 399 mg Sodium, 40.5 g Carbohydrate, 5.8 g Fibre, 9 g Sugars, 0 g Added Sugars, 12.2 g Protein
Carbohydrate Choices: 2

ASPARAGUS

Asparagus has been called the Harbinger of Spring, which is your first tip-off as to when locally grown asparagus is available: it's in the Spring. If it's the dead of winter and asparagus is available at your local grocery store, it came to Canada on the Asparagus Bus from distant shores. I prefer locally grown seasonal asparagus not only for the flavour but in support of asparagus farmers right across Canada. I make the most of local asparagus when it arrives to market in May and June and eat my fill for those two short months.

ASPARAGUS TIPS:

• To trim asparagus, bend the asparagus toward the bottom of the stalk. The asparagus spears will naturally snap and break at the point where the stalks become tough. Reserve the woody stalks for use in homemade vegetable stock or add to your compost bin.

• When purchasing asparagus, look for bright green stalks that are crisp, straight and have tightly closed, compact tips. There is no difference in tenderness between slender and thick asparagus spears, but you should select uniform size to ensure even cooking.

• To store fresh asparagus, cut 1/4 inch (6 mm) off the bottom of the spears and stand upright in an inch (2.5 cm) of water. Cover loosely with plastic and refrigerate OR wrap trimmed ends in damp paper towels and refrigerate in a plastic bag.

INGREDIENTS

1 clove garlic, minced

1 Tbsp (15 mL) canola oil

1 onion, chopped

5 medium carrots, scrubbed well
and chopped

1 Tbsp (15 mL) minced fresh
ginger

1 Tbsp (15 mL) curry paste, hot or
mild (see note)

4 cups (1 L) no salt added chicken
or vegetable broth

1/2 cup (125 mL) dried red lentils,
rinsed and drained

1/2 tsp (2 mL) iodized salt

1/4 tsp (1 mL) freshly ground
black pepper

Chopped cilantro (optional)

INGREDIENT NOTE:

Curry Paste—Curry paste
provides an authentic rounded
flavour. There are various ones
available from mild to hot—your
choice.

Curried Carrot Soup Fall/Winter

Barb Holland, PHEc

This lovely golden-hued soup is easy to prepare, economical and heart healthy. Serve with rustic whole grain bread or naan.

METHOD

1. Heat a large saucepan over medium heat; add oil, onion and carrots and sauté for 5 minutes or until lightly softened.
2. Stir in ginger, garlic and curry paste and sauté 30 seconds.
3. Add the broth and lentils. Bring to a boil, cover, reduce heat and simmer 20 minutes or until carrots are tender.
4. Remove from heat; using a hand-held immersion blender, puree the soup OR transfer to a blender or food processor and puree in smaller batches and return soup to saucepan.
5. Reheat if necessary. Season to taste with salt and pepper. Garnish each serving with cilantro if desired. Serve.

Makes 6 cups (1.5 L) One serving = 1 1/2 cups (375 mL)
Per serving: 188 Calories, 4.3 g Total Fat, 0.4 g Saturated Fat, 0.1 g Trans Fat, 484 mg Sodium, 32 g Carbohydrate, 5.4 g Fibre, 10.5 g Sugars, 0 g Added Sugars, 7.7 g Protein
Carbohydrate Choices: 2

CARROTS

If any of these varieties rings a bell—Caropak, Cellobunch, Chancellor, Six-Pak, Avenger, Apache or Caro-chief —you, my friend, must be a Canadian carrot farmer.

Traditional French Onion Soup Fall/winter

Mairlyn Smith, PHEc

Go ahead and dig out the old French onion soup bowls you received as
a wedding gift back in the 1970's, because everything old is new again.
No onion soup bowls? Scour garage sales, flea markets or second-hand
stores, or use oven-safe high-sided bowls instead.

METHOD

1. Heat a large pot over medium-low heat; add oil or butter and
   onions, sautéing until the onions are very (I repeat, very) soft, about
   20 to 25 minutes (if they start to stick or look dry you might have to
   add another 1 Tbsp/15 mL oil or butter). Stir very often (I know, I
   know, there's a lot of sweat equity in this recipe, but it's all worth it).
2. Add flour, salt and pepper, stirring to coat the onions. Add garlic,
   parsley and thyme. Stir well. Add broth, wine and sherry, bring to
   the boil and cover. Reduce heat to low and gently simmer for 45
   minutes, stirring occasionally. When the soup is ready, remove from
   heat.
3. To toast baguette slices, preheat broiler and place a wire rack inside
   a rimmed baking sheet, place baguette slices on top and toast each
   side of the bread until browned. Takes all of 1 to 3 minutes.
4. Spoon soup into bowls. Place 2 toasted baguette pieces on top of
   the soup and top with one-fifth of the cheese per bowl. Place under
   broiler until the cheese is melted and lightly browned. Serve.

Makes 8 cups (2 L) One serving = 1 1/2 cups (375 mL)
Per serving: 334 Calories, 14.6 g Total Fat, 5.9 g Saturated Fat, 0 g Trans Fat, 486 mg Sodium, 28 g
Carbohydrate, 2.4 g Fibre, 6.4 g Sugars, 0 g Added Sugars, 13.2 g Protein
Carbohydrate Choices: 2

INGREDIENTS

4 large onions, thinly sliced
2 Tbsp (30 mL) canola oil or
  unsalted butter
2 Tbsp (30 mL) all-purpose flour
1/2 tsp (2 mL) iodized salt
Pinch of pepper
3 large cloves garlic, minced
1 Tbsp (15 mL) chopped fresh
  parsley
1 tsp (5 mL) dried thyme leaves
4 cups (1 L) no salt added chicken
  broth
1 cup (250 mL) dry Canadian
  VQA white wine
2 Tbsp (30 mL) Canadian sherry
10 thin slices whole wheat
  baguette (approx. 1/2 a
  baguette)
1 1/2 cups (375 mL) shredded
  Canadian Gruyere

1 Tbsp (15 mL) canola oil

1 leek, cleaned and sliced (see note p. 63)

2 garlic cloves, minced

1 lb (450 g) white button mushrooms, sliced

1 lb (450 g) assorted wild mushrooms, sliced

4 cups (1 L) low sodium chicken broth

1 Tbsp (15 mL) chopped fresh tarragon

2 tsp (10 mL) apple cider vinegar

1 can (370 mL) evaporated skim milk

1/2 tsp (2 mL) iodized salt

Mushroom Soup Fall/Winter

Cathy Ireland, PHEc

"I love to entertain friends and family. This soup is a great starter recipe and sets the stage for the rest of the meal to come." —Cathy

METHOD

1. Heat a large skillet over medium, heat oil and add the sliced leek. Cook and stir until softened, about 5 minutes. Stir in garlic and cook until fragrant, about 1 minute. Add mushrooms. Cook and stir until mushrooms lose moisture, about 15 to 20 minutes. Reserve 1/4 cup (60 mL) mushrooms for garnish.

2. Add broth and tarragon and bring to a boil. Reduce heat and simmer uncovered an additional 10 minutes to develop flavours. Add apple cider vinegar and remove from heat.

3. Use a hand-held immersion blender to puree the soup *or* transfer to a blender or food processor and puree in smaller batches, then return soup to saucepan.

4. Add milk and salt and simmer 5 minutes until heated through.

5. Garnish with reserved mushrooms. Serve.

Makes 7 cups (1.75 L) One Serving = 3/4 cup (185 mL) as a starter
Per serving: 75 Calories, 1.8 g Total Fat, 0.1 g Saturated Fat, 0 g Trans Fat, 195 mg Sodium, 11.4 g Carbohydrate, 1.5 g Fibre, 7.4 g Sugars, 0 g Added Sugars, 6.2 g Protein
Carbohydrate Choices: 1/2

MUSHROOMS

Mushrooms are readily available all year long, thanks to Canadian Mushroom Growers and Mushrooms Canada. There are over 100 mushroom farms in Canada with over 200 million pounds grown every year. Ontario tops the list, producing 50 percent of all the mushrooms produced. BC produces 35 percent, the Prairie Provinces collectively produce 10 percent, and Quebec and the Maritimes share five percent of production.

The varieties we grow in Canada that are available at your local grocery store are white button, cremini, portobello, shiitake, oyster, enoki and king oyster. At farmers' markets you can find miatake and chanterelles. All mushrooms are immune enhancing and are the only vegetable that contains vitamin D, naturally.

For more mushroom love, check out www.mushrooms.ca.

PHEC TIP:
Add 1/3 cup (80 mL) dry red wine or sherry for an extra special addition.

INGREDIENTS

2 Tbsp (30 mL) canola oil

1 Tbsp (15 mL) unsalted butter

1 cup (250 mL) diced ham **or** back bacon

2–3 shallots, chopped

3 medium potatoes, scrubbed well and diced

2 stalks celery, thinly sliced on the diagonal

2 cups (500 mL) low sodium chicken or vegetable broth

One 14 oz (398 mL) can creamed corn

1 1/2 cups (375 mL) skim or 1% milk

1 cup (250 mL) finely chopped celery leaves **or** a chiffonade made from Brussels sprouts, kale or beet greens (see note)

Salt and pepper to taste

Corn Chowder Multi-seasonal Diane O'Shea, PHEc

"My now-grown children, all four of them, say this recipe was their very favourite from their childhood and teen years. For over 25 years our farm produced high-quality vegetables such as sweet corn and potatoes to be sold at farmers' markets in Stratford, St. Mary's, Grand Bend and Exeter. Chowders like these are "forgiving" recipes, as exact ingredient quantities are not a major concern. For example, in-season vegetables such as red, yellow and green peppers can easily be added. Corn chowder should be hearty fare with plenty of chopped vegetables in a creamy broth, and with a little ham or bacon for colour and flavour." —**Diane**

For the harried time crunchers out there, this recipe is super quick, easy to make and delicious.

METHOD

1. In a large heavy saucepan over medium heat, warm oil. Add butter and allow it to melt without browning.
2. Add ham or back bacon and sauté until browned. Add shallots and sauté until soft, about 2 to 3 minutes.
3. Add potatoes and celery. Toss well to coat. Add broth, bring to a boil and cover. Reduce heat and simmer until all the vegetables are very soft, about 15 to 20 minutes.
4. Stir in creamed corn and milk and heat through. Add your favourite green—we tried it with kale to rave reviews. Heat through until the greens are wilted; serve. Salt and pepper to taste.

Makes approx. 6 cups (1.5 L) One serving = 1 cup (250 mL)
Per serving: 232 Calories, 9.1 g Total Fat, 2.3 g Saturated Fat, 0.2 g Trans Fat, 538 mg Sodium, 28.5 g Carbohydrate, 2.3 g Fibre, 9.5 g Sugars, 0 g Added Sugars, 10.4 g Protein
Carbohydrate Choices: 2

BACK BACON

Bob and Doug MacKenzie, a couple of Canuck hosers from SCTV, are famous for putting the *Great White North* on the comedy map and Back Bacon aka Canadian Bacon or Peameal Bacon on the foodie radar.

Not your average bacon, back bacon is a larger cut that includes both the pork loin and the pork belly, making it leaner than regular bacon.

PHEC TIPS:

• When your local fresh sweet corn is in season, cut kernels from 2 or 3 cobs and add to step 3 to bump up the flavour.

• In the fall, when red, yellow and green peppers are abundant, add 1 cup (250 mL) finely diced bell pepper for colour, texture and flavour.

2 slices bacon

2 tsp (10 mL) canola oil

1 tsp (5 mL) unsalted butter

1 large onion, diced

4 large cobs of fresh, local sweet
   corn *or* 4 cups (1 L) frozen
   corn

4 cups (1 L) low sodium
   vegetable broth

1/4 tsp (1 mL) iodized salt

Pepper to taste

1 bay leaf

Silky Summer Corn Bisque Summer

Emily Kichler, OHEA Student Member

This soup is perfect to make in the peak of corn season when it's fresh, sweet and tender. It's elegant enough to entertain with, but simple enough to make any day of the week.

METHOD

1. In a large soup pot over medium heat, sauté the bacon until crisp, remove with a slotted spoon and place on a paper towel. Set aside.

2. Drain any excess fat and discard. Return pot to stove and heat over medium-low heat. Add oil and butter and heat until melted. Reduce heat to low, add onion and sauté until very soft and translucent but not browned, about 8 to 10 minutes.

3. Meanwhile, husk the corn. Remove kernels from the cobs to yield 4 cups (1 L) corn kernels. If using frozen corn, place in a colander and rinse under hot water to thaw. Set aside to drain.

4. When the onion is soft, add the corn, broth, salt, pepper and the bay leaf. Bring to a boil, cover, reduce heat to low and simmer for 15 to 20 minutes or until the corn kernels are tender. Discard the bay leaf.

5. Crumble cooked bacon and set aside. When the corn is tender, remove from heat. Using a hand-held immersion blender, puree the soup *or* transfer to a blender or food processor and puree in smaller batches, then return soup to saucepan.

6. Reheat if necessary, ladle into bowls and garnish with bacon bits. Serve.

Makes 6 cups (1.5 L) 1 Serving = 1 1/2 cups (375 mL)
Per serving: 244 Calories, 6.4 g Total Fat, 1.6 g Saturated Fat, 0.1 g Trans Fat, 279 mg Sodium, 47.3 g Carbohydrate, 5.6 g Fibre, 12.8 g Sugars, 0 g Added Sugars, 7.4 g Protein
Carbohydrate Choices: 3

Maple Parsnip Soup Multi-seasonal

Wendi Hiebert, PHEc

"Parsnips are one of my favourite vegetables. I love the flavour of this soup because of the sweetness that comes from the parsnips and maple syrup, contrasted with the subtle bite from the Dijon mustard. It's a delicious way to enjoy parsnips and the flavourful maple syrup (aka liquid gold!) produced in Quebec, Ontario and the Maritime provinces."—Wendi

METHOD

1. Heat oil in a large saucepan over medium heat; add parsnips, onion and garlic. Cook, stirring frequently, for 5 minutes.
2. Add broth; bring to a boil, cover, reduce heat and simmer until parsnips are tender, about 20 minutes.
3. Remove from heat; using a hand held immersion blender, puree the soup *or* transfer to a blender or food processor and puree in smaller batches, then return soup to saucepan.
4. In a small bowl, whisk together the milk, maple syrup and mustard until thoroughly blended. Add mixture to the soup, whisking to combine. Add salt and gently reheat soup.
5. Spoon soup into serving bowls. If desired, garnish with a drizzle of maple syrup and/or croutons.

Makes 8 cups (2 L) One serving = 1 1/3 cups (330 mL)
Per serving: 165 Calories, 2.9 g Total Fat, 0.3 g Saturated Fat, 0.1 g Trans Fat, 267 mg Sodium, 31.4 g Carbohydrate, 4 g Fibre, 18 g Sugars, 9.8 g Added Sugars, 4.4 g Protein
Carbohydrate Choices: 1

INGREDIENTS

1 Tbsp (15 mL) canola oil
1 lb (450 g) parsnips, scrubbed, trimmed and cut into 1/2-inch (1 cm) slices (see note)
1 large onion, chopped
2 cloves garlic, minced
6 cups (1.5 L) no salt added chicken broth
3/4 cup (185 mL) 1% milk or evaporated skim milk
1/3 cup (75 mL) pure maple syrup
2 Tbsp (30 mL) grainy or regular Dijon mustard
1/4 tsp (1 mL) iodized salt
Drizzle of pure maple syrup (optional)
½ cup (125 mL) croutons (optional)

INGREDIENT NOTE:

Parsnips—The lowly parsnip is loaded with blood pressure-lowering potassium. Locally grown parsnips can be bought loose or in 1 lb (450 g) bags. This recipe uses an entire bag.

INGREDIENTS

8 slices bacon, diced (low sodium recommended)

1 onion, diced

1 large carrot, scrubbed well and diced

2 cloves garlic, minced

2 tsp (10 mL) dried thyme

1/4 tsp (1 mL) freshly ground black pepper

1 bay leaf

2 medium potatoes, peeled and cubed

1 1/2 cups (375 mL) dried spilt peas, rinsed and drained

1 tsp (5 mL) iodized salt

7 cups (1.75 L) no salt added vegetable broth

1/4 cup (60 mL) finely chopped green onions (optional)

Quebec Style Pea Soup Early Spring, Fall and Winter

Carol Frail, PHEc

"What's more Canadian than visiting a sugar shack in the spring? In Quebec, it's not just about the tire au sirop d'érable (hot maple syrup poured over fresh snow, then rolled on a Popsicle stick—yum!), it's also about the all-you-can-eat feast! Traditional pea soup is made with ham hock and lard, both of which I have omitted to make this soup healthier, but without making it any less delicious." —Carol

METHOD

1. In a large soup pot over medium heat, sauté the bacon until crisp, remove with a slotted spoon and place on a paper towel. Set aside.

2. Add onion and carrots and sauté until the onion is translucent. Add the minced garlic, thyme, black pepper, bay leaf, cubed potatoes, split peas and salt. Sauté for 1 minute.

3. Add the broth and bring to a boil. Cover, reduce the heat to a simmer and cook for approximately 45 minutes or until the peas and potatoes are very soft.

4. Remove soup from the heat and remove the bay leaf; using a hand held immersion blender, puree the soup *or* transfer to a blender or food processor and puree in smaller batches, then return soup to saucepan.

5. If needed, add additional water or broth. Reheat if necessary. Sprinkle bacon over soup, stir in and serve. Sprinkle with green onion, if using.

Makes 8 cups (2 L) One serving = 1 cup (250 mL)
Per serving: 211 Calories, 10.3 g Total Fat, 3.7 g Saturated Fat, 0 g Trans Fat, 445 mg Sodium, 24.2 g Carbohydrate, 2.4 g Fibre, 7 g Sugars, 0 g Added Sugars, 7 g Protein
Carbohydrate Choices: 1 1/2

Red Lentil and Kale Soup Fall/Winter Marinoush Megardichian, PHEc

"One of my goals when I was going to Teachers College was to make all of my own meals. As a student, cost, time and nutrition were the main factors when it came to these home cooked creations. This Middle Eastern inspired soup fits the bill on all accounts. It's delicious, nutrient dense, economical, easy to make and was heart-warming during those cold winter months."—**Marinoush**

METHOD

1. Rinse kale leaves. Remove the stalks using a knife or just tear the leaves away from the stalks; discard stalks. Thinly slice leaves and set aside.

2. Heat a medium saucepan over medium heat; add oil and onion. Sauté for 3 to 5 minutes or until lightly browned.

3. Add lentils, garlic, salt, pepper, turmeric and curry powder and stir well. Add broth and water and bring to a boil. Cover, reduce heat to medium-low and simmer for 10 to 15 minutes, stirring occasionally. Test for doneness; the lentils should be very soft.

4. Add kale and stir until wilted. Serve.

Makes 5 cups (1.25 L) One serving = 1 cup (250 mL)
Per serving: 294 Calories, 7.2 g Total Fat, 0.7 g Saturated Fat, 0.1 g Trans Fat, 503 mg Sodium, 43.7 g Carbohydrate, 8 g Fibre, 3.3 g Sugars, 0 g Added Sugars, 16.4 g Protein
Carbohydrate Choices: 2 1/2

INGREDIENTS

5 large kale leaves
2 Tbsp (30 mL) canola oil
1 onion, chopped
1 1/2 cups (375 mL) dried red lentils, rinsed and drained
2 cloves garlic, minced
1 tsp (5 mL) iodized salt
1 tsp (5 mL) cracked black pepper
1/2 tsp (2 mL) turmeric
1/2 tsp (2 mL) curry powder
2 cups (500 mL) no salt added vegetable broth
2 cups (500 mL) water

NATIONAL KALE DAY

Co-founded by Dr. Kathleen Kevany and Meggie MacMichael, National Kale Day on October 14, 2014 was a kale celebration done up right. They turned a good old-fashioned Gaelic Ceilidh (pronounced kay-lee) into a Kale-leigh, celebrating kales's extraordinary health benefits along with demonstrations of how to cook it. The festival is linked to the Rural Research Centre (RRC) at Dalhousie University, a research institute focused on rural research and making connections between research and the people who shape rural life in Nova Scotia. You can join the Kale-leigh via social media—it's the first Wednesday of October every year, so don't miss out on the kalextravaganza.

1 tsp (5 mL) cracked black pepper

1 tsp (5 mL) turmeric

1 tsp (5 mL) ground cumin

1 tsp (5 mL) cinnamon

1/4 tsp (1 mL) ground allspice

2 Tbsp (30 mL) canola oil

4 large shallots, diced

3 stalks celery, diced

4 cloves garlic, minced

1 tsp (5 mL) fresh grated ginger

One 28 oz (796 mL) can diced no
   salt added tomatoes

4 cups (1 L) no salt added chicken
   broth

1 cup (250 mL) cold water

1 cup (250 mL) dry red lentils,
   rinsed and drained

8 dried apricots, coarsely chopped

1/2 tsp (2 mL) iodized salt

Spicy Red Lentil Soup Fall/Winter

Mairlyn Smith, PHEc (with permission from *Healthy Starts Here!* [Whitecap 2011])

Love spice? This soup has your name on it. Instead of using a premade curry powder, this soup uses a blend of spices to create a signature spice blend. Hearty and economical, one serving provides you with 15 grams of protein.

METHOD

1. Mix together cracked black pepper, turmeric, cumin, cinnamon and allspice in a small bowl and set aside.

2. Heat a large pot over medium heat; add oil and shallots. Sauté for 5 minutes or until golden brown. Add celery and continue to sauté until slightly soft.

3. Add garlic, ginger and the spice mixture. Sauté for 1 minute—the smell will hit you in the face, it's wonderful.

4. Add tomatoes, broth, water, lentils, apricots and salt. Bring to a boil, cover, reduce heat to simmer and cook for 35 to 40 minutes or until the lentils have "melted" into the soup, stirring occasionally. Serve. Can be made up to 2 days in advance and stored in the fridge.

Makes 8 cups (2 L) One serving = 2 cups (500 mL)
Per serving: 249 Calories, 3.3 g Total Fat, 0.8 g Saturated Fat, 0 g Trans Fat, 435 mg Sodium, 42.9 g Carbohydrate, 8.6 g Fibre, 15.2 g Sugars, 0 g Added Sugars, 15 g Protein
Carbohydrate Choices: 2

LENTILS

Lentils are a part of the legume family thought to have originated in the East. They are one of the oldest cultivated plants in human history, dating back 20,000 years, and Canada is currently the world's largest exporter of lentils to the global marketplace. That's right—we are growing some of the world's best lentils right here in our own country, with Saskatchewan being the leading lentil-growing province.

Red lentils are smaller and cook faster than their bigger cousins, the green and brown lentils. The lentils most commonly found in our grocery stores are large green lentils (also known as Laird-type lentils) and split red lentils. Budget friendly and packed with fibre, B vitamins, iron and protein, Canadian lentils are winners and belong in your pantry. They have a double win/win factor: low in fat and calories, but high in protein. Their low glycemic index (GI) values and resistant starch content (see page 193) make them ideal for people living with diabetes.

For everything you ever wanted to know about Canadian lentils check out www.lentils.ca

INGREDIENTS

3 Tbsp (45 mL) canola oil, divided

2 cup (500 mL) fresh or frozen corn kernels

1 small onion, chopped

4 medium carrots, scrubbed well and chopped

4 cloves garlic, minced

2 tsp (10 mL) mild yellow curry powder (if you like spicy, go with hot)

1 tsp (5 mL) smoked paprika

1/4 tsp (1 mL) freshly ground black pepper

1 Bartlett pear, cored and chopped

6 large red bell peppers, roasted (see p. 151) *or* 1 1/2 cups (375 mL) jarred roasted red peppers, drained

5 cups (1.25 L) no salt added chicken broth

1/2 cup (125 mL) 0% MF Greek style yogurt

1/4 cup (60 mL) finely chopped fresh parsley

Roasted Red Pepper, Pear, Corn and Carrot Soup
Summer/Fall Trevor Arsenault, PHEc

"I'm a fan of thick, pureed soups because I make less of a mess eating them compared to broth soups. This roasted red pepper soup not only provides me with a convenient way to eat a couple servings from the Vegetable and Fruit food group, it does so with a playful combination of smoky and sweet flavours."—Trevor

METHOD

1. Heat a large saucepan over medium-low heat; add 1 Tbsp (15 mL) oil plus the corn kernels and sauté for 5 to 6 minutes until they turn golden brown. Remove from saucepan and set aside, making sure to scrape up any browned corn kernels at the bottom of the saucepan.

2. Return the saucepan to heat; add remaining oil, onion and carrots and sauté for 4 to 6 minutes until starting to turn light brown.

3. Add garlic, curry powder, paprika and pepper and sauté for another minute until fragrant and starting to brown. (Don't even think about leaving the stove—the garlic and spices can go from great to burnt in seconds.)

4. Add pear, roasted peppers and broth. Scrape bottom of saucepan with a wooden spoon or spatula to loosen any stuck bits of fabulous flavour enhancers.

5. Continue to cook over medium-low heat for 20 to 25 minutes until vegetables are tender. Remove from heat. Using a hand held immersion blender, puree the soup *or* transfer to a blender or food processor and puree in smaller batches, then return soup to saucepan.

6. Add corn and stir well. Make sure the soup is still hot, then ladle into soup bowls; top each with 1 Tbsp (15 mL) yogurt and sprinkle with parsley.

Makes 8 cups (2 L) One serving = 1 cup (250 mL)
Per serving: 185 Calories, 6.3 g Total Fat, 0.5 g Saturated Fat, 0.1 g Trans Fat, 78 mg Sodium, 29 g
Carbohydrate, 5.3 g Fibre, 12.7 g Sugars, 0 g Added Sugars, 5.6 g Protein
Carbohydrate Choices: 1 1/2

HOW TO ROAST A RED PEPPER

1. Place oven rack at centre position and Preheat oven to 500°F (260°C). Line a rimmed baking pan with aluminum foil—you'll thank us.
2. Place peppers in the pan, leaving space between each of the peppers as well as the sides of the pan. Roast for 20 minutes.
3. Using tongs, give peppers a 1/4 turn (ninety degrees for all you math majors). Reduce heat to 450°F (230°C) and roast for another 20 minutes.
4. Give peppers another 1/4 turn and roast another 20 minutes or until skin is dark brown or black and the flesh is very soft. Peppers should be difficult to lift without tearing and leaking water.
5. Remove pan from oven. Move all peppers to the centre of the pan and cover with an inverted mixing bowl to steam and cool for 20 minutes.
6. When cool enough to handle, make 1 slice from stem to bottom in each pepper and spread them flat, skin-side down. Tear out stem and seeds. Use a paper towel to wipe away any stray seeds.
7. Flip peppers over and peel off skin. Use a spoon to help remove any tough spots.
8. Chop peppers and set aside if making soup immediately, or refrigerate for later use.
9. Yields approximately 1 1/2 cups (375 mL). Roasted, seeded and peeled pepper can be frozen in zippered sandwich bags for later use. Label the bag with the number of peppers it contains.

INGREDIENTS

6 slices 100% whole grain
  bread (optional, for shamrock
  croutons)

1 large bunch broccoli

1 Tbsp (15 mL) unsalted butter

3 garlic cloves, minced

1 onion, chopped

1/2 tsp (2 mL) iodized salt

1/2 tsp (2 mL) freshly ground
  black pepper

2 medium potatoes, peeled and
  chopped

4 cups (1 L) low sodium
  vegetable or chicken broth

2 cups (500 mL) skim milk

1/2 cup (125 mL) shredded
  Canadian Havarti, mozzarella
  or cheddar cheese

Shamrock Soup Multi-seasonal

Jennifer MacKenzie, PHEc (with permission from Dairy Farmers of Canada)

Canada is a melting pot of cultures and traditions. Next St. Patrick's Day, when we celebrate all things Irish, serve this lovely, lightly green-coloured soup, even if you aren't from the Emerald Isle.

METHOD

1. If you are making the shamrock croutons, take a shamrock cookie cutter or a sharp paring knife and cut shamrock shapes from bread. Place on a baking sheet and set aside.
2. Cut broccoli tops from stalks. Peel stalks and chop coarsely, then set aside. Cut tops into small florets and set aside. Keep in mind that you are going to cook the broccoli stalks and florets separately.
3. In a large pot over medium heat, add butter and sauté garlic and onion for about 5 minutes or until softened. Add salt and pepper. Add broccoli stalks and potatoes and sauté for 1 minute.
4. Pour in broth and bring to a boil over high heat. Reduce heat, cover and boil gently for about 10 minutes or until potatoes are almost tender. Add broccoli florets and boil gently, uncovered, for about 5 minutes or until florets are tender. Remove from heat.

5. Using a hand held immersion blender, puree the soup until smooth *or* transfer to a blender or food processor and puree in smaller batches, then return soup to saucepan.

6. Reheat if necessary and stir in the milk; heat over medium-low heat, stirring often, just until steaming (do not let boil). Remove from heat; stir in the cheese until melted.

7. Just before serving, preheat broiler; broil croutons on each side until toasted.

8. Ladle soup into bowls and top with croutons.

Makes 9 1/2 cups (2.25 L) One serving = 1 1/2 cups (375 mL)
Per serving: 208 Calories, 5.9 g Total Fat, 3.4 g Saturated Fat, 0.1 g Trans Fat, 423 mg Sodium, 28.7 g Carbohydrate, 3.5 g Fibre, 8.5 g Sugars, 0 g Added Sugars, 10.9 g Protein
Carbohydrate Choices: 2

INGREDIENTS

PHEC TIP:
To make the soup ahead, transfer it to a container after puréeing and let cool. Cover and refrigerate for up to 2 days or freeze for up to 2 months. Let thaw in the refrigerator overnight. Reheat in a saucepan over medium heat until hot and bubbling before adding the milk and cheese. (source: Dairy Farmers of Canada)

INGREDIENTS

1/2 lb (250 g) small beets
(approx. 4–5; see note)

2 Tbsp (30 mL) canola oil

1 onion, chopped

2 large cloves garlic, minced

2 medium potatoes, scrubbed
well, cubed and rinsed to
remove excess starch

3 celery stalks with leaves,
chopped

2 carrots, scrubbed well, finely
chopped or julienned into
matchstick pieces no longer
than 1 inch (2.5 cm)

1/4 small cabbage, shredded into
slivers no longer than 1 inch
(2.5 cm)

8 cups (2 L) no salt added
vegetable broth or (if you
aren't a vegetarian) beef broth

1 bay leaf

1 tsp (5 mL) caraway seeds

1 tsp (5 mL) dried basil leaves

1 tsp (5 mL) dried sage leaves

1/2 tsp (2 mL) freshly ground
black pepper

One 19 oz (540 mL) can lima
beans, well rinsed and drained

1/3 cup (80 mL) chopped fresh
parsley

1 Tbsp (15 mL) balsamic vinegar

1/2 tsp (2 mL) iodized salt

Borscht Multi-seasonal Maria McLellan, PHEc

*"I'm a Canadian of Ukrainian heritage who grew up in the West
End of Toronto. I enjoyed many traditional Ukrainian foods, but
borscht (beet soup) always had tremendous colour, eye appeal and
tasted so good! I tried many recipes over the years that came from Ukrainian
cookbooks or adaptations of traditional recipes, but
decided that I wanted to create a recipe that was nutrient rich
and contained the particular flavours I enjoyed. This borscht
recipe is meatless, but full of flavourful vegetables along with garlic,
lima beans, parsley and caraway seeds. Try it once and then adapt it
to suit your own tastes, if you like."* —Maria

METHOD

1. Rinse beets under cold running water; trim any green ends and
   place unpeeled beets in a medium saucepan. Cover with water and
   bring to the boil. Reduce heat, cover with a lid and simmer until
   tender, about 30 to 35 minutes. Drain. When cool to the touch, peel
   and cube, set aside.

2. In a large soup pot over medium heat, add oil, onion and garlic,
   sauté for 3 to 4 minutes or until softened but not browned.

3. Add potatoes, celery, carrots and cabbage and sauté for 1 minute.
   Add stock, bay leaf, caraway seeds, basil, sage, pepper and stir until

INGREDIENT NOTE:

Beets—To avoid beet-red fingertips, peel and cut cooked beets wearing rubber gloves. Cut into cubes on waxed or parchment paper to avoid staining the cutting board. In a hurry? Go ahead and use 4 to 5 small canned beets.

combined. Bring to a boil, cover and reduce heat to simmer, cooking for 15 minutes or until vegetables are tender.

4. Remove bay leaf, add lima beans, parsley, vinegar and reserved beets. Bring back to a boil, then reduce to simmer. When the soup is heated through, serve. Soup can be made the day before, and flavour improves when refrigerated and reheated the next day.

Makes 12 cups (3 L) One serving = 1 1/2 cups (375 mL)
Per serving: 175 Calories, 4 g Total Fat, 0.4 g Saturated Fat, 0.1 g Trans Fat, 411 mg Sodium, 31.8 g Carbohydrate, 5.3 g Fibre, 10.2 g Sugars, 0 g Added Sugars, 5.2 g Protein
Carbohydrate Choices: 2

SUGAR BEETS

Did you know that Canada produces sugar from locally grown sugar beets? The bulk of sugar beets are grown in southern Alberta with the remainder grown in Ontario.

Sugar beets are harvested in the fall, then processed to extract the sugar and separate it from the fibre, water and other non-sugar materials. Major by-products include sugar beet molasses and beet pulp, which is used to produce a highly nutritious animal feed.

Vegetables—
Make Room on Your Plate

161 What Does a Serving Size Look Like?

162 Roasted Brussels Sprouts with Cranberries

165 Baked Tomato Spinach Spaghetti Squash

166 Stir Fried Baby Bok Choy

167 Ratatouille

168 Not Your Regular Mashed Potatoes

170 Roasted Sweet Potatoes and Cranberries

172 Easy Rutabaga (or Turnip) and Sweet Potato Casserole

175 Grilled Corn

178 Asian-Style Eggplant

180 Gourmet Poutine, Eh!?

183 New Potatoes with Shallots and Mint

VEGETABLES

If there is one food group you should never give up it's Mother Nature's superstars, the vegetable and fruit family. Think multi-coloured: deep greens, reds, oranges, even purples—the deeper the colour the better.

As a keynote speaker I've been lucky to have travelled across Canada many times, in all kinds of weather. In each and every talk I always spell out what a serving of vegetables and fruits is (see below) and then ask via a show of hands how many people have eaten their seven to ten servings the day before. On average only about one to two percent of my audience hold up their hands. *Insert my silent scream* No wonder we have health issues.

Is it the fibre, the vitamin and mineral content, the antioxidants? Or is it the fact that your hunger is satisfied when you've eaten your seven to ten? We don't really know, but I believe it's a combination of all of these reasons. The bottom line is that eating vegetables and fruits is always a good idea. Steam, roast, grill, stir-fry, throw them in a soup or make a salad; all vegetables can be prepared in a number of ways for a quick nutrient-dense side dish.

WHAT DOES A SERVING SIZE LOOK LIKE?

Size matters. We always knew that. But what really matters is portion sizes.

Most people don't know what a serving of vegetables and fruits is. As Professional Home Economists, we are here to make your life easier. Check out what a serving size is according to Canada's Food Guide:

VEGETABLES AND FRUITS

- 1/2 cup (125 mL) fresh, frozen or canned vegetables or fruit (size of your cupped hand)
- 1/2 cup (125 mL) 100% juice, vegetable or fruit (size of your cupped hand)
- 1 cup (250 mL) leafy raw vegetables: spinach, arugula, etc. (size of your fist)
- 1/2 cup (125 mL) cooked leafy vegetables: spinach, kale, bok choy, etc. (size of your cupped hand)
- 1 cup (125 mL) mixed green salad (size of your fist)
- 1 piece of medium sized fruit (size of a tennis ball)
- 1/4 cup (60 mL) dried fruit (size of two golf balls)

FRUIT MATTERS TOO!

Findings from the Nurses' Health study (following over 85,000 women) have suggested that a greater consumption of whole fruits—especially blueberries, grapes and apples—is associated with a lower risk of type 2 diabetes.

INGREDIENTS

Brussels Sprouts

1 lb (450 g) Brussels sprouts,
   bottoms trimmed, cut in half
   (see note)

2/3 cup (150 mL) fresh or frozen
   cranberries

2 Tbsp (30 mL) canola oil

Iodized salt and pepper to taste

Dressing

1 tsp (5 mL) whole grain Dijon
   mustard

2 Tbsp (30 mL) pure maple syrup

1 Tbsp (15 mL) apple cider
   vinegar

INGREDIENT NOTE:

Brussels Sprouts—Choose
Brussels sprouts that are dark
green and are tightly closed and
dense for their size. Wrap them
loosely in a paper towel and then
place then in a plastic bag in your
vegetable crisper. They should
remain fresh for up to 2 weeks.
When trimming Brussels sprouts,
peel or pull away any blemished
or bruised leaves.

Roasted Brussels Sprouts with Cranberries Fall/Winter

Anastasia Meeks, OHEA Student Member

"I was on a mission to change my family's minds about having Brussels sprouts as a Christmas dinner side dish—they were nay, and I was yay. They all loved this recipe so much that they requested for it to make an appearance at next year's dinner. Mission accomplished." —**Anastasia**

METHOD

1. Preheat oven to 350°F (175°C). Line a large, rimmed baking sheet with parchment paper.
2. Place Brussels sprouts and cranberries on the prepared pan. Drizzle with oil and season lightly with salt and pepper. Gently toss to coat with oil and seasonings.
3. Bake 20 to 30 minutes or until the Brussels sprouts have browned and tenderized and the cranberries have softened. Shake the pan periodically.
4. Make the dressing in a large bowl, whisking together the mustard, maple syrup and vinegar.
5. When Brussels sprouts and cranberries are done, place in the large bowl with the dressing and toss until coated. Serve.

Makes 4 cups (1 L) One serving = 1/2 cup (125 mL)
Per serving: 73 Calories, 3.7 g Total Fat, 0.3 g Saturated Fat, 0.1 g Trans Fat, 25 mg Sodium,
9.5 g Carbohydrate, 2.8 g Fibre, 4.6 g Sugars, 3.1 g Added Sugars, 2 g Protein
Carbohydrate Choices: 1/2

BRUSSELS SPROUTS

Brussels sprouts were cultivated in England and France, and if I was a betting person I'd wager these nutrient-dense little cabbages made it over to Canada via our English and French ancestors. However, historically, Thomas Jefferson gets all the credit for introducing them into North America in the early 1800's. Grown throughout Canada they are considered a Canadian minor crop. BC is the biggest producer, followed by Ontario and Québec.

Baked Tomato Spinach Spaghetti Squash Fall/Winter
Jennifer Hill, PHEc

"I've always been fascinated with spaghetti squash. I was first introduced to this unique vegetable as a high school student when my family studies teacher pulled apart the squash strands with a fork. A few years later I began a gluten-free diet and started replacing my spaghetti noodles with spaghetti squash. This is my spin on a recipe my mom used to make." —Jennifer

METHOD

1. Using a fork, pierce the squash in several places. Place whole in the microwave and cook on high for 10 to 20 minutes depending on size. Check at 10 minutes and roll over. To test for doneness, pierce with a fork; if the fork slides easily, it's done. Carefully remove from the microwave using oven mitts. Wrap in a clean tea towel or paper towel and let rest.

2. Preheat oven to 350°F (180°C). Lightly oil a 9-inch (23 cm) glass baking pie plate. Set aside.

3. When the squash is cool enough to handle, cut in half. Remove seeds and discard. Using a fork lengthwise, scrape the insides of the squash to separate the flesh from the thick peel. It should start to look like spaghetti strands. Set aside.

4. In a medium bowl, beat together the eggs and pepper. Add the garlic, tomatoes, spinach, onion and feta and mix well.

5. Add the squash and mix until the squash is fully coated. Spoon the mixture into the prepared pan. Bake for 35 minutes or until the eggs have set.

6. Let cool for 5 minutes, cut into 8 wedges and serve.

Makes one 9-inch (23 cm) pie plate One serving = 1/8 pie
Per serving: 112 Calories, 6 g Total Fat, 3.5 g Saturated Fat, 0 g Trans Fat, 260 mg Sodium, 10 g Carbohydrate, 1.7 g Fibre, 2.4 g Sugars, 0 g Added Sugars, 10.2 g Protein Carbohydrate Choices: 1/2

INGREDIENTS

1 small spaghetti squash, scrubbed

2 omega-3 eggs

1 tsp (5 mL) freshly ground black pepper

3 cloves garlic, minced

1 cup (250 mL) diced fresh tomatoes, drained

2 cups (500 mL) chopped fresh baby spinach

1 small onion, diced

1 cup (250 mL) crumbled Canadian goat feta cheese

PHEC TIP:

One of our major PHEc principles is that anytime you can add a leafy green to up the flavour, you're upping the nutrient profile too, so it's a culinary double whammy.

1/4 cup (60 mL) lower sodium
    vegetable or chicken broth
1 Tbsp (15 mL) lower sodium soy
    sauce
1/4 tsp (1 mL) red pepper flakes
1 tsp (5 mL) cornstarch
2 cloves garlic, minced
1 lb (450 g) baby bok choy (see
    note)
1 Tbsp (15 mL) canola oil

INGREDIENT NOTE:

Bok Choy—If you can't find
baby bok choy choose regular
bok choy and chop into 1-inch
(2.5 cm) pieces. Choose perky
looking bright green coloured
bok choy leaves that have no
bruises on the white stalk.

PHEC TIP:

This easy side dish goes well with
poultry and fish, especially if they
have an Asian flair.

Stir Fried Baby Bok Choy Spring/Summer

Mairlyn Smith, PHEc

Bok choy is an Asian leafy green and an excellent source of folate
and vitamin C. It is also a source of fibre, potassium, calcium and
magnesium. Grown in many places in Canada, Holland Marsh, just
north of Toronto, produces Bok Choy as well as Napa Cabbage, Chinese
Broccoli, Chinese Spinach and Mustard Cabbage.

METHOD

1. In a small bowl, whisk together broth, soy sauce, red pepper flakes
   and cornstarch. Whisk in garlic and set aside.
2. Place bok choy in a colander and wash under cold running water.
   Let drain. Cut off approx. 1/2 inch (1 cm) of the bottom stalk where
   the leaves are attached and discard it.
3. Heat a large non-stick frying pan over medium heat; add oil and
   bok choy. Stir-fry until the green part of the bok choy starts to wilt.
4. Whisk sauce mixture and pour over bok choy. Stir until the sauce
   starts to boil. Serve.

Makes 2 1/2 cups (625 mL) One serving = 1/2 cup (125 mL)
Per serving: 45 Calories, 3 g Total Fat, 0.2 g Saturated Fat, 0.1 g Trans Fat, 188 mg Sodium,
g Carbohydrate, 1 g Fibre, 1.5 g Sugars, 0 g Added Sugars, 2 g Protein
Carbohydrate Choices: less than 1

Ratatouille **Summer** Joyce Ho, PHEc

"Ratatouille is an easy to make, traditional French dish. I like to add an Italian twist to it at the end by sprinkling some Parmesan on top, adding extra flavour." —Joyce

METHOD

1. Heat oil in a large skillet over medium heat. Add eggplant and zucchini and sauté for 7 to 9 minutes or until softened.

2. Add pepper, tomatoes, salt and pepper. Sauté for 5 to 7 minutes or until the peppers are softened. Sprinkle fresh herbs and toss. Sprinkle with parmesan *or* remove from heat, let sit room temperature and then add fresh herbs and cheese to serve. Goes well with Creamy Herbed Polenta (see page 105 for a picture of both).

Makes 6 cups (1.5 L) One serving = 1 cup (250 mL) without polenta
Per serving: 111 Calories, 4 g Total Fat, 1 g Saturated Fat, 0.1 g Trans Fat, 172 mg Sodium, 9.2 g Carbohydrate, 4.4 g Fibre, 4.2 g Sugars, 0 g Added Sugars, 3.8 g Protein
Carbohydrate Choices: less than 1

PARMESAN CHEESE

Did you know that Canada makes its own Parmesan? Fox Hill Cheese out of the Annapolis Valley, Nova Scotia and BioBio out of Quebec are just two of the cheese companies creating a Canadian version of Parmesan. Find them in cheese specialty stores or Loblaws or the Great Canadian Superstore.

INGREDIENTS

1 Tbsp (15 mL) canola oil

1 large eggplant, chopped into 1/2-inch (1 cm) chunks (approx. 6 cups/1.5 L)

2 medium zucchini chopped into 1/2-inch (1 cm) chunks (approx. 2 1/2 cups/625 mL)

1 large orange pepper, cut into 1/2-inch (1 cm) chunks

3 plum tomatoes, chopped

1/4 tsp (1 mL) iodized salt

1/8 tsp (0.5 mL) freshly ground black pepper

3 Tbsp (45 mL) finely chopped or torn fresh basil

1 Tbsp (15 mL) fresh thyme leaves

1 Tbsp (15 mL) fresh oregano leaves, finely chopped

1/4 cup (60 mL) Canadian Parmesan, shaved

INGREDIENTS

1 lb (450 g) peeled and cubed
    rutabaga
2 carrots, scrubbed well and
    chopped into equal-sized
    chunks
2 lb (900 g) Russet or baking
    potatoes, peeled and
    quartered (see note)
1/2 cup (125 mL) frozen corn
1/2 cup (125 mL) chopped green
    onion
1/2 cup (125 mL) buttermilk,
    more if necessary
1 Tbsp (15 mL) unsalted butter
1/4 tsp (1 mL) iodized salt
1/4 tsp (1 mL) freshly ground
    pepper

Not Your Regular Mashed Potatoes Fall/Winter

Amy Whitson, PHEc

Adding turnip and carrot to mashed potatoes gives that *same old same old* a whole new flavour and nutrition boost.

METHOD

1. To cook vegetables, place cubed rutabaga and carrots in a large saucepan. Add enough water to barely cover veggies; bring to a boil, cover, reduce heat to medium and lightly boil for 12 minutes.
2. Add potatoes and cook for 12 to 15 minutes or until all vegetables are tender. Check the water levels to ensure the pot doesn't boil dry, adding boiling water if needed.
3. Drain well, reduce heat to low, return the pot uncovered to the element and let sit for 1 to 2 minutes to dry.
4. Mash the vegetables using a potato masher until smooth. Stir in the corn, green onion, buttermilk, butter, salt and pepper. Add more buttermilk if too dry. Adjust seasonings to taste. Serve.

Makes 6 cups (1.5 L) One serving = 3/4 cup (185 mL)
Per serving: 148 Calories, 1.8 g Total Fat, 1 g Saturated Fat, 0.1 g Trans Fat, 115 mg Sodium, 30.8 g Carbohydrate, 3.8 g Fibre, 6.2 g Sugars, 0 g Added Sugars, 3.6 g Protein
Carbohydrate Choices: 2

POTATOES

As the leader in potato production, Prince Edward Island potato producers are the potato stars in Canada, growing one quarter of all of the potatoes grown in our home and native land. Manitoba, New Brunswick and Alberta come in second, third and fourth respectively.

Some of the most popular potato varieties grown and enjoyed in Canada are:

- Russets: *the go to* potato for its versatility, with a dark skin and white flesh. Great baked, mashed, fried or scalloped.
- Whites: these vary in size and shape, with a beige peel and white flesh. They can be used in soups, stews, salads or mashed, and are commonly used to make potato chips. The small round varieties harvested in early summer are sometimes called new potatoes and have a thinner skin.
- Reds: red potatoes have a rosy, red skin and white flesh. Great for roasting, boiling or steaming due to their moist, firm texture. Leave the peel on for added fibre and colour.
- Yellows: yellow potatoes have a golden yellow flesh and a mildly yellow skin. The most common variety is the Yukon Gold. Roast, boil or steam.
- Mini or nugget: smaller versions of whites, reds or yellows. Roast, boil, steam or grill.
- Heirloom varieties: these include Warba New Nugget potatoes and Kennebec, both available in BC. Roast, boil or grill.

(Source: Statistics Canada [22-008-X, January 2010, January 2011])

INGREDIENT NOTE:

Potatoes—Store potatoes in a cool dark dry place (and that doesn't mean your vegetable drawer). The only types of potatoes that love your fridge are new potatoes or minis. Discard any potato that has a green tinge to it. This is called solanine and it is toxic.

2 lb (1 kg) chopped sweet
  potatoes (approx. 4 medium or
  large sweet potatoes, scrubbed
  well and cut into 1-inch/2.5
  cm cubes)

1 Tbsp (15 mL) canola oil

1/4 tsp (1 mL) cinnamon

2 cups (500 mL) fresh or frozen
  cranberries

1/2 cup (125 mL) dried
  cranberries

1 cup (250 mL) natural apple
  juice (see note)

1 Tbsp (15 mL) pure maple syrup

INGREDIENT NOTE:

Natural Apple Juice—Natural
apple juice is made from whole
apples, including the peel,
making it a more nutrient dense
choice. Usually found where fresh
cold juice is sold.

Roasted Sweet Potatoes and Cranberries Fall/winter
Mairlyn Smith, PHEc

The perfect side dish for Thanksgiving or Christmas. Depending on
the size of your turkey and how much oven space you have, this festive
vegetable dish can be made the day of—or up to two days in advance—
then warmed up in the oven while your turkey is having its "time out."
It's also worth noting that this recipe can easily be halved.

METHOD

1. Preheat oven to 425°F (220°C). Line a 12 1/2- × 13 1/2-inch (3.5 L)
   covered casserole dish with wet parchment paper (see page 388).
2. In a large bowl toss together the sweet potatoes with oil and
   cinnamon. Add fresh or frozen cranberries and dried cranberries,
   toss.
3. Tip into prepared pan. Pour the apple juice over. Drizzle with maple
   syrup. Cover with the lid or parchment paper and bake in the oven.
4. Bake for 60 to 85 minutes or until the sweet potatoes are very soft.
   Serve.

Makes approx. 6 cups (1.5 L) One serving = 1/2 cup (125 mL)
Per serving: 121 Calories, 1.4 g Total Fat, 0.1 g Saturated Fat, 0 g Trans Fat, 47 mg Sodium,
26.8 g Carbohydrate, 3.6 g Fibre, 10.8 g Sugars, 3.7 g Added Sugars, 1.4 g Protein
Carbohydrate Choices: 1 1/2

IS IT A SWEET POTATO OR A YAM?

One of my personal pet peeves is the incorrect labelling of sweet potatoes and yams. Yams are covered in slightly hairy fibres and are native to China and Africa. Sweet potatoes are native to Central and South America and are grown mostly in Ontario. They have a beige, orange, yellow or purple flesh. Nutrient-dense and full of fibre, sweet potatoes need to be stored in a cool dark place, not in the fridge which will harden them. Available all year long at your local grocery store.

PHEC TIPS:

• You can prepare this recipe a day or two in advance of serving; ignore step 4 and bake for 40 to 45 minutes, or until the sweet potatoes are just tender. Remove from the oven and cool, refrigerating for up to two days. On the day you want to serve, finish cooking in the oven and bake for 20 to 40 minutes, or until the sweet potatoes are very soft and the dish has heated through.

• If you're *not* using a stainless steel knife, the sweet potatoes may turn brown when you cut them.

1/2 medium rutabaga or 1 large turnip, peeled and cut into 1-inch (2.5 cm) cubes

2 medium sweet potatoes, peeled, cut into 1-inch (2.5 cm) cubes

2 Tbsp (30 mL) unsalted butter

1/2 tsp (2 mL) freshly grated nutmeg

Freshly ground pepper

Easy Rutabaga (or Turnip) and Sweet Potato Casserole
Fall/Winter Mary Carver, PHEc

"My Mother was a great cook! However, she always added brown sugar to mashed turnips, which (although delicious) added unnecessary sugar and extra calories. I have chosen to cook turnips with sweet potato—the natural sweetness from the sweet potato eliminates the need for sugar."—Mary

Mary originally sent in this recipe using turnips, but due to a long-standing vegetable identification mix up (see picture for the visual clarification) the recipe was tested using a rutabaga. If you are fan of turnips, feel free to use 1 large turnip instead of the rutabaga.

METHOD

1. Place cubed rutabaga (or turnip) and sweet potatoes in a large saucepan; add enough water to just cover the vegetables and bring to a boil. Cover, reduce heat to medium and cook until vegetables are tender.

2. Remove from heat and drain. Save vegetable water for a homemade soup, if desired.

3. Preheat oven to 350°F (175°C). Line 9-inch (2.5 L) square baking pan with wet parchment paper (see page 388).

4. Mash vegetables together, using a potato masher or a fork. Add butter, nutmeg and pepper; mash gently.

5. Transfer mixture to a shallow casserole dish and bake for 15 minutes. PHEc tip: You can also refrigerate for 2 days, then bake.

Makes 4 cups (1 L) One serving = 1/2 cup (125 mL)
Per serving: 63 Calories, 3 g Total Fat, 2 g Saturated Fat, 0.1 g Trans Fat, 23 mg Sodium, 8.6 g Carbohydrate, 1.6 g Fibre, 2.7 g Sugars, 0 g Added Sugars, 0.8 g Protein
Carbohydrate Choices: 1/2

TURNIPS AND RUTABAGAS

White turnips or "neeps" are smaller than rutabagas, have a tangier flavour and are best mashed or added to soups or stews. The Fraser Valley delta in BC has the longest growing season in Canada, allowing them to harvest fresh turnips in mid-July (see picture).

Rutabagas are more intimidating than the wee turnip, both in flavour and size. Grown in many provinces, they are harvested and then waxed, making them available year round. Try raw rutabaga with dip or in soups, stews or mashed with carrots.

Grilled Corn Summer/Fall Trevor Arsenault, PHEc

"Fresh corn has a sweetness and aroma that canned or frozen corn just can't rival. The season for sweet corn lasts only a few weeks, so I try to make the most of it by purchasing ears the same day they are harvested and grilling them with different flavour combinations every time. It's one of the best parts of summer for me." —Trevor

METHOD

1. Preheat barbecue to medium. Make sure your grill is clean.
2. In a small bowl, stir together oregano, basil, sage and salt. Set aside.
3. Place 6 sheets of foil on the counter, one per cob. Brush cobs with melted butter or canola oil and sprinkle with the dried seasonings. Wrap tightly in the foil.
4. Place cobs on grill parallel with the grates so that they don't roll. Cook corn for 5 minutes then rotate 1/4 turn. Continue to cook and rotate until kernels are bright yellow and plump, approximately 20 minutes. Be careful to not overcook or corn will become chewy. When done, remove from the grill and serve.

Makes 6 cobs One serving = 1 cob
Per serving: 117 Calories, 3.5 g Total Fat, 1.4 g Saturated Fat, 0.1 g Trans Fat, 51 mg Sodium, 21.8 g Carbohydrate, 2.6 g Fibre, 4.7 g Sugars, 0 g Added Sugars, 3.6 g Protein
Carbohydrate Choices: 1

INGREDIENTS

1/2 tsp (2 mL) dried oregano
1/2 tsp (2 mL) dried basil
1/4 tsp (1 mL) ground dried sage
Pinch of iodized salt
6 fresh local cobs of corn, husked with silky threads removed (see note)
1 Tbsp (15 mL) unsalted butter, melted **or** canola oil
1/4 tsp (2 mL) cracked black pepper

INGREDIENT NOTE:

Corn—Corn cobs can be cleaned, seasoned and wrapped ahead of time. Store in the fridge until ready to grill. If you have leftover corn after the meal, trim the kernels away from the cob with a sharp knife and store them in the fridge or freezer for later use.

PHEC TIP:

This recipe can easily be adapted to suit almost any flavour combination. Try mixing some of the following together in place of the suggested spice mix: 1/2 tsp (2 mL) garlic powder, 1/4 tsp (1 mL) onion powder and a pinch of salt and pepper; 1/8 tsp (0.5 mL) cumin, 1/4 tsp (1 mL) chili powder and 1/4 tsp (1 mL) smoked paprika; 1/2 tsp (2 mL) ground ginger, 1/4 tsp (1 mL) aniseed, 1/4 tsp (1 mL) coriander and a pinch of salt.

HOW TO BUY FRESH CORN:

- When buying fresh corn look for bright green, firm, moist husks.
- The silk should be stiff, dark and moist, not dried out.
- For the best flavour, sweet corn should be eaten the same day as it was picked; as the corn ages the sweetness goes down and the starchiness goes up.

1/2 cup (125 mL) no salt added chicken broth

2 Tbsp (30 mL) diced fresh ginger

2 Tbsp (30 mL) reduced sodium soy sauce

1 Tbsp (15 mL) Thai chili garlic sauce

1 Tbsp (15 mL) canola oil

1 lb (450 g) Asian eggplant (or either Mirabel, Vernal or Mini Fingers eggplant)

Asian Style Eggplant Summer/Fall Mairlyn Smith, PHEc

"The first time I visited New York I had an eggplant dish in Chinatown that was so amazing I ate most of it myself, even though I was sitting at a table with eight other people whom I had just met—seriously, it was so good that I completely lost my manners. I knew the first thing I would make when I got home was that dish, and I was lucky, on only my second attempt at reproducing it I came up with this recipe."—**Mairlyn**

Recipe note: You need a non-stick skillet with a tight-fitting lid.

METHOD

1. Make the sauce in a small bowl; whisk together chicken broth, ginger, soy sauce, chili garlic sauce and oil. Set aside.
2. Rinse eggplant. Slice off top and bottom. Slice into 1/4-inch (5 mm) coins.
3. Heat a large non-stick skillet over medium heat and add eggplant in batches. There isn't any oil because you're toasting the eggplant, not frying. Flip the coins over and keep toasting them until they are lightly browned, about 3 to 4 minutes. Remove and add the second batch. When all of the eggplant has been toasted, reduce heat to medium-low. Add all of the toasted eggplant back to the skillet.
4. Whisk sauce once more and add to eggplant. Quickly cover the pan with a lid. When you add the sauce it's going to bubble up but don't worry, just get the lid on fast and continue cooking until the eggplant is soft, about 2 to 3 minutes. Remove the lid and let the sauce reduce until it is slightly thick and not watery. Serve.

Makes 2 cups (500 mL) One serving = 1/2 cup (125 mL)
Per serving: 70 Calories, 3.8 g Total Fat, 0.3 g Saturated Fat, 0.1 g Trans Fat, 327 mg Sodium, 8 g Carbohydrate, 0.4 g Fibre, 3.7 g Sugars, 0 g Added Sugars, 2 g Protein
Carbohydrate Choices: 1/2

ASIAN EGGPLANT

Asian eggplant is sometimes called Chinese eggplant and are the long skinny variety. Other Asian style varieties are Mirabel, Vernal and Mini Fingers. Readily available in larger grocery stores, you will definitely find them in an Asian grocery store. Store them unwrapped in the fridge, and use within 3 to 5 days of purchasing.

DEVELOPING CROPS FOR CANADA'S CLIMATE

Vineland Research and Innovation Centre, located in the Niagara Region in Ontario on 90 acres of land, is an independent, not-for-profit organization, funded in part by Growing Forward 2, a federal-provincial-territorial initiative. They are dedicated to developing and sustaining new and innovative crops that can be grown in Canada as well as developing more productive crops. They are responsible for developing such ethnic-cultural crops as Ontario-grown Asian eggplants and okra.

GREENHOUSE PRODUCE

With the demand for more locally grown produce year round, the Canadian greenhouse industry has been growing in leaps and bounds. Greenhouse grown peppers, tomatoes, lettuce, cucumbers and eggplants are produced primarily in BC and Ontario.

INGREDIENTS

Fries

4 medium baking potatoes, scrubbed, cut into skinny fries and patted dry (see note)

2 tsp (10 mL) canola oil

1 tsp (5 mL) garlic powder

1 tsp (5 mL) onion powder

1 tsp (5 mL) paprika

Dash of black pepper

Toppings

4 cloves garlic, minced

2 tsp (10 mL) canola oil

1 onion, quartered thinly sliced

One 8 oz (227 g) pkg Cremini mushrooms, halved and thinly sliced

4 cloves garlic, minced

1 onion, quartered and thinly sliced

1/4 cup (60 mL) red or white wine vinegar (see note)

1 cup (250 mL) no salt added chicken broth

Poutine Sauce

1 tsp (5 mL) canola oil

2 tsp (10 mL) corn starch

2 tsp (10 mL) water

2 Tbsp (30 mL) fresh or frozen green peas, thawed

1/4 cup (60 mL) Quebec curds or grated strong white cheddar (see note)

1 Tbsp (15 mL) chopped fresh parsley

Dash of black pepper

Gourmet Poutine, Eh!? Multi-seasonal

Cristina Fernandes, PHEc, RD

"Whether pronounced pooh-tin or pooh-teen, poutine's deliciousness can't be denied. Several communities in Quebec claim to be the birthplace of the great Poutine, and with good reason. One often-cited tale is that of Fernand Lachance, who claims that poutine was invented in 1957; Lachance is said to have exclaimed, "ça va faire une maudite poutine" meaning, "it will make a damn mess" when asked to put a handful of curds on french fries. Traditionally, poutine consists of classic fries, cheese curds and sauce; however, as with any cuisine, poutine has found many different expressions." —Cristina

METHOD

1. Preheat oven to 425°F (220°C). Line two large rimmed baking sheets with parchment paper and set aside.

2. In a large bowl or a resealable bag, toss together the cut potatoes and the 2 tsp (10 mL) oil to evenly coat. Add garlic powder, onion powder, paprika and black pepper. Toss or shake until evenly coated.

3. Place fries on prepared pans and bake for 30 minutes or until golden brown.

4. Meanwhile, add 2 tsp (10 mL) oil and mushrooms to a medium skillet and cook over medium heat until the mushrooms are lightly browned and tender. Add garlic and onions and continue sautéing until the onions are soft and lightly browned. Remove from pan and set aside. (Reheat in microwave or keep warm in the oven until serving time.)

5. To make the sauce, pour the white wine vinegar into a small saucepan. Add the broth and a dash of pepper and bring to a boil. Simmer for 10 minutes.

6. Whisk the water and corn starch in a small bowl. Stir into the sauce until bubbly and thickened. Reduce heat to low and set aside, stirring occasionally until you're ready to serve.

7. When fries are baked, place in a large serving dish or in individual serving dishes as we did in the picture on the previous page. Add peas and cheese curds (or grated cheddar, if using). Pour sauce on top to warm peas and melt cheese. Top with onion and mushroom mixture and sprinkle with parsley. Serve.

Makes 6 cups (1.5 L) One serving = 1 cup (250 mL)
Per serving: 191 Calories, 6.2 g Total Fat, 1.7 g Saturated Fat, 0.2 g Trans Fat, 63 mg Sodium, 29.3 g Carbohydrate, 2.7 g Fibre, 3.2 g Sugars, 0 g Added Sugars, 4.7 g Protein
Carbohydrate Choices: 2

INGREDIENT NOTES:

Potatoes—Use a tea towel to dry the cut potatoes prior to adding the oil and seasonings. If a crispier fry is desired, try soaking the cut potatoes in ice water for 20 to 30 minutes prior to drying and seasoning.

Vinegar—If you love vinegar you are going to love this recipe; for everyone else, feel free to reduce the amount to 2 Tbsp (30 mL).

Curds—Quebec curds (white cheddar) can be substituted with a lower fat cheese such as a low fat cheddar, mozzarella or even with a dry curd cottage cheese.

New Potatoes with Shallots and Mint Spring/Summer
Rachel Johnstone, OHEA Student Member

METHOD

1. Put potatoes in a steamer basket and place inside a medium saucepan with approx. 4 inches (10 cm) water. Place over high heat, bring to a boil, reduce heat to medium-high and steam for about 10 to 20 minutes or until done (depends on the size of the potatoes). To check for doneness, insert a small knife into one of the potatoes. If it goes in smoothly and feels soft, then they are done.

2. When the potatoes are fully cooked, remove from steamer basket, discard water, put back into saucepan and toss with the shallots, mint, butter and oil. Season with salt and pepper to taste and serve.

Makes approximately 3 cups (750 mL) One serving = 1/2 cup (125 mL)
Per serving: 139 Calories, 6.4 g Total Fat, 2.7 g Saturated Fat, 0.3 g Trans Fat, 33 mg Sodium, 19.3 g Carbohydrate, 1.7 g Fibre, 0.7 g Sugars, 0 g Added Sugars, 2 g Protein

INGREDIENTS

1 lb (450 g) new, mini new or nugget potatoes, rinsed well and cut into quarters

2 shallots, diced

16 fresh mint leaves, chiffonade (see sidebar p. 143)

2 Tbsp (30 mL) butter

1 Tbsp (15 mL) cold pressed canola oil

Salt and pepper, to taste

Salads—Salute to the Leafy Green

188 Waste Less and Enjoy More Fresh Produce

190 Beet Apple Coleslaw

192 Festive Fruit and Nut Coleslaw

193 Winter Pea Salad

194 Maple Brussels Sprout Slaw

196 Bohemian-Style Cucumber Salad

198 Apple Hemp Heart Salad

200 Lentil and Roasted Sweet Potato Salad

201 Shaved Zucchini and Summer Squash Salad

202 Sweet and Red Potato Salad

204 Kale Tossed Salad with Roasted Garlic Dressing

207 Grilled Vegetable, Barley & Feta Salad

208 Four Fabulous Dressings

208 Birch Syrup Salad Dressing

210 Ice Syrup Salad Dressing

211 Honey Mustard Salad Dressing

211 Fresh Ginger Maple Syrup Dressing

212 Tips for Farmers' Marketing

Canada's Food Guide recommends that each and every Canadian eat one serving of leafy greens a day. That's a mere 1 cup (250 mL) or a large handful (visualize the size of your fist). One of the best ways to make sure you're getting your leafy greens is to have a salad every day.

There are eleven fabulous and unique salads to tantalize you in this chapter, plus as a bonus feature for the plain, "spring mix" salad crowd, there are two all-Canadian salad dressings, one family friendly salad dressing and one with an Asian spin to sprinkle over your bowl of leafy greens. Note: sprinkle is the verb, not pour, drown or smother. It's a salad dressing not a salad drowning.

WASTE LESS AND ENJOY MORE FRESH PRODUCE
by Teresa Makarewicz, PHEc

It's a fact! Canadians waste food—especially fresh produce. However, with careful planning and proper storage, families can save money and time and always have nutritious produce on hand for quick and healthy meals.

Here are a few tips to reduce waste, save money and enjoy more produce:

- Think ahead. Plan meals, make a grocery list and stick to it. See page 214-215 for Grocery Shopping 101.
- Buy only what you need and use it in reasonable time. A 20 lb (9 kg) bag of potatoes is no bargain if it spoils.
- Visit farmers' markets early in the day; freshly picked greens and herbs wilt rapidly in the sun.
- Keep produce cool. Take a cooler along to safely transport produce home in a hot car.
- Before storing, remove elastic bands or twist ties to avoid bruising of produce.
- Store produce unwashed. With the exception of leafy greens, fresh fruits and veggies have a natural protective coating and washing before storing speeds up spoilage.
- Separation of fruits and vegetables is vital. As fruits ripen, they produce a colourless, odourless, tasteless gas called ethylene that triggers ripening and causes vegetables to spoil.
- Pack produce loosely in perforated plastic bags. To perforate, snip several holes into bags with scissors.
- Check refrigerated produce regularly. Remove spoiling items. It's true! One bad apple can spoil the whole bunch.

Some fruits and vegetables need special attention:

- Apples ripen 10 times faster at room temperature. Store in a perforated bag in the crisper.
- Keep unripe fruits, such as peaches, nectarines, plums, pears and melon on the counter at room temperature—but out of direct sunlight—until they yield to gentle pressure, then refrigerate.
- Avoid bitter carrots by storing them away from apples.
- Leave corn husks on and refrigerate cobs in a perforated plastic bag. Husk when ready to use.
- Store onions and potatoes in a cool, dark, dry place, but not side by side. Potatoes decrease the shelf life of onions, causing them to rot prematurely. Light causes potatoes to turn green and bitter.
- Sweet potatoes should not be refrigerated as the core will harden. For longer storage, keep cool around 55°F to 60°F (13°C to 16°C) or at room temperature for 1 week.
- Broccoli and cauliflower can be stored whole in a perforated plastic bag, or cut into florets and stored (unwashed) in a plastic bag for quick use.
- Store tomatoes at room temperature away from direct sunlight. Refrigeration changes their texture and flavour.
- Cover herbs with a damp cloth or paper towel and refrigerate in a sealable bag or container. Or trim ends, place in a jar with water, cover loosely and refrigerate. Remember to change the water every couple of days;
- Can, pickle or freeze produce at its peak of freshness.
- If you do need to throw out produce, compost it back to the soil or use a green bin.
- Make a nutritious pot of soup to use up veggies and avoid waste.

INGREDIENTS

Dressing

1/4 cup (60 mL) apple cider
   vinegar
3 Tbsp (45 mL) canola oil (cold
   pressed for an even bigger
   flavour spin)
2 Tbsp (30 mL) pure maple syrup

Coleslaw

1/4 large green cabbage
1 large carrot, scrubbed well, peel
   left on
2 medium beets, peeled (see
   note)
1/2 Granny Smith apple, scrubbed
   (peel on), cored and cut into
   1-inch (2.5 cm) slices
6–8 radishes, cut into 1-inch (2.5
   cm) slices
Salt & pepper to taste (optional)

Beet Apple Coleslaw Summer/Fall

Spencer Finch-Coursey, PHEc

"I know many people are intimidated by beets, either because of the colour and the fear of staining or because they've only had pickled beets and they didn't like them. I like beets now, but it was an acquired taste. Raw beets taste different than pickled, so if you have never has a raw beet, please try this coleslaw, I'm sure it will change your mind." —Spencer

METHOD

1. In a large bowl, whisk vinegar, oil and maple syrup together to make the dressing. Set aside.
2. Wash cabbage and remove outer leaves, then slice into quarters lengthwise and core.
3. Grate cabbage, carrot and beets using either the grater attachment on a food processor or a box grater. Transfer to the large bowl and add apple and radishes.
4. Toss together and season with salt and pepper, if desired. Serve.

Makes 6 Cups (1.5 L) One Serving = 1/2 cup (125 mL)
Per serving: 60 Calories, 3.6 g Total Fat, 0.3 g Saturated Fat, 0.1 g Trans Fat, 21 mg Sodium,
7 g Carbohydrate, 1 g Fibre, 5 g Sugars, 2 g Added Sugars, 0.7 g Protein
Carbohydrate Choices: 1/2

HEALTH BITE

Fresh raw beets have a great flavour, are high in fibre, potassium, magnesium, iron, vitamin A, B & C and folic acid; that's quite the pedigree.

BEETS

Beets are grown in most provinces in Canada, loving our cooler climates and rich soil. They store well in plastic bags or loosely wrapped in dry paper towels in your vegetable drawer. Locally grown beets from BC can be purchased year round. The only months that local beets aren't available in Ontario are May and June.

INGREDIENT NOTE:

Beets—Use rubber gloves while peeling and cutting beets to prevent your hands from turning purple. For a different colour spin, try using yellow, white or even candy cane beets, which are available at farmers' markets or higher-end grocery stores or speciality produce stores.

INGREDIENTS

Dressing

1/2 cup (125 mL) apple cider
    vinegar
1/4 cup (60 mL) canola oil (use
    cold pressed for an even
    bigger flavour spin)
2 Tbsp (30 mL) liquid honey
Pinch salt and pepper

Coleslaw

1/2 medium green cabbage
1 large carrot, scrubbed well,
    grated
1/2 cup (125 mL) chopped
    walnuts
1/2 cup (125 mL) dried
    cranberries or blueberries
2 medium red-skinned apples,
    scrubbed well and diced with
    the peel left on
1/2 cup (125 mL) raw pumpkin
    seeds

PHEC TIP:

Like all coleslaws, this tastes
even better the next day. A great
make-ahead for that big family
get together.

Festive Fruit and Nut Coleslaw Fall/Winter

Emily Dobrich, OHEA student member

*"Coleslaw is a favourite with my family. Whether the occasion is a family
dinner, a potluck with friends or a Christmas feast, everyone looks forward
to a serving of this classic comfort food. Over the years my mother has
developed several variations on it, and this version is my particular
favourite."*—**Emily**

METHOD

1. In a large bowl, whisk the vinegar, oil, honey, salt and pepper
    together to make the dressing. Set aside.
2. Wash cabbage and remove the outer leaves; slice in half lengthwise
    and core. Cut one half of the cabbage in two and slice into thin
    strips from the inside cut edge *or* use a food processor with the
    thinnest slicing attachment. Transfer to the bowl.
3. Add carrot, walnuts, cranberries (or blueberries, if using) and diced
    apple; toss well.
4. Sprinkle with pumpkin seeds and toss. Serve.

Makes 8 cups (2 L) One serving = 1/2 cup (125 mL)
Per serving: 123 Calories, 8.4 g Total Fat, 0.9 g Saturated Fat, 0.1 g Trans Fat, 48 mg Sodium,
11.6 g Carbohydrate, 2 g Fibre, 8.2 g Sugars, 4.2 g Added Sugars, 2.6 g Protein
Carbohydrate Choices: 1/2

Winter Pea Salad Winter

Mairlyn Smith, PHEc, adapted from *Healthy Starts Here!* (Whitecap 2011)

Okay, you're dying for a fresh green salad and all the lettuce in your crisper has turned to slime. What's a cook to do? When there's not a lettuce leaf to find in your fridge, my secret weapon is frozen peas.

METHOD

1. Rinse the frozen peas in a colander under cold water until they feel fresh. Don't over rinse; they actually taste really great when they are still cold. Drain well.
2. In a medium bowl, whisk together mayo and vinegar.
3. Add peas, celery, parsley and shallots and toss well. Serve.

Makes 4 cups (1 L) One serving = 1/2 cup (125 mL).
Per serving: 69 Calories, 2.2 g Total fat, 0 g Sat Fat, 0 g Trans Fat, 76 mg Sodium, 10 g Carbohydrate, 3 g Fibre, 3.1 g Sugars, 0 g Added Sugars, 3 g Protein
Carbohydrate Choices: 1/2

RESISTANT STARCH:

More than just a convenient frozen vegetable in the winter months, peas are a good source of resistant starch. There are three speeds starch is digested at: fast, slow and resistant. Both the fast and slow varieties are digested in the small intestine, but the resistant *resists* being digested and makes its way into the large intestine. Here's where the health benefits happen. The starch begins to ferment, which in turn becomes food for the good bacteria in your large intestine, known in the GI-tract business as a "prebiotic." Aside from long-term GI health, this can affect weight loss in a positive way. Other Canadian sources of resistant starch are lentils, beans and oats.

INGREDIENTS

2 1/2 cups (625 mL) frozen peas
1/4 cup (60 mL) low fat mayo
2 Tbsp (30 mL) apple cider vinegar
2 large stalks celery, sliced thinly
1/2 cup (125 mL) finely chopped fresh parsley
1 shallot, minced

Dressing

1/3 cup (80 mL) apple cider
  vinegar

1/4 cup (60 mL) pure maple syrup

2 Tbsp (30 mL) grainy Dijon
  mustard

2 Tbsp (30 mL) prepared
  horseradish (mild or hot)

1/2 tsp (2 mL) iodized salt

1/2 tsp (2 mL) fresh ground black
  pepper

1/4 cup (60 mL) canola oil (use
  cold pressed for an even
  bigger flavour spin)

Slaw

4 cups (1 L) Brussels sprouts,
  trimmed

6 radishes, trimmed

1 large carrot, scrubbed well

4 green onions, finely chopped

1/3 cup (80 mL) dried cranberries
  (optional)

Maple Brussels Sprout Slaw Fall/Winter

Amy Whitson, PHEc

*"Your family will love this tangy slaw and (if you don't tell them)
they won't even know that they are eating Brussels sprouts;
they'll think it's cabbage."* —Amy

METHOD

1. In a large bowl, whisk vinegar, maple syrup, mustard, horseradish,
    salt and pepper together to make the dressing. Whisk in the oil
    until smooth and set aside.

2. To make the salad, use either the grating attachment on a food
    processor or a box grater to shred the sprouts, radishes and carrot.
    Transfer to the bowl.

3. Add the onions and cranberries (if using) and toss well to coat. Let
    the salad stand for 15 minutes to meld flavours. Taste and adjust
    seasonings as needed. Serve.

Makes 5 to 6 cups (1.25 to 1.5 L) One serving = 1/2 cup (125 mL)
Per serving: 87 Calories, 5.9 g Total Fat, 0.5 g Saturated Fat, 0.1 g Trans Fat, 14 mg Sodium,
8 g Carbohydrate, 2.5 g Fibre, 3.6 g Sugars, 2.4 g Added Sugars, 1.7 g Protein
Carbohydrate Choices: 1/2

HEALTH BITE

Brussels sprouts are a nutrient dense member of the cruciferous family
of super vegetables. According to the American Institute for Cancer
Research, several components within this family of veggies have been
linked to a reduction of cancer risk.

INGREDIENTS

2 large English cucumbers, scored and sliced thinly (see note)

1 tsp (5 mL) iodized salt

1/4 cup (60 mL) granulated sugar, less if desired

1/4 cup (60 mL) white wine vinegar or regular

1–2 Tbsp (15–30 mL) finely chopped fresh dill + extra for garnish

1/2 cup (125 mL) 0% MF Greek style yogurt

INGREDITENT NOTE:

Cucumber—To score a cucumber, place tines of a fork on the peel of the cucumber and drag towards you. This will leave long thin lines on the cucumber, which will help absorb flavours.

Bohemian Style Cucumber Salad Summer/Fall

Mary Johnston, PHEc

"I grew up on a dairy farm eating skim milk yogurt, long before it became a dairy section staple. My father always made his own yogurt with our own milk. He ordered the culture from Quebec, and every month a new culture would arrive. He'd carefully heat the milk, stir in the culture and then incubate the mixture. Each week he would make a new batch using some of the previous week's batch as the culture, until the new culture arrived."—**Mary**

Make this light, cool, fresh salad in the summer when there are lots of fresh local cucumbers in your garden, in farmers' gardens and at your local grocery store.

METHOD

1. Place sliced cucumber in a colander.
2. Place colander in the sink, sprinkle with salt and let stand for at least 1 hour. Squeeze as much of the liquid out as possible. Pat dry with a clean tea towel or paper towel. Note: This process wilts the cucumber slices.
3. Place cucumbers into a bowl with the sugar, vinegar and dill. Toss well to mix.
4. The salad can be prepared to this point and stored covered in the refrigerator for up to 3 days. Drain before the next step.
5. Just before serving, stir in the yogurt. Garnish with fresh dill.

Makes 4 cups (1 L) One serving = 1/2 cup (125 mL)
Per serving: 47 Calories, 0.1 g Total Fat, 0 g Saturated Fat, 0 g Trans Fat, 305 mg Sodium, 10.2 g Carbohydrate, 0.6 g Fibre, 8 g Sugars, 6.6 g Added Sugars, 1.7 g Protein
Carbohydrate Choices: 1/2

YOGURT

Quick—name the food trend of the decade. If you said yogurt give yourself a pat on the back. Yogurt has become so popular among Canadians in recent years that it was awarded this title by Joël Grégoire, Food and Beverage Industry Analyst from The NPD Group, Canada.

More than 1.76 million lb (800,000 kg) of yogurt are eaten each day in Canada, with the average Canadian consuming 17 1/2 lb (8 kg) of yogurt every year on average. (Source: Stats Canada 2012)

Greek style yogurt has more than two times the protein content as regular yogurt. One 3/4-cup (175 g) serving weighs in with 2/3 oz (18 g) protein. Available from zero fat to full fat since its introduction in the early 2000's, Canadians have been flocking to it.

Some popular Canadian companies producing yogurt are Danone, Ultima, Parmalat, Liberte, Iogo and Olympic.

INGREDIENTS

Dressing

1/4 cup (60 mL) 0% MF Greek-
   style yogurt

1 Tbsp (15 mL) apple cider
   vinegar

1/2 tsp (2 mL) ground cinnamon

1 Tbsp (15 mL) liquid honey

Salad

3 large apples, scrubbed well,
   diced to equal approx. 2 1/2
   cups (625 mL) (see note)

1 stalk celery, chopped

1/2 cup (125 mL) dried
   cranberries or blueberries

1/2 cup (125 mL) walnuts,
   chopped

3 Tbsp (45 mL) raw shelled hemp
   hearts (see note)

Apple Hemp Heart Salad Summer/Fall

Janet Buis, PHEc

"This modern twist on the traditional Waldorf salad is a healthy hit with my family. Fresh apples from our local orchard add a great seasonal touch to this nutrient-rich salad."—Janet

METHOD

1. In a large bowl, whisk together yogurt, vinegar, cinnamon and honey.
2. Add apples, celery, cranberries (or blueberries, if using), walnuts and hemp hearts and gently toss.
3. Serve immediately, or cover and refrigerate.

Makes 4 cups (1 L) One serving= 1 cup (250 mL) using dried cranberries
Per serving: 264 Calories, 13.7 g Total Fat, 1.4 g Saturated Fat, 0 g Trans Fat, 21 mg Sodium, 33.4 g Carbohydrate, 5 g Fibre, 24.4 g Sugars, 12.4 g Added Sugars, 6.4 g Protein
Carbohydrate Choices: 2

HEALTH BITE

Hemp hearts are a source of Omegas 6 and 3 fatty acids, protein and fibre. They add a mild nutty texture to salads, yogurt, cereal, smoothies, stir fries and baking. For more information see page 199.

HEMP HEARTS

The edible insides of the hemp seed, hemp hearts might just be the new flaxseed. They contain soluble and insoluble fibres, making them heart and gastrointestinal tract healthy. Factor in omega-3 fatty acids and a string of vitamins and minerals, and you have yourself another Canadian superstar food. What sets it apart from flaxseed is its protein content. Three Tbsp (45 mL) hemp hearts contains 1/3 oz (10 g) of protein, which is about three times higher than ground flaxseed. The majority of edible Canadian hemp is grown in the Prairies and Ontario.

HEALTH BITE

Apple peel is potent; it contains ursolic acid, which boasts a host of health benefits from building muscle to helping with weight control. It also keeps cholesterol and blood sugar under control. Scrub apples well, dry and enjoy the added health benefits.

INGREDIENT NOTES:

Apples—For this recipe choose a crispy firm apple such as a Gala, Honey Crisp, Empire or Granny Smith.

Hemp Hearts—Hemp hearts are available in the health food section of many grocery stores as well as at Costco and most health food stores. Store hemp hearts in your refrigerator or freezer. For this recipe we used Manitoba hemp hearts.

INGREDIENTS

1 large sweet potato, peeled and
diced into 1/2-inch (1 cm)
pieces

1/4 cup + 2 tsp (70 mL) canola
oil, divided

1/4 tsp (1 mL) iodized salt

1/2 tsp (2 mL) fresh ground black
pepper, divided

2 Tbsp (30 mL) red wine vinegar

1 Tbsp (15 mL) pure maple syrup

1/2 tsp (2 mL) ground cumin

1/2 tsp (2 mL) ground coriander

1/2 tsp (2 mL) curry powder

1/4 tsp (1 mL) iodized salt

1 can (540 mL) lentils, well rinsed
and drained

1 cup (250 mL) cooked edamame,
fresh or frozen

1/2 cup (125 mL) chopped red
onion

1/3 (75 mL) cup dried cranberries

1/4 cup (50 mL) chopped fresh
coriander

Lentil and Roasted Sweet Potato Salad Multi-seasonal

Rosemarie Superville, PHEc

"When I was growing up in Trinidad, my Mom served a lentil stew as a side dish that was a family favourite. I had no idea then how versatile and nutritious lentils were or that they grew in Canada. Now I have my own signature lentil dish that I prepare quite regularly in the early fall; it's especially great at barbeques." —Rosemarie

METHOD

1. Preheat oven to 400°F (200°C). Line a rimmed baking sheet with parchment paper.

2. In a large bowl, toss together sweet potato, 2 tsp (10 mL) oil, salt and 1/4 tsp (1 mL) pepper.

3. Spread evenly onto the prepared pan and roast for 20 to 25 minutes, stirring occasionally, until browned and tender. Cool slightly.

4. In a large bowl, whisk together 1/4 cup (60 mL) oil, vinegar, maple syrup, cumin, coriander, curry powder, salt and 1/4 tsp (1 mL) pepper.

5. Add cooled roasted sweet potato, lentils, edamame, red onion and cranberries; toss to coat.

6. Add chopped coriander and toss. Chill at least 1 hour to blend flavours. Serve.

Makes 4 1/2 cups (1.125 mL) One serving = 3/4 cup (185 mL)
Per serving: 265 Calories, 12.2 g Total Fat, 1 g Saturated Fat, 0.2 g Trans Fat, 293 mg Sodium, 31.7 g Carbohydrate, 5.9 g Fibre, 10.5 g Sugars, 5.3 g Added Sugars, 8.2 g Protein
Carbohydrate Choices: 2

Shaved Zucchini and Summer Squash Salad Summer

Erin MacGregor, PHEc, RD

If you're one of those backyard vegetable gardeners who planted zucchini this year and are now desperately trying to find recipes that will use your bumper crop before it takes over the rest of your yard— this is a recipe for you.

METHOD

1. Wash and pat dry the summer squash and the zucchini. Use a Y-shaped vegetable peeler or a mandolin to shave or peel the squash and zucchini into flat ribbons. Transfer into a bowl.
2. Toss squash and zucchini with salt and let sit for 10 minutes. Using a colander, drain excess water from the bowl. If still really wet, gently squeeze any excess water out with your hands.
3. To make the dressing, whisk together oil and vinegar in a small bowl. Pour over salad and toss gently.
4. Add basil and feta and toss gently until well combined. Season to taste.

Makes 5 cups (1.25 L) Each serving = approx. 3/4 cup (185 mL)
Per serving: 48 Calories, 3.7 g Total Fat, 1.2 g Saturated Fat, 0 g Trans Fat, 164 mg Sodium, 2.5 g Carbohydrate, 0.7 g Fibre, 2.1 g Sugars, 0 g Added Sugars, 1.8 g Protein
Carbohydrate Choices: less than 1

INGREDIENTS

2 small yellow summer squash
2 small zucchini
1/4 tsp (1 mL) iodized salt + extra for seasoning
1 Tbsp (15 mL) canola oil (use cold pressed for an even bigger flavour spin)
1 Tbsp (15 mL) white wine vinegar
2 Tbsp (30 mL) chopped fresh basil
3 oz (75 g) feta cheese, finely crumbled
Fresh ground black pepper to taste

INGREDIENT NOTE:

Basil—Depending where you live in Canada you may be able to grow your own basil. With the many varieties of basil available, experiment and use Thai basil, purple basil, Italian flat leaf basil or the smaller variety. You might even end up with a bumper crop, in which case: puree basil in a food processor with canola oil until you have a green paste. Spoon into freezer bags, flatten, seal bag and freeze. Add to your favourite pasta dishes and soups all winter long.

INGREDIENTS

2 1/2 cups (625 mL) chopped medium-sized sweet potatoes (approx. 2 potatoes), scrubbed well and cut into 1-inch (2.5 cm) cubes

1 1/4 cups (310 mL) medium-sized red potatoes (approx. 2 potatoes), scrubbed well and cut into 1-inch (2.5 cm) cubes

1/2 cup (125 mL) low-fat mayonnaise

1/3 cup (80 mL) skim milk

1 Tbsp (15 mL) apple cider vinegar

1 tsp (5 mL) prepared mustard

1 tsp (5 mL) iodized salt

Freshly ground black pepper to taste

2 Tbsp (30 mL) finely diced sweet onion

3 celery stalks, including leaves, thinly sliced

1/4 cup (60 mL) chopped fresh parsley

Sweet and Red Potato Salad Late Summer/Fall

Linda Lichtenberger, PHEc

This combination of sweet potatoes and regular potatoes is innovative and delicious.

METHOD

1. Place the potatoes and sweet potatoes in separate saucepans and just cover with water. Bring to a boil, cover, reduce heat to medium-low and cook until the potatoes are tender: red potatoes about 5 minutes, sweet potatoes 3 to 4 minutes. Remove from heat, drain well and let cool in the saucepan uncovered.

2. In a large bowl, whisk together mayo, milk, vinegar, mustard, salt and pepper; set aside.

3. When the potatoes are at room temperature, tip into the bowl with the dressing and gently toss. Add onion, celery and parsley and gently toss again. Serve or refrigerate until serving time. Can be stored in the fridge for up to 2 days.

Makes 6 cups (1.5 L) One serving = 1/2 cup (125 mL)
Per serving: 254 Calories, 3.8 g Total Fat, 0.6 g Saturated Fat, 0 g Trans Fat, 314 mg Sodium, 17.6 g Carbohydrate, 2.5 g Fibre, 4.7 g Sugars, 0 g Added Sugars, 2.2 g Protein
Carbohydrate Choices: 1

INGREDIENTS

Roasted Garlic Dressing

1 bulb garlic (see note)

1/4 cup (60 mL) canola oil + 1/4
    tsp (1 mL), divided

Salt and pepper to taste

1/3 cup (80 mL) plain Balkan-
    style 1% MF yogurt

1/4 tsp (1 mL) dry mustard
    powder

1/4 cup (60 mL) grated Parmesan
    cheese

1 tsp (5 mL) finely chopped fresh
    parsley

Salad

1 large bunch kale, ribs removed
    and sliced into 1/2-inch (1 cm)
    thick ribbons

1 cup (250 mL) grated carrot

1 large red bell pepper, cut into
    1/2-inch (1 cm) cubes

1 English cucumber, thinly sliced

INGREDIENT NOTE:

Garlic—Choose local garlic
when possible. Buy local at your
farmers' market in the fall and
store it in a cool dark place over
the winter months. Once roasted,
garlic keeps for up to 3 days in
the refrigerator.

Kale Tossed Salad with Roasted Garlic Dressing
Late Summer/Autumn/Early Winter Camille Lacey Naranjit, PHEc

*"I always grow herbs and shallots, so one year I decided to try growing garlic.
I rooted a few garlic bulbs and planted them outside in the spring so that by
the start of the fall I had bulbs of green garlic. I dried the garlic by twisting
the shoots and hanging them in the sun for two days, then I dried them in
my dark basement for a couple of months until they were cured and ready to
use. That was just a few bulbs—imagine thousands of pounds. I have a new-
found respect for garlic growers."*—Camille

METHOD

1. Preheat oven to 375°F (190°C).
2. Cut approx. 1/4 inch (6 mm) off the top of garlic bulb and remove
    the very outer papery leaves. Drizzle with 1/4 tsp (1 mL) canola oil
    and sprinkle with a pinch of salt and pepper.
3. Wrap bulb in foil (or put in a terracotta garlic baker, covering with
    the lid) and put in the preheated oven. Bake for 50 minutes or until
    the garlic bulb is a nice golden-brown colour with the cloves being
    soft and "spreadable."
4. When cool to the touch, hold the garlic bulb and squeeze out
    softened flesh into a mini food processor. Add yogurt, mustard,
    1/4 cup (60 mL) oil, Parmesan cheese and parsley and puree until
    dressing is blended and smooth. Season with pepper to taste and
    set aside.
5. In a large bowl, toss together the kale, carrot, pepper and
    cucumber. Pour the dressing over top toss well to coat. Serve.

Makes 8 cups (2 L) One serving = 1 cup (250 mL)
Per serving: 180 Calories, 8.4 g Total Fat, 1.2 g Saturated Fat, 0.2 g Trans Fat, 84 mg Sodium,
9 g Carbohydrate, 1.8 g Fibre, 3 g Sugars, 0 g Added Sugars, 3.5 g Protein
Carbohydrate Choices: 1/2

VITAMIN K:

Vitamin K is a fat-soluble vitamin whose key role is in blood clotting. It is also important for bone health. The richest source of this essential vitamin is found in natto, a fermented soy product eaten in the Japanese diet. The richest sources of vitamin K in a typical Canadian diet are dark green leafy vegetables, green vegetables and extra old cheddar cheese.

WHAT ARE WE GOING TO DO WITH ALL THAT ZUCCHINI?

As any backyard gardener can attest, zucchini is really easy to grow. Maybe too easy to grow—my first zucchini patch overtook my garden in about 40 seconds! I turned my back and boom, the entire garden was all zucchini. Okay, I am exaggerating but it came as no surprise that commercially grown zucchini is not only popular but abundantly grown right across Canada.

Choose small firm zucchini that have no bruises or dents, store them in the fridge in a plastic bag for up to five days.

Grilled Vegetable, Barley and Feta Salad Summer
Mary Johnston, PHEc

Cook the barley the night before to speed up the process. Feeling creative? This seasonal salad can morph into many variations depending on what vegetables are available.

METHOD

1. In a medium saucepan over high heat, combine barley and broth and bring to a boil. Reduce heat, cover and simmer 30 to 35 min, or until barley is cooked to desired tenderness. Remove from heat, fluff with a fork and let sit covered for 5 minutes. Remove lid and let cool to room temperature.
2. Preheat barbecue or grill to medium-high.
3. In a large bowl, add the red pepper, zucchini, eggplant and mushroom; drizzle with oil and toss well. Place vegetables directly on the grill or in a grill basket and cook for 8 to 10 minutes or until slightly blackened but not overcooked or mushy. Cool for 5 minutes or until you can touch them. Cut peppers, zucchini and eggplant into strips. Cut mushrooms into quarters.
4. Place feta cheese on grill and cook until golden and crisped, about 3 to 4 minutes, turning once. Cut cheese into 1/2-inch (1 cm) pieces.
5. In a large bowl, whisk together the vinegar, mustard, maple syrup, garlic and oil. Add barley and vegetables and toss well. Add spinach, basil and feta and toss again. Serve right away.

INGREDIENTS

- 1 cup (250 mL) pearl barley, rinsed using a wire strainer
- 2 cups (500 mL) no salt added vegetable broth
- 1 large red pepper, quartered and seeded
- 1 medium zucchini, cut lengthwise into planks 1/2-inch (1 cm) thick
- 1 small eggplant, sliced into 1/2-inch (1 cm) thick rounds
- 10 cremini mushrooms
- 1/2 lb (250 g) block feta cheese, cut into 1/2-inch (1 cm) slices
- 1 Tbsp (15 mL) canola oil
- 1/4 cup (60 mL) white wine vinegar
- 1/2 tsp (2 mL) dry mustard
- 1 Tbsp (15 mL) pure maple syrup
- 1 clove garlic, minced
- 1/4 cup (60 mL) cold pressed canola oil
- 4 cups (1 L) lightly packed baby spinach
- 1/4 cup (60 mL) chopped fresh parsley or basil

Makes 10 cups (2.5 L) One serving = 1 cup (250 mL)
Per serving: 189 Calories, 12.8 g Total Fat, 4.3 g Saturated Fat, 0.1 g Trans Fat, 302 mg Sodium, 14 g Carbohydrate, 3.2 g Fibre, 6.2 g Sugars, 1.2 g Added Sugars, 5.9 g Protein
Carbohydrate Choices: 1

1 Tbsp (15 mL) canola oil (use
   cold pressed for an even
   bigger flavour spin)
1 Tbsp (15 mL) birch syrup
1 Tbsp (15 mL) balsamic vinegar
1 tsp (5 mL) Dijon mustard
1 Tbsp (15 mL) minced shallots

FOUR FABULOUS DRESSINGS

Here are four fantastic salad dressings for your all-Canadian salad.
Want a smoother creamier salad dressing? Give it a whirl in an
immersion blender. Want to double or triple the recipe? Go ahead.
Just remember—for food safety, Health Canada recommends that all
homemade salad dressings be stored in the coldest part of the fridge for
no longer than 4 to 7 days.

Birch Syrup Salad Dressing Mairlyn Smith, PHEc

(Birch syrup dressing is on the right and ice syrup salad dressing is on the left)

Birch syrup is produced exactly like maple syrup but has a bolder
flavour; it gives this salad dressing a hint of caramel and molasses and
I am a fan. Birch syrup is produced in Ontario, Manitoba and parts
of Quebec. I have tried Boreal Birch Syrup out of Thunder Bay, Rocky
Lake Birchworks Syrup out of Manitoba (www.rockylakebirch.com)
and Escuminac out of Quebec.

   You can find birch syrup at boutique, speciality or higher-end
grocery stores, or you can contact the supplier directly.

METHOD

1. Whisk together the oil, birch syrup, vinegar and mustard in a small
    bowl. Stir in shallots. Store dressing in fridge for 4 to 7 days.

Makes 1/4 cup (60 mL). One serving = 1 Tbsp (15 mL)
Per serving: 51 Calories, 3.6 g Total Fat, 0.3 g Saturated Fat, 0.1 g Trans Fat, 26 mg Sodium,
4.5 g Carbohydrate, 0.3 g Fibre, 3.1 g Sugars, 2.5 g Added Sugars, 0.2 g Protein
Carbohydrate Choices: 1/2

1 Tbsp (15 mL) canola oil (use
cold pressed for an even
bigger flavour spin)
1 Tbsp (15 mL) Ice Syrup
1 Tbsp (15 mL) apple cider
vinegar
1 tsp (5 mL) Dijon mustard
1 small clove garlic, minced

Ice Syrup Salad Dressing
Mairlyn Smith, PHEc

Created and produced in the Niagara region of Ontario, Ice Syrup has some amazing flavour notes, similar to its big sister icewine. There is a wonderful balance of sweetness and acidity that lends itself to a salad dressing or a glaze on meat or poultry. Ice Syrup is the brain child of Niagara-on-the-Lake grower Steve Murdza, and is sold online or at boutique, speciality or higher-end grocery stores. It's amazing. See www.icesyrup.com for more information.

METHOD
Whisk together the oil, ice syrup, vinegar, mustard and garlic in a small bowl. Store dressing in fridge for 4 to 7 days.

Makes 1/4 cup (60 mL). One serving = 1 Tbsp (15 mL)
Per serving: 44 Calories, 3.6 g Total Fat, 0.3 g Saturated Fat, 0.1 g Trans Fat, 22 mg Sodium, 3 g Carbohydrate, 0.3 g Fibre, 2.3 g Sugars, 2.3 g Added Sugars, 0.2 g Protein
Carbohydrate Choices: less than 1

Honey Mustard Salad Dressing

Mairlyn Smith, PHEc

Trust me, kids will eat more salad if this dressing is on it.

METHOD

Whisk together the oil, vinegar, mustard and honey in a small bowl. Store dressing in fridge for 4 to 7 days.

Makes 1/4 cup (60 mL). One serving = 1 Tbsp (15 mL)
Per serving: 58 Calories, 3.5 g Total Fat, 0.3 g Saturated Fat, 0.1 g Trans Fat, 43 mg Sodium, 7 g Carbohydrate, 0.5 g Fibre, 6.6 g Sugars, 6.6 g Added Sugars, 0.2 g Protein
Carbohydrate Choices: 1/2

Fresh Ginger Maple Syrup Dressing

Margot Cummings Hodgins, PHEc

This fresh dressing is great to use on a green salad or as a coleslaw, dipping sauce or marinade for fish, chicken or duck.

METHOD

Whisk together the maple syrup, vinegar and oil in a small bowl. Grate the ginger into the mixture and mix well. Store dressing in fridge for 4 to 7 days.

Makes 1/3 cup (80 mL). One serving = 1 Tbsp (15 mL)
Per serving: 39 Calories, 2 g Total Fat, 0.2 g Saturated Fat, 0 g Trans Fat, 1 mg Sodium, 5.7 g Carbohydrate, 0 g Fibre, 5 g Sugars, 4.9 g Added Sugars, 0 g Protein
Carbohydrate Choices: less than 1

INGREDIENTS

HONEY MUSTARD

1 Tbsp (15 mL) canola oil (use cold pressed for an even bigger flavour spin)

1 Tbsp (15 mL) apple cider vinegar

2 tsp (10 mL) Dijon mustard

1 1/2 Tbsp (22 mL) liquid honey

INGREDIENTS

GINGER MAPLE

2 Tbsp (30 mL) pure maple syrup

2 Tbsp (30 mL) apple cider vinegar

2 tsp (10 mL) canola oil (use cold pressed for an even bigger flavour spin)

1 Tbsp (15 mL) grated fresh ginger (see note p.134)

TIPS FOR FARMERS' MARKETING

Shopping at farmers' markets is a wonderful way to embrace local seasonal foods and the farms that produced them. The total impact of farmers' markets on the Canadian economy, reported in an Agriculture and Agri-Food Canada report in 2009, was $3.09 billion. With the growth and popularity of farmers' markets the numbers are only getting higher.

My favourite time of the food calendar year is when the farmers' market at my neighbourhood civic centre opens. I leap out of bed on that first Tuesday of the third week in May, arriving sans makeup with my trusty reusable bags or bundle buggy to sprint across the lawn and discover the season's new treasures. Rain or shine, I show up with my change purse to shop, chat, learn what's coming into season and get ideas on how to cook unusual fruits and vegetables. It's like going to Foodie Disneyworld—no rides, but thrills nonetheless.

Sometimes I play *Plan Your Dinner Party* around what's available, other times I just let the smells and sights dictate the entire week's menus. Local, just-picked produce is so incredibly fresh, it's more nutrient dense and it lasts longer in your fridge.

If you're a newbie to shopping at a farmers' market, I've assembled some tips to help you navigate this wonderland.

BEFORE YOU LEAVE HOME:

- Pack a cooler and a cold source—those just-picked blackberries will smoosh if you don't take care of them on the way home.
- Bring small change and small bills—don't expect a farmer to be thrilled as he's giving you change for a fifty when you only spent fifty cents on some radishes.
- Pack your own bags. Embracing a farmers' market isn't just about the freshness and flavours of homegrown produce, it's also about keeping our environment green. So put your money where your mouth is and bring your own bags.
- A buggy, wagon or teenager are all great to bring with you for the heavy stuff. Sure the teen may grumble, but after the first whiff of a cinnamon bun from the bake shop vendor, they'll be putty in your hands.
- Arrive early to avoid disappointment. I missed the first crop of asparagus the one morning I slept in.

WHEN YOU ARRIVE:

- Take a walkabout before you get caught up in the farmers' market flurry. Circle the market to see what's available, what looks fantastic and who has the best price.
- Buy the heavy stuff first, that way you won't squash the tomatoes when you put your Hubbard squash on top.
- Experiment with fruits and veggies you have never tried; the farmers are only too happy to share a recipe or cooking tip.
- Become a regular and get to know your farmers. I love chatting with my "heirloom tomato guy" Ron Thiessen from Thiessen Farms in Jordan Station, Ontario. The day those heirloom tomatoes appear I am in tomato heaven. Like all *real* farmers he knows about the variety he's selling, tips on storage, handling and serving ideas. Check out thiessenfarms.com

It was always a sad day when the farmers packed up their treasures for the winter, until I discovered local all-season markets. In Toronto we have the St. Lawrence Market and my new favourite community Market, the Wychwood Barns. Then it's seasonal produce all winter long. Lucky Vancouverites have Granville Market all year long, but then they don't really have winter, do they?

For a list of farmers' markets right across Canada (listed by province) check out http://www.farmersmarketsincanada.com/

Legumes—The Big Bang
from the Prairies

218 BEANS, LEGUMES, PULSES: WHO'S WHO AND WHAT'S WHAT

221 COOKING FROM SCRATCH

224 FALAFEL PATTIES WITH TAHINI SAUCE AND PICKLED ONIONS

228 FRENCH-INSPIRED VEGETARIAN SHEPHERD'S PIE

230 SLOW COOKER BAKED BEANS

232 CHICKPEA BURGERS

234 CHIPOTLE BLACK BEAN CHILI

237 CHICKPEA AND CAULIFLOWER CURRY

238 HUMMUS, CANADIAN STYLE

240 ASIAN-STYLE EDAMAME AND CORN SALAD

LEGUMES

Pop Quiz: What do we grow on Prairies that is nutrient-dense, loaded with protein, loaded with both soluble and insoluble fibre, has a plethora of B vitamins, can help your GI tract, is heart healthy and diabetes friendly and a vegetarian's best friend? If you answered legumes give yourself an A+.

BEANS, LEGUMES, PULSES: WHO'S WHO AND WHAT'S WHAT

Legumes are the protein-rich plant family containing soybeans, peanuts, fresh peas, fresh beans, dried beans, dried peas, dried chickpeas and dried lentils.

All beans and pulses are heart healthy and very good for you. What separates the "big" kids from the others is their fat and protein content:

- Soybeans are nutrient dense and are considered a complete protein, which means all of the protein building blocks (amino acids) are in place. They also contain fat.
- Peanuts are not technically a nut, they're a legume (a piece of trivia to wow your friends with the next time you're playing Jeopardy!). Lower in protein and higher in fat than the rest of the family members, but still in the clan.
- Fresh beans and peas are much lower in protein and have little to no fat.

- Pulse is the term we use for dried seeds—beans, split peas, chickpeas and lentils—and they are nutrient-dense treasure troves of Mother Nature's best. Heart healthy and extremely low in fat (plus gluten free), pulses are loaded with protein, fibre, B vitamins, iron, zinc and antioxidants; a veritable cornucopia of health in a tiny dried seed.

So why don't people eat soybeans and pulses every day? I think it's because they might give you gas.

My advice is: Get over it! There are so many countries in the world who celebrate gas. We should be one of them because it's "Better to fart and save your heart." Eat them with friends and loved ones, just never on Valentine's Day.

March 5 is National Farting Day—a totally fabricated day I created back in 2011. In my continued zeal to encourage Canadians to eat beans, split peas and lentils, the popular Toronto daytime TV program Cityline agreed to let me bring media attention to National Farting Day on the show and it was a riveting success. Bless them and the lovely Tracy Moore who's the host; we had a wonderful time debunking bean myths and debating the entire subject of flatulence. Since then National Farting Day has become an essential annual tradition, so mark March 5 down on your calendar and get ready to have a (heart-healthy) gas!

SUPPORT YOUR LOCAL PULSE FARMER

Pulse Canada (www.pulsecanada.com) knows a thing or two about growing pulses. Their goal is to spread the news that dried beans, peas, chickpeas and lentils are healthy for your body and our planet. Every time you choose a pulse you're not only giving your body a boost in the health department, you are supporting a Canadian pulse farmer.

THE YEAR OF THE BEAN

Cue the fireworks and start eating legumes ASAP because the United Nations has declared 2016 as the International Year of the Bean! How are you going to celebrate?

HEALTH BITE

Beans are touted as one of the best nutritional all-stars out there. The Mayo clinic, one of the most reputable hospitals and research clinics in the world, rates it as one of their top ten foods.

COOKING FROM SCRATCH

Dried pulses including soybeans can be stored in a cool dark place for up to one year. After that, they don't go bad, but will be very dry and will require a longer cooking time. My advice? Use within one year of purchasing.

To prepare your pulse or soybeans, measure it out and place in a strainer. Rinse well under cold running water and pick through to remove any stones or shrivelled beans. Soak every 1 cup (250 mL) of dried beans with 3 cups (750 mL) cold water. Pulse Canada recommends soaking beans, whole peas and chickpeas for at least 12 hours or overnight in the refrigerator, whereas dried lentils and split peas just need a rinse. Before cooking, rinse and drain under cold running water (this helps in the tooting department). They are now ready to be used in a recipe.

In a hurry? For a quick soak, combine every 1 cup (250 mL) dried beans with 3 cups (750 mL) cold water in a large pot, bring to a boil, reduce heat to medium and gently boil for 2 minutes. Remove from heat, cover and let sit for 1 hour. Rinse well—your pulse is now ready to be cooked in a recipe.

Place presoaked, rinsed beans in a large heavy-bottomed saucepan (most pulses double or even triple their size) with enough water to cover them by 2 inches (5 cm). Bring to a boil, cover, reduce heat to simmer and cook *gently* just until the pulse is tender. Don't go for mushy. The beans are done when they are tender to the bite. Here are some guidelines for cooking times from Pulse Canada. Time will vary with the type and age of the pulses, as well as with altitude and the hardness of the water. PHEC Tips:

- Never add salt to beans until *after* they are cooked. Adding salt too soon increases their cooking time and can toughen them up. Rule of thumb: soak, cook, then salt with iodized salt.

- For convenience, you can always use canned beans. Placing them in a strainer and rinsing under cold running water until the water runs clear will reduce sodium levels by about 40 percent. Or buy low sodium canned beans; you can still drain and rinse them to reduce the sodium levels even further. Better yet, buy no-salt-added beans and add your own iodized salt to control the amount and type of sodium, as well as the iodine in your diet.

Pulse	Soaking Requirement	Cooking Time
Beans	Yes	45–60 minutes
Peas		
Whole	Yes	40–45 minutes
Split	No	1–1 1/2 hours
Lentils		
Whole Green	No	30–45 minutes
Split Red	No	10–15 minutes
Chickpeas	Yes	1–1 1/2 hours

One 19 oz (540 mL) can chick
peas, well rinsed and drained

2 green onions, chopped

1 large clove garlic, minced

1/2 cup (125 mL) coarsely
chopped parsley

1/4 cup (60 mL) coarsely chopped
cilantro

2 tsp (10 mL) ground cumin

1/2 tsp (2 mL) ground coriander

Pinch cayenne

1/2 tsp (5 mL) iodized salt

1 omega-3 egg

1/4 cup (60 mL) 100% whole
wheat bread crumbs or Panko
crumbs

1 Tbsp (15 mL) canola oil

Four 100% whole wheat pitas

Tahini Sauce (recipe follows)

1 cup (250 mL) shredded lettuce
(approx.)

1 cup (250 mL) diced tomatoes
(approx.)

Pickled Red Onion slices (recipe
follows)

PHEC TIP:

You can make the patties ahead,
cover and refrigerate until ready
to cook.

Falafel Patties with Tahini Sauce and Pickled Onions
Multi-seasonal Barb Holland, PHEc

Falafel Patties

Bye-bye deep-frying. A quick pan-fry in a skillet and you've got a quick
and healthy vegetarian meal. To serve falafels, stuff them into whole
wheat pitas and add a variety of toppings—Tahini sauce, Pickled Red
Onions, diced tomatoes and shredded lettuce.

METHOD

1. In food processor, combine chick peas, green onions, garlic, parsley,
   cilantro, cumin, coriander, cayenne and salt. Pulse for 5 seconds
   and scrape down with a rubber spatula. Add egg and process until
   you have a chunky but even texture (not a smooth paste, you aren't
   making baby food). Scrape down as needed.

2. Place mixture in a large bowl. Fold in the panko crumbs, don't over-
   mix.

3. Form the mixture into 8 patties, each approx. 3 inches (8 cm) wide
   and 1/2 inch (1 cm) thick.

4. In a large non-stick skillet, heat oil over medium heat. When hot,
   add 4 patties and cook until firm and golden on both sides, about 4
   to 5 minutes per side.

5. Transfer to a plate and repeat with the remaining patties.

6. To serve, cut pitas in half crosswise. Place 1 falafel patty into each half.

7. Serve each falafel with 2 Tbsp (30 mL) Tahini sauce, lettuce,
   tomatoes and 1/4 cup (60 mL) Pickled Red Onions.

Makes 8 patties One serving = 1 pita, 2 Falafel patties, 1/4 cup (60 mL) Pickled Red Onion and 2
Tbsp (30 mL) Tahini Sauce
Per serving: 570 calories, 14.8 g Fat, 2.1 g Sat. Fat, 0 g Trans Fat, 859 mg Sodium,
61.5 g Carbohydrates, 7.7 g Fibre, 11.4 g Sugars, 9.4 g Added Sugars, 15.5 g Protein
Carbohydrate Choices: 3.5

Pickled Red Onions

METHOD

1. Peel and thinly slice red onion. If you have a mandolin, use it, if not slice the onion really thinly and ask Santa for a mandolin for Christmas.
2. Separate rings and place onions in a clean 2-cup (500 mL) Mason jar.
3. In a small saucepan or large glass microwave-safe measuring cup, combine vinegar, sugar and salt. Bring to a boil. Remove from heat and stir to dissolve sugar. Pour over onion slices into the Mason jar.
4. Cool to room temperature, then cover and refrigerate. Will keep up to 1 month refrigerated.

Makes approx. 1 1/2 cups (375 mL) One serving = 2 Tbsp (30 mL)
Per serving: 24 Calories, 0 g Total Fat, 0 g Saturated Fat, 0 g Trans Fat, 96 mg Sodium,
5.4 g Carbohydrate, 0.2 g Fibre, 4.7 g Sugars, 0.1 g Protein
Carbohydrate Choices: less than 1

Tahini Sauce

METHOD

1. In a small bowl, mix together the yogurt, tahini, vinegar and garlic. Season with salt and pepper to taste. Add hot sauce if desired.

Makes 1/2 cup (125 mL) One serving = 1 Tbsp (15 mL)
Per serving: 47 Calories, 3.8 g Total Fat, 0.6 g Saturated Fat, 0 g Trans Fat, 11 mg Sodium, 2.6 g Carbohydrate, 0.7 g Fibre, 0.6 g Sugars, 0.1 g Protein

Carbohydrate Choices: less than 1

INGREDIENTS

1/4 cup (60 mL) plain 1% MF yogurt
1/4 cup (60 mL) tahini
1 Tbsp (15 mL) apple cider vinegar
1 small clove garlic, minced
Salt and pepper to taste
Hot sauce to taste (optional)

INGREDIENTS

Filling

2 Tbsp (30 mL) canola oil

1 large onion, finely chopped

4 cloves of garlic, minced

3 medium carrots, scrubbed well
and diced

1 celery stalk, diced

1 lb (450 g) cremini mushrooms,
cleaned and sliced

Two 19 oz (540 mL) cans brown
lentils, well rinsed and drained

One 12 oz (340 g) pkg original
veggie ground round

1 1/2 cups (375 mL) no salt
added vegetable broth

1/2 cup (125 mL) Canadian VQA
dry red wine

1/3 cup (80 mL) chopped fresh
dill

1/4 cup (60 mL) fresh parsley,
chopped

2 tsp (10 mL) fresh thyme, minced

1/4 tsp (1 mL) iodized salt

1/4 tsp (1 mL) freshly ground
pepper

2 Tbsp (30 mL) apple cider
vinegar

1 Tbsp (15 mL) soft unsalted
butter *or* no salt added non
hydrogenated margarine

1 Tbsp (15 mL) all-purpose flour

1/2 cup (125 mL) skim milk

French-Inspired Vegetarian Shepherd's Pie
Multi-seasonal Jennifer Goodwin, PHEc

This hearty dinner option is not just for vegetarians—even your meat-eating friends and family will be asking for seconds. Serve with Festive Fruit and Nut Coleslaw on page 192 or a mixed green salad to round out your plate.

METHOD

1. Heat a large heavy saucepan over medium heat. Add oil, onion and garlic; sauté for 5 minutes. Add carrots and celery and sauté for 2 minutes.
2. Add mushrooms and sauté for 2 to 5 minutes, stirring occasionally.
3. Add lentils, veggie ground round, vegetable broth, red wine, dill, parsley, thyme, salt and pepper. Stir in well and simmer for 20 to 25 minutes, stirring occasionally. Stir in apple cider vinegar.
4. In a small dish, combine soft butter (or margarine, if using) and flour until it forms a paste. Add to the lentil mixture and stir for 5 minutes until the liquid is thickened to a gravy-like consistency.
5. Pour in milk and stir well to combine.
6. Transfer lentil mixture into prepared pan and set aside.
7. Preheat oven to 350°F (180°C) and lightly oil a 9- × 13-inch (3.5 L) casserole pan.

8. To make the topping, cook potatoes in a partially covered saucepan with just enough water to cover them. Cook until tender, about 15 to 25 minutes. Drain. Mash potatoes, add milk and mash again until fluffy. Season to taste.

9. Spoon mashed potatoes over the lentil mixture and gently spread to cover. (The dish can be prepared to this point, refrigerated overnight and baked the following day, though the baking time will be longer if the mixture is cold.)

10. Bake for 20 minutes until the mixture is bubbly and the potatoes are beginning to turn golden.

11. Remove from the oven and sprinkle with grated cheddar cheese. Return to the oven for 5 to 10 minutes and bake until cheese is melted.

12. Remove from the oven. Sprinkle with sliced green onions and salt and pepper to taste. Serve.

Makes 8 servings One serving = 1 cup (250 mL)
Per serving: 523 calories, 13.8 g Fat, 6 g Sat. Fat, 0.2 g Trans Fat, 628 mg Sodium, 69.4 g Carbohydrates, 10.8 g Fibre, 8.8 g Sugars, 0 g Added Sugars, 27.5 g Protein
Carbohydrate Choices: 4

INGREDIENTS

Topping

3 lb (1.4 kg) baking potatoes, peeled and chopped
1/2 cup (125 mL) skim milk
1 1/2 cups (375 mL) shredded Canadian old cheddar cheese
2 green onions, thinly sliced
Salt and pepper to taste (optional)

PHEC TIPS:

• Plan ahead by splitting the recipe in half and baking in 2 smaller casserole dishes, or in 2 single-serving baking dishes. Cool, label with date and freeze. Reheat in the microwave.

• Cooking for vegans? Substitute cow's milk with soy or rice beverage and replace the butter with vegetable-based margarine and cheese. Watch labels for casein and whey, which are milk proteins and therefore not vegan.

INGREDIENTS

2 1/2 cups (625 mL) dried white
pea or navy beans

4 1/2 cups (1.125 L) boiling
water, divided

One 5 1/2 (156 mL) can tomato
paste

3 Tbsp (45 mL) pure maple syrup

3 Tbsp (45 mL) molasses

2 Tbsp (30 mL) Worcestershire
sauce

1 Tbsp (15 mL) sodium-reduced
soy sauce

2 tsp (2 mL) dry mustard

2 onions, diced

1/4 tsp (1 mL) iodized salt
(optional) added at the end of
cooking time

Slow Cooker Baked Beans Multi-seasonal

Marla Nicholls, PHEc & Mairlyn Smith, PHEc

*"This economical, nutritious recipe has long been a family favourite.
Each March, our family purchases the maple syrup that is used
in this recipe at a local sugar bush, and white pea beans, called
navy beans in the USA, thrive in southwestern Ontario where growing
conditions are ideal. Canada is one of the world's top five
exporters of beans."* —**Marla**

Recipe development is a like a choreographed dance—ingredients
enter and exit until the entire routine/recipe is a perfectly balanced
performance. Some performances are a combination of ingredients and
ideas like this recipe. Two PHEcs + two similar but slightly different
recipes = one fabulous dance, I mean recipe.

METHOD

1. Rinse beans and place into the bowl of a large slow cooker. Add 7
   cups (1.75 L) cold water. Soak overnight or for at least 12 hours in
   the fridge.
2. The next morning, drain the beans well, rinse and place them back
   into the slow cooker.

3. In a medium bowl, whisk together 2 cups (500 mL) boiling water, tomato paste, maple syrup, molasses, Worcestershire, soy sauce and mustard. Pour over beans.
4. Add onions and the rest of the boiling water. Mix well, cover and cook on low for 8 to 10 hours or high for 4 to 5 hours. Stir occasionally.
5. If the beans start to look dry add another 1/2 cup (125 mL) boiling water and stir in well. Taste before serving and add 1/4 tsp (1 mL) iodized salt if desired.

Makes approximately 8 cups (2 L) One serving = 1 cup (250 mL)
Per serving: 305 calories, 1.1 g Fat, 0.1 g Sat. Fat, 0 g Trans Fat, 123 mg Sodium, 59 g Carbohydrates, 12.5 g Fibre, 15 g Sugars, 7.9 g Added Sugars, 16.2 g Protein
Carbohydrate Choices: 3

PHEC TIP:
Homemade beans are more economical than buying a can of baked beans, plus, more importantly, you get to control the amount of salt and sugar added.

One 19 oz (540 mL) can chickpeas, well rinsed and drained

1 clove of garlic, minced

1/2 onion, diced

1/4 cup (60 mL) natural wheat germ

2 Tbsp (30 mL) canola oil, divided

1 Tbsp (15 mL) water

1 Tbsp (15 mL) BBQ sauce (low sodium if possible)

1 tsp (5 mL) Worcestershire sauce *or* apple cider vinegar

1 Tbsp (15 mL) fresh chopped parsley

1 tsp (5 mL) cumin

1 tsp (5 mL) dried thyme

1 tsp (5 mL) dried mustard

1/2 tsp (5 mL) iodized salt

Six 100% whole wheat buns (optional)

PHEC TIP:

This recipe can be doubled.

Chickpea Burgers Multi-seasonal

Marnie Van Esbroeck, OHEA Student Member

"I had never eaten a chickpea before I became a vegetarian, but once I had I began trying many new dishes and quickly developing a love for all things chickpea—they are a very versatile little pulse! The secret ingredient in my burgers is wheat germ, which I find helps hold the patties together. I find store-bought veggie burgers to be dry, but these burgers have a lot of flavour and have been given the seal of approval by my meat-eating husband and friends."—Marnie

METHOD

1. In a large bowl, mash the chickpeas with a potato masher until they are almost pasty.
2. Add garlic, onion, wheat germ, 1 Tbsp (15 mL) oil, water, BBQ sauce, Worcestershire sauce (or apple cider vinegar, if you are cooking for vegetarians), parsley, cumin, thyme, mustard and salt, and blend together until all of the ingredients are well incorporated.
3. Divide into 6 equal patties. (Patties can be frozen at this point and then thawed for a future dinner.)
4. Heat a large skillet over medium-high heat. Add the remaining 1 Tbsp (15 mL) oil, place 3 patties in the pan and cook each side until golden brown, approximately 3 to 4 minutes per side. Repeat until all 6 patties are cooked.
5. Serve as is or on toasted 100% whole wheat buns with your choice of toppings.

Makes 6 burgers One serving = 1 patty (does not include bun or condiments)
Per serving: 87 calories, 3.6 g Fat, 0.4 g Sat. Fat, 0 g Trans Fat, 272 mg Sodium, 11.2 g Carbohydrates, 2.2 g Fibre, 1.3 g Sugars, 0 g Added Sugars, 3 g Protein
Carbohydrate Choices: 1/2

One serving = 1 patty with whole wheat hamburger bun (no condiments)
Per serving: 227 calories, 6 g Fat, 0.8 g Sat. Fat, 0 g Trans Fat, 572 mg Sodium, 36.2 g Carbohydrates, 4.2 g Fibre, 3.3 g Sugars, 8 g Protein
Carbohydrate Choices: 2

MAKE MY SNACK CHICKPEAS, PLEASE

Want a great tasting, nutrient dense snack? Try roasting chickpeas. Line a large baking sheet with parchment paper, toss a can of rinsed and drained chickpeas with 2 Tbsp (30 mL) canola oil and add up to 1 Tbsp (30 mL) of your favourite seasonings. Roast in a 400°F (200°C) oven for 30 to 40 minutes, or until chickpeas are golden brown and crunchy. Cool and serve right away.

You can also check out Three Farmers' Roasted Chickpeas, produced in Saskatchewan and available right across Canada at threefarmers.ca.

INGREDIENTS

2 tsp (10 mL) canola oil

3 cloves garlic, minced

1 large onion, chopped

1 red pepper, chopped

2 carrots, scrubbed well and diced

2 Tbsp (30 mL) chili powder

1 Tbsp (15 mL) paprika

1 tsp (5 mL) dried oregano

1 tsp (5 mL) ground cumin

Two 19 oz (540 mL) cans black
   beans, well rinsed and drained,
   divided

One 28 oz (796 mL) can crushed
   tomatoes

1 1/2 cups (375 mL) fresh or
   frozen corn, no need to thaw

1/2 cup (125 mL) water

2 Tbsp (30 mL) pureed canned
   chipotle pepper with adobo
   sauce (see note)

Suggested toppings: thinly sliced
   green onions, chopped fresh
   cilantro, plain yogurt, shredded
   Canadian old Cheddar cheese

Chipotle Black Bean Chili Fall/Winter

Teresa Makarewicz, PHEc

Chili is pure comfort food and so easy to prepare. It's delicious served over cooked barley, or spooned over a baked or microwaved sweet potato and serve with one or more of the suggested toppings below.

METHOD

1. Heat a large pot over medium heat; add oil, garlic, onion, red pepper and carrots; sauté for 10 minutes or until the onion is softened and slightly browned. Stir in chili powder, paprika, oregano and cumin; sauté for 1 minute or until fragrant.

2. Puree 1 cup (250 mL) of the beans in a food processor or mash well with a potato masher. Add the pureed and whole beans, tomatoes, corn, water and chipotle pepper to the pot, bring to a boil, cover, reduce heat to medium and simmer uncovered for 20 to 30 minutes or until the carrots are tender, stirring occasionally.

3. Serve with your choice of topping.

Makes 9 cups (2.25 L) One serving = 1 1/2 cups (375 mL) without toppings
Per serving: 221 calories, 3.2 g Fat, 0.3 g Sat. Fat, 0 g Trans Fat, 347 mg Sodium,
40 g Carbohydrates, 10.6 g Fibre, 10 g Sugars, 0 g Added Sugars, 9 g Protein
Carbohydrate Choices: 2

INGREDIENT NOTE:

Chipotle Peppers—Look for canned chipotle peppers in adobo sauce in the Mexican section of most grocery stores. To freeze leftovers, puree the entire can of chipotles with adobo sauce until smooth. Spoon 1 Tbsp (15 mL) portions on a parchment-lined baking sheet and freeze until firm; transfer to an airtight container and freeze to use for the next spicy chili attack.

PHEC TIPS:

- Freeze leftover chili for up to 3 months and keep it ready for a lunch or busy weeknight dinner option.
- Upon standing, this chili will thicken. When reheating, add more water if you like and thin to desired consistency.
- The family that eats together stays together, so make dinner a family friendly event by setting out small bowls of any of the suggested toppings and then let everyone create their own signature bowl of chili.

Chickpea and Cauliflower Curry Fall/Winter

Mairlyn Smith, PHEc

OHEA meetings usually involve a learning component. At a meeting in May, 2014, we were lucky to have as our guest instructor Raghavan Iyer, 2014 President of the International Association of Culinary Professional (IACP) and the 2004 IACP Award of Excellence winner for Cooking Teacher of the Year. He taught a class on curry in which we learned that curry is all about the layering of flavours, as well as how to use individual spices instead of commercial curry blends, about slow cooking, and enough about curry to fill another cookbook. Based on his class I went home and redid all of my curry recipes. This is one of the recipes that has had a Raghavan/Mairlyn makeover.

METHOD

1. In a small bowl, combine the coriander, cumin, turmeric, red pepper flakes, cinnamon, cloves and salt. Set aside.
2. Heat a large skillet over medium heat; add oil and onion and sauté until soft, about 3 to 5 minutes. Add garlic and ginger and sauté for 1 minute; add in spice mixture and sauté for another 2 minutes; the aroma should hit you on the face. You'll know it when it happens.
3. Stir in canned tomatoes, chickpeas and cauliflower. Bring to a boil, cover and reduce heat to medium-low; cook for 15 minutes, stirring occasionally. Reduce heat to simmer and cook 15 to 20 minutes, or until cauliflower is cooked through and the beans are soft. Sprinkle with cilantro, stir in and serve.

Makes 8 cups (2 L) One serving = 1 1/2 cups (375 mL)
Per serving: 220 calories, 9.7 g Fat, 0.8 g Sat. Fat, 0.2 g Trans Fat, 248 mg Sodium, 28.1 g Carbohydrates, 8.5 g Fibre, 9.4 g Sugars, 0 g Added Sugars, 7.2 g Protein
Carbohydrate Choices: 1

INGREDIENTS

Spice Mixture
2 tsp (10 mL) ground coriander seed
2 tsp (10 mL) ground cumin
1 tsp (5 mL) turmeric
1 tsp (5 mL) red pepper flakes
1/2 tsp (2 mL) cinnamon
1/4 tsp (1 mL) ground cloves
1/4 tsp (1 mL) iodized salt

Curry
3 Tbsp (45 mL) canola oil
1 small onion, chopped
3 cloves garlic, minced
1 Tbsp (15 mL) freshly grated ginger
One 28 fl oz (796 mL) canned diced tomatoes, no salt added
One 19 fl oz (540 mL) can lower sodium chickpeas, well rinsed and drained
1 small cauliflower, cut into small florets
1 1/2 cups (310 mL) frozen green peas
1/2 cup (125 mL) chopped cilantro

INGREDIENTS

One 19 oz (540 mL) can
    chickpeas, well rinsed and well
    drained

2 Tbsp (30 mL) apple cider
    vinegar

1/4 cup (60 mL) tahini

2 cloves garlic

2 Tbsp (30 mL) cold pressed
    canola oil (if you only have
    regular, no worries)

3 Tbsp (45 mL) water

1 large or 2 small roasted red
    peppers (I use bottled)

1/8 tsp (0.5 mL) iodized salt

Dash of ground paprika

Hummus, Canadian Style Multi-seasonal

Amy Whitson, PHEc

Where's the lemon? Well we don't grow lemons in Canada, so this hummus uses apple cider vinegar instead, creating a homegrown version of a traditional, heart-healthy vehicle for eating more vegetables.

METHOD

1. Combine chickpeas, vinegar, tahini, garlic, oil, water, red peppers, salt and paprika in a food processor and pulse until smooth, scraping the bowl as needed. Let stand for at least 20 minutes before serving to meld flavours. Store leftovers in the fridge for up to 3 days.

Makes 2 cups (500 mL) One serving = 1/4 cup (60 mL)
Per serving: 132 calories, 7.7 g Fat, 0.8 g Sat. Fat, 0 g Trans Fat, 106 mg Sodium, 7.2 g Carbohydrates, 1.7 g Fibre, 0.5 g Sugars, 0 g Added Sugars, 2.7 g Protein
Carbohydrate Choices: 1/2

APPLE CIDER VINEGAR

When we said bye-bye to lemon and lime juice (because we don't grow any citrus fruits in Canada) we had to find an alternative for that acidic zing that so many recipes need. So it was hello to apple cider vinegar.

    With the amount of apples grown in Canada it was a no brainer that we would make apple cider vinegar. Apple cider vinegar is made from apples that have been fermented and then diluted with water to an acidity of about 5 percent. Most commercial apple cider vinegars are filtered, leaving them clear, but a more natural apple cider vinegar is cloudy, containing a sign of fermentation (strands of protein and enzymes called the "mother"), and is touted as having more health benefits than clear apple cider vinegar. Unfiltered natural apple cider vinegar has become a niche market made by artisans and available at many local orchards, farms and health food stores.

In Quebec, the family-owned business Vinaigrerie Gingras has a rich history in farming. Charles Gingras left France in 1669 to settle in Canada, and in 1671 he was granted a piece of land in Saint-Augustin-de-Desmaures where he established himself as a farmer. Four generations later, his great-great-great- (think I'm running out of greats) grandson Pierre took over the family business and started making high quality apple cider vinegar. Next time you are in Rougemont, Quebec, visit their family orchards and store (or order online).

In New Brunswick check out La Fleur du Pommier in Chemin Cocagne Sud, Uris Williams & Sons in St-Antoine or Verger Belliveau Orchard in Memramcook. In Ontario, Filsinger's Organic Foods and Orchards make a high quality apple cider vinegar and have a store locator on their website that will help you find a store near you. Or try Cider Keg, a family-run business in Norfolk County near Vittoria, Ontario. They sell cider both at their home farm and at Springridge Farm in Milton, Ontario. In BC check out Silverhill Orchard in Mission.

INGREDIENTS

Dressing

1 Tbsp (15 mL) apple cider vinegar

1 Tbsp (15 mL) sodium-reduced soy sauce

1 Tbsp (15 mL) no salt or sugar rice vinegar

2 tsp (10 mL) red miso paste

1 tsp (5 mL) canola oil

2 cloves garlic, minced

1 Tbsp (15 mL) minced fresh ginger

Salad

2 cups (500 mL) frozen shelled edamame

1 cup (250 mL) fresh or frozen corn, thawed

1 red pepper, diced

4 green onions, sliced thinly

Makes 4 cups (1 L) One serving = 1 cup (250 mL) Per serving: 166 Calories, 6.2 g Total Fat, 0.7 g Sat Fat, 0 g Trans Fat, 233 mg Sodium, 21.2 g Carbohydrates, 6.1 g Fibre, 5.2 g sugar, 0 g Added Sugars, 11.3 g Protein Carbohydrate Choices: 0

Asian-Style Edamame and Corn Salad
Late Summer/Early Fall Mairlyn Smith, PHEc

The Japanese have been eating edamame (pronounced ey-dah-MAH-meh) for over 2,000 years. These delicious, albeit mild-tasting green soybeans can be found either at farmers' markets, the frozen vegetable section (or frozen health food section) in larger supermarkets or at any Asian store worth its salt in seaweed. Edamame is grown in Ontario and some parts of Canada (see below). Look for the "Product of Canada" label when buying frozen.

METHOD

1. In a small bowl, whisk together apple cider vinegar, soy sauce, rice vinegar, miso, oil, garlic and ginger. Store in fridge until serving time.
2. In a small pot, bring 1 cup (250 mL) of water to a boil. Add the edamame, bring back to a boil, reduce heat, cover and simmer for 3 to 4 minutes. *Don't overcook*—they tend to go soggy if they have been overcooked. When cooked, drain and place in a medium bowl.
3. Toss together the edamame, thawed frozen corn, diced red pepper and green onions.
4. Store covered in the fridge until well chilled, about 1 to 2 hours or until serving time.
5. Remove from fridge, pour on dressing and toss well. Serve immediately.

EDAMAME

MacKellar Farms in Alvinston, Ontario is the only farm in Canada that grows edamame on a commercial level. They have taken it beyond the farmers' market and now offer Canadians a locally grown, 100% all-natural frozen edamame, sold in larger grocery stores from sea to sea. For a store locator, check out their website mackellarfarms.ca.

Pork and Lamb—The Other Guys

245 A Crash Course in Cooking Pork

248 Herb-Stuffed Pork Loin Roast

251 Maple Pulled Pork

252 Pork Tenderloin with Wild Rice Stuffing

254 Canadian Cassoulet

256 Lettuce Cups

258 Food Safety in the Home

261 Curried Lamb Stew with Fall Vegetables

263 Lamb Chops

PORK AND LAMB

When it comes to pork, Canada is a leader in the international pork industry, ranking third in export volume and seventh in production. Although there are pig farms right across Canada, the biggest pig farms are located in areas that also produce grains, which become feed for the farms. So, you guessed it, those provinces would be: Alberta, Saskatchewan, Manitoba, Quebec and Ontario, with Quebec on the leader board, producing the most pork in Canada.

Sheep are also raised right across Canada. The main sheep producing provinces are Ontario, Quebec, Alberta and Saskatchewan. Raised for meat, wool and milk, there are approximately one million sheep in Canada with 11,000 producers. The majority of those producers are hobbyists who run small *mom-and-pop* type farms.

A CRASH COURSE IN COOKING PORK:

When I was growing up, my mother would routinely cook the living daylights out of Brussels sprouts, turkey and pork. The Brussels were grey blobs of grey green and her turkey and pork dishes were both dry and tasteless. (Insert *sorry mom for outing your cooking*) The reason my mom and mothers all over Canada were cooking their pork until it was *well done* came from their understanding of Trichinosis, a disease caused by a parasite. Happily for this generation, as of January 2000, the Public Health Agency of Canada removed Trichinosis from its national surveillance list. With science and the use of food thermometers, we now know that this microbe is destroyed at 137°F (58°C), which is well under the accepted cooked temperature for pork, 160°F (71°C). Invest in a food thermometer and say hello to tender, juicy pork.

Andrea Villneff, PHEc, with Ontario Pork writes:

> *I often get questions asking me the best way to cook pork. Using a meat thermometer is important, not only for food safety but also to make sure that you do not overcook your pork. Pork is juicy, delicious and tender when cooked properly.*

- Lean cuts such as cuts from the loin and tenderloin should be cooked to the minimum internal temperature of 160°F (71°C). Take these cuts out of the oven at an internal temperature of 155°F (68°C), then tent for 5 minutes while it comes up to proper temperature. Remember that in these cuts a hint of pink is ideal.
- "Tough cuts" (or "flavourful cuts" as I like to call them), such as shoulder and ribs are tough because of a protein called collagen. This protein is dissolved when cooked slowly at a low temperature. With these cuts, don't worry so much about hitting the minimum

internal cooking temperature; you should go past it! You will know when these cuts are done because you should be able to take a fork and pull the meat away easily. This is how you get fall-apart juicy ribs or a perfectly tender pork shoulder roast.

- Ground pork products, like sausage, need to be fully cooked till no pink remains 160°F (71°C); this is true for all ground meat products.

QUICK AND EASY LOCAL PORK

Deb Campbell, PHEc, from Huron County, Ontario, aka Ontario's West Coast, writes:

Huron County is noted for the best sunsets in the world and some very flavourful commodities like local pork form Metzger Meats in Hensall. Grill thick cut bone-in smoked pork chops, then serve with a sauce made from equal amounts Dijon mustard and maple syrup or honey.

HEALTH BITE

Pork is an excellent source of protein, vitamin B-12, vitamin B-6, thiamin, niacin, selenium, zinc and phosphorus, all the essential nutrients for your long-term health. When looking for lean cuts of pork, choose pork tenderloin, pork chops, pork steaks trimmed of visible fat, pork roasts, pork leg (or ham), pork cutlets/pork Scaloppini.

There are no hormones licensed for Canadian pork production. As a double safeguard, the meat is federally inspected on a random basis, to ensure that the meat is hormone (and antibiotic) free at the packers. (Source: Put Pork on Your Fork) For more information about the Canadian Pork industry or for recipes using pork, check out www.putporkonyourfork.ca.

INGREDIENTS

Stuffing

1 Tbsp (15 mL) canola oil, divided

1 onion, finely chopped

2 stalks celery, finely chopped

2 cloves garlic minced

1 cup (250 mL) 100% whole
   wheat Panko crumbs *or* 3
   slices whole grain bread, cut
   into small cubes

1/2 cup (125 mL) sodium-reduced
   chicken broth

1 Tbsp (15 mL) finely chopped
   fresh rosemary

1/4 tsp (1 mL) ground sage

1/2 cup (125 mL) dried
   cranberries

Pork Roast

2 lb (900 g) boneless rib end pork
   roast, excess fat trimmed

1 Tbsp (15 mL) balsamic vinegar

1 1/2 cups (375 mL) loosely
   packed baby spinach leaves

Herb Stuffed Pork Loin Roast Fall/Winter

Bridget Wilson, PHEc

*"The herbed stuffing adds wonderful flavour to this attractive pork roast.
Serve with roasted vegetables and potatoes for a hearty meal."*—Bridget

METHOD

1. Preheat oven to 350°F (175°C).

2. To make the stuffing, heat 1 tsp (5 mL) oil in non-stick medium skillet. Add onion and celery; cook and stir on medium heat for 5 minutes or until softened. Stir in garlic and cook 1 minute longer. Remove from heat. Add panko crumbs (or breadcrumbs, if using), broth, rosemary, sage and cranberries; toss and set aside.

3. To prepare the roast, place roast on a clean cutting board (for more information about cutting boards see page 258 on Food Safety in the Home) with short ends at 12 and 6 o'clock. Holding a sharp knife parallel to the work surface, make a cut 1/2 inch (1 cm) deep lengthwise through underside of roast, pulling back meat with your free hand and unrolling it as you continue to cut through roast. Cover meat with plastic wrap and pound to even thickness, approx. 1/3 inch (8 mm) thick. It's a great way to get rid of aggression: either use a meat pounder or the bottom of a heavy-bottom small saucepan. (Tip: You should end up with a piece of meat that is approx. 1/2 inch (1 cm) thick and 3 times the size of the original roast.)

4. Whisk remaining 2 tsp (10 mL) oil with vinegar in a small bowl. Brush half of the mixture over the cut side of pork. Place spinach in an even layer over pork, and top with the stuffing mixture, leaving a 1-inch (2.5 cm) border. Press stuffing mixture down and roll up tightly like a jelly roll, starting at one short side. Tie closed with kitchen string. Place in roasting or shallow pan.

PHEC TIP:

Replace dried cranberries with the same amount of chopped dried apricots or raisins, if desired.

5. Roast for 1 hour and 10 minutes or until internal temperature reaches 160°F (71°C), brushing with the oil and balsamic mixture at the 40 minute mark. When done, remove from the oven, cover with foil and let rest 10 minutes before slicing to serve.

Makes 8 servings One serving = 1/8 roast
Per serving: 261 Calories, 9.5 g Total Fat, 2.7 g Saturated Fat, 0 g Trans Fat, 116 mg Sodium, 16.6 g Carbohydrate, 2 g Fibre, 7 g Sugars, 4 g Added Sugars, 26.8 g Protein
Carbohydrate Choices: 1

BALSAMIC VINEGAR

You don't have to go to Italy to get genuine balsamic vinegar; Giordano and Marilyn Venturi make a dark, sweet, tart gift from the Vinegar Gods in Cobble Hill on Vancouver Island, BC. They grow their own grapes and then make the vinegar in oak barrels that were made for them near Modena, Italy, the home of balsamic vinegar. Available online or for all those lucky people living on Vancouver Island or in Vancouver, available in many higher end grocery stores. I met Giordano and Marilyn years ago when I was doing Harrowsmith Country Life and they are definitely two Canadian food treasures.

Maple Pulled Pork Fall/Winter

Linda Lichtenberger, PHEc

"When I was a kid my aunt and uncle would take me on a horse-drawn sleigh to the sugar bush near their home in Lucknow, Ontario, to experience the process of making maple syrup. It's always been a familiar and comfortable food item in my kitchen." —Linda

METHOD

1. Place sweet potato, tomato and onion into slow cooker. Remove any visible fat from the pork and set over vegetables.
2. In a medium bowl, stir together the dry mustard, brown sugar, crushed rosemary and hot pepper flakes (if using). Stir in the maple syrup, vinegar, water and minced garlic. Pour over the pork.
3. Cook on high for 3 1/2 to 4 hours, or on low for 5 to 6 hours.
4. When ready to serve, remove meat to plate. Mash vegetables right in the slow cooker.
5. Pull pork apart with two forks to separate into small pieces; return meat to slow cooker and mix with the mashed vegetables.
6. If more liquid is needed, use water, apple cider or apple juice, your choice. Serve.

Makes 6 cups (1.5 L) One serving = 1/2 cup (125 mL)
Per serving: 149 Calories, 1.2 g Total Fat, 0.5 g Saturated Fat, 0 g Trans Fat, 68 mg Sodium, 14.8 g Carbohydrate, 0.7 g Fibre, 11 g Sugars, 9.6 g Added Sugars, 19 g Protein
Carbohydrate Choices: 1

INGREDIENTS

1 medium sweet potato, scrubbed well and sliced into 1/2-inch (1 cm) pieces
1 medium tomato, diced
1 onion, diced
2 lb (900 g) pork tenderloin
1 tsp (5 mL) dry mustard
1 Tbsp (15 mL) packed dark brown sugar
1/4 tsp (1 mL) crushed dried rosemary
1/2 tsp (2 mL) hot pepper flakes (optional)
1 Tbsp (15 mL) Worcestershire sauce
1/2 cup (125 mL) pure maple syrup
1/4 cup (60 mL) apple cider vinegar
1/4 cup (60 mL) water
2 cloves garlic, minced
Apple cider or apple juice (if more liquid is needed)

PHEC TIP:

Heap each serving over a baked potato, or serve with a crusty roll.

Stuffing

1/2 cup (125 mL) wild rice

2 cups (500 mL) no salt added
   vegetable broth

1/4 tsp (1 mL) iodized salt

1 Tbsp (15 mL) canola oil

1 onion, finely diced

1 stalk celery, finely diced

1 clove of garlic, minced

1/4 cup (60 mL) dried cranberries

1/4 cup (60 mL) chopped walnuts

1 tsp (5 mL) dried rosemary

1 tsp (5 mL) dried thyme

Pork Tenderloin

1 lb (450 g) pork tenderloin

Salt and pepper (for seasoning)

Pork Tenderloin with Wild Rice Stuffing Multi-seasonal

Andrea Villneff, PHEc

"A roast with stuffing is always a showstopper. It looks regal and no one has to know how easy it was to do. Wild Rice stuffing is a fun and easy way to spice up a meal, and is a trick my mom used often." —Andrea

For people who love rosemary and pork, this recipe has your name written all over it.

METHOD

1. In a saucepan over high heat, bring wild rice, vegetable broth and salt to a boil. Reduce heat, cover and simmer until most of the rice is split and tender, about 45 minutes. Remove rice from heat and let stand, covered, for 5 minutes. Drain any excess liquid.

2. Preheat oven to 375°F (190°C) and line a 9- × 13-inch (3.5 L) baking dish with parchment paper, set aside.

3. In a medium frying pan over medium-high heat, add oil, onion and celery and sauté for 5 minutes or until the onion and celery are translucent. Add the garlic and sauté for 2 minutes, then remove from heat.

4. In a medium bowl, combine cooked wild rice, onion and celery mixture, cranberries, walnuts, rosemary and thyme. Set aside.

5. Cut any excess fat from the pork tenderloin. On a clean cutting

board, butterfly the pork tenderloin and place the stuffing in the cavity of the tenderloin. Tightly roll the tenderloin up like a jelly roll, so that the stuffing is well contained. Season the outside with salt and pepper.

6. Place on prepared pan and roast for 20 to 35 minutes or until a meat thermometer reads 160°F (71°C). Let stand for 10 minutes, cut into 12 equal slices and serve.

Makes 6 servings (12 slices in total) One Serving = 2 slices
Per serving: 229 Calories, 7 g Total Fat, 1 g Saturated Fat, 0 g Trans Fat, 163 mg Sodium, 20.2 g Carbohydrate, 2.2 g Fibre, 6.8 g Sugars, 2.7 g Added Sugars, 21.8 g Protein
Carbohydrate Choices: 1

CRANBERRIES

Native to our Atlantic provinces, cranberries grow wild and are sometimes known as "marsh apples." Canada is the world's second-largest producer of this tart little red fruit. They are grown in cranberry bogs and love wet soil. Harvesting is performed by flooding the bog and then, using a mechanical beater, knocking the cranberries into the water. As they float on the water, they are pumped into trucks.

British Columbia is Canada's largest cranberry producer. Check out the Fort Langley Cranberry Festival in BC or the Bala Cranberry Festival in Ontario.

PHEC TIP:
To avoid overcooking the pork tenderloin, remove from the oven when it reaches an internal temperature of 155°F (68°C) with a meat thermometer. Cover or tent the roast with foil and let it rest it for 10 minutes; it will continue to cook and will reach 160°F (71°C).

Filling

1 lb (450 g) lean ground pork

1 onion, chopped

1 carrot, scrubbed well and diced

1 celery stalk, diced

4 cloves garlic, minced

2 tsp (10 mL) herbes de Provence–style herb blend (see note)

1/2 tsp (2 mL) fennel seed

1/2 tsp (2 mL) iodized salt

1/2 tsp (2 mL) fresh ground black pepper

Pinch hot pepper flakes (or to taste)

One 28 oz (796 mL) can no salt added plum tomatoes

1 cup (250 mL) no salt added chicken broth

1/2 cup (125 mL) Canadian VQA dry white wine or additional chicken broth

4 cups (1 L) cooked white pea, navy or white kidney beans (see p. 221-222) *or* two 19 oz (540 mL) cans white kidney beans, well rinsed and well drained

6 cups (1.5 L) finely chopped fresh or frozen kale, spine removed

Canadian Cassoulet Fall/Winter

Amy Whitson, PHEc

A spin on the traditional Cassoulet using Canadian pork and pulses.

METHOD

1. Crumble the pork into a large, non-stick skillet set over medium heat. Add the onion, carrot, celery, garlic, herb blend, fennel, salt, pepper and hot pepper flakes.
2. Cook, stirring and breaking up the meat until well browned. Add the tomatoes, broth and wine (or additional broth, if using) and simmer for 15 minutes (break up the whole tomatoes using a potato masher).
3. Preheat oven to 375°F (190°C). Lightly oil 9- × 13-inch (3.5 L) casserole dish.
4. Stir in the beans and kale and transfer to a prepared pan. Cover and bake for 30 minutes.

5. For the topping, pulse the bread with the Parmesan, parsley and oil in a food processor until it is a fine crumble. Sprinkle evenly over the pork mixture. Bake for an additional 15 minutes or until browned and bubbling.

Makes 10 cups (2.5 L) One serving = 1 1/4 cups (310 mL)
Per serving: 346 calories, 14.5 g Fat, 5 g Sat. Fat, 0 g Trans Fat, 608 mg Sodium,
28.4 g Carbohydrates, 7 g Fibre, 5.5 g Sugars, 23 g Protein
Carbohydrate Choices: 1 1/2

INGREDIENT NOTE:

Herbes de Provence—Make your own herbes de Provence blend by combining equal parts dried savoury, marjoram (and/or oregano), rosemary and thyme. Dried lavender can also be included.

INGREDIENTS

Topping

2 slices whole grain bread, torn into chunks

1/2 cup (125 mL) grated Canadian Parmesan cheese

1/4 cup (60 mL) lightly packed parsley leaves

1 Tbsp (15 mL) canola oil

INGREDIENTS

2 omega-3 eggs

Pepper (optional)

2 Tbsp (30 mL) canola oil, divided

2/3 lb (350 g) pork tenderloin, chopped into 1/2-inch (1 cm) pieces

1/2 onion, chopped

4 shiitake mushrooms, caps only (see note)

2 cloves garlic, minced

1 small jalapeño, finely chopped, (optional)

1/2 cup (125 mL) frozen green peas (no need to thaw)

4 cups (1 L) bean sprouts, rinsed and blanched (see note)

2 Tbsp (30 mL) lower sodium soy sauce

8 Boston lettuce leaves (see note)

1/2 cup (125 mL) chopped cilantro

Lettuce Cups Multi-seasonal
Diana Huey, PHEc

"As a kid, I enjoyed eating lettuce wraps prepared by my mom. It made dinner fun and I enjoyed building my own meal. Celebrate local produce and Canadian pork all at the same time." —Diana

METHOD

1. Beat eggs in a medium bowl. Add pepper if desired.
2. In a medium skillet over medium high heat, add 1 tsp (5 mL) oil. Pour in eggs, tilting pan to cover bottom, and cook until set. Remove from pan, roll up like a cigar and set aside. Slice into thin ribbons when cool enough to touch.
3. In the same skillet, add 1 Tbsp (15 mL) oil and sauté pork until fully cooked, about 5 minutes. Remove from pan and set aside.
4. Back in the same pan, heat remaining oil and sauté the onion, mushrooms, garlic and jalapeño (if using). Add frozen peas, blanched bean sprouts, cooked pork and egg ribbons.
5. Add soy sauce and divide filling among the lettuce leaves, approx. 1/2 cup (125 mL) per lettuce leaf. Top each lettuce cup with 1 Tbsp (15 mL) cilantro and serve.

Makes 8 lettuce cups One serving= 2 lettuce cups
Per serving: 266 Calories, 11.2 g Total Fat, 2 g Saturated Fat, 0.2 g Trans Fat, 352 mg Sodium, 15 g Carbohydrate, 3.2 g Fibre, 6.8 g Sugars, 0 g Added Sugars, 27.3 g Protein
Carbohydrate Choices: 1

INGREDIENT NOTES:

Shiitake Mushrooms—The stems from shiitake are tough; use the caps or tops only. Use stems for soup stocks or compost.

Bean Sprouts—Sprouts are a healthy food, but can become contaminated with E. Coli and/or Salmonella, which can lead to food poisoning. For this reason Health Canada advises that all sprouts be cooked before eating them. You can find bean sprouts in most grocery stores where they sell either lettuce or herbs. To blanch, rinse bean sprouts well, add to boiling water for 3 minutes, then drain.

Lettuce—To make it easier to separate lettuce leaves, cut a head of Boston lettuce in half and cover with cold water. Soak for about 15 minutes.

FOOD SAFETY IN THE HOME

Food poisoning usually includes stomach pains, nausea, vomiting and even fever. With over 4 million Canadians getting food poisoning every year, home cooks can practice some basic food safety rules to protect their families.

CLEAN

- Make sure your hands and the counters are clean before and after touching food.
- Wash hands for at least 20 seconds with soap and water, sing a chorus of "Happy Birthday" to yourself or pretend you are in an episode of *Grey's Anatomy* just before a surgical procedure.
- Designate a cutting board for fruits and vegetables and a separate one for meat, including pork, fish and poultry. Wash well with hot soapy water after use. Air dry.
- Never transfer cooked meat, fish or poultry onto a plate that was used for raw meat, fish or poultry.
- Avoid kitchen sponges, they are a breeding ground for bacteria
- Wipe counters with paper towels *or* change your dishcloth daily. Wash the dishcloth in hot soapy water and air dry.
- To sanitize counters, use Health Canada's recommendation of 1 tsp (5 mL) bleach to 10 cups (2.5 L) water. Store in a spritz bottle.
- Wash your reusable grocery bags, often.
- Wash out your cooler bags, often.
- Wash out reusable lunch bags every day.
- Rinse all produce under cold running water just before use, including hard peeled vegetables and fruits like watermelon, squash, etc.
- Use a vegetable brush on skinned produce like potatoes, apples, pears, etc.

CHILL

- Let the food safety rule "Keep hot foods hot and cold food cold" become your food safety mantra.
- Food safety starts in your refrigerator—keep your fridge at 40°F (4°C) or lower and your freezer at -18°C (0°F) or lower
- Bring raw meat, fish or poultry home from the grocery store and refrigerate it as soon as possible (up to 2 hours in the cold winter months, immediately in the summer).
- Store raw meat, fish and poultry away from other foods in separate containers to prevent any raw juices dripping on other foods. Best place to store them is on the bottom shelf.
- Store raw meat, fish and poultry no longer than 2 to 3 days in the refrigerator; for longer periods, freeze and thaw as needed.
- When freezing foods, place in a freezer bag or container to avoid freezer burn and label with the date.
- Don't overcrowd your fridge; you need proper cold air circulation to maintain optimum storage. If you haven't seen the back of your fridge since Pierre Trudeau (Justin's dad) was the Prime Minister, the storage times need to be reconsidered.
- Even though your mom may have thawed frozen meat, fish and poultry on the kitchen counter, doesn't mean it gets the green light. *Never* thaw anything on the kitchen counter. Thaw in the fridge, in the microwave or in a sink full of cold water, changing the water every 30 minutes.

COOK

- The only way to tell that meat, fish and poultry are properly cooked is with a food thermometer. Investing in one is a great idea, as it's one of the most important tools in food safety you can buy. Check page 305 for a chart detailing the ideal internal temperatures for

cooked poultry, and page 344 for the ideal internal temperatures for cooked beef.

- Have a pot of chili on the stove for serving to a crowd? Keep hot foods at or above 60°C (140°F).
- Cooked meat, fish and poultry should be stored in separate containers within 1 to 2 hours of being cooked, and eaten within 2 to 4 days. Remember, you can't smell bacteria until it's so far gone that food poisoning is almost a foregone conclusion. Didn't label what and when you put it in the fridge? *When in doubt, throw it out.*

HAVE FOOD WILL TRAVEL, SAFELY

Transporting a dish to a party? Keep it cold or hot using thermal bags. For cold foods, place freezer packs on top of the food and on the sides of the thermal bag. For hot foods, keep the food hot until just before you leave your home and heat as soon as you arrive. If the drive is more than 30 minutes, don't even think about packing hot food. If you are driving from Winnipeg to Brandon, Manitoba, or Vancouver to Abbotsford, BC, offer to bring something cold or a cake....

Curried Lamb Stew with Fall Vegetables Fall/Winter
Janet Butters, PHEc

"I love making stews in the fall and winter. They are thick and hearty and able to satisfy big appetites. This recipe is a variation of the beef stew my late father always made when I was young. His father, Cyril Butters, Steward, worked in food services on his ship, the HMS Glorious, and was one of the 1207 who lost their lives when the Glorious went down on June 8, 1940, in the Norwegian Sea. This recipe is dedicated to them both." —**Janet**

METHOD
1. In a large pot, combine lamb pieces (including any bones) with rosemary and just enough water to cover. Bring to the boil, cover, reduce heat and simmer for 30 minutes.
2. Drain and let cool slightly. Trim excess fat and cut the lamb into bite-sized pieces. Discard the bones and fat.
3. Rinse out the pot, add 6 cups (1.5 L) water and bring to the boil.
4. In a large non-stick pan over medium heat, brown the lamb pieces in butter and oil, add curry powder and sauté. When the water comes to the boil, add the browned lamb pieces.
5. Add garlic, shallot, onion, potatoes, rutabaga, carrots, celery, bouillon cubes, allspice and the bay leaf. Bring back to the boil,

INGREDIENTS

2 lb (900 kg) fresh lamb shoulder, cut into quarters
2 large sprigs fresh rosemary
2 tsp (10 mL) butter
1 tsp (5 mL) canola oil
3 Tbsp (45 mL) curry powder, mild or hot
2 large garlic cloves, crushed
1 large shallot, finely chopped
1 large onion, finely chopped
6 medium potatoes, peeled and cut into 1/2-inch (1.5 cm) chunks
1/2 small rutabaga, peeled and diced
4 carrots, peeled and diced
3 celery stalks, diced
2 low sodium vegetable bouillon cubes
6 whole allspice berries
1 small bay leaf
2 Tbsp (30 mL) cornstarch
2 Tbsp (30 mL) cold water
5 large mint leaves, coarsely chopped
1 1/2 cups (375 mL) frozen peas

PHEC TIP:

Serve in individual pumpernickel bread bowls along with crustless bread torn or cut into bite-sized chunks for dipping. You'll want to sop up every drop.

cover, reduce heat to medium-low and cook for 45 minutes.

6. In a small bowl, whisk together cornstarch and 2 Tbsp (30 mL) cold water to make a loose paste. Stir into lamb mixture until it comes to a boil and thickens. Add the mint and peas and cook another 5 minutes to warm through. Remove bay leaf and serve.

Makes 14 cups (3.5 L) One Serving = 1 1/2 cups (375 mL)
Per serving: 381 Calories, 14.6 g Total Fat, 6.2 g Saturated Fat, 0.8 g Trans Fat, 210 mg Sodium, 31.4 g Carbohydrate, 4.8 g Fibre, 5 g Sugars, 0 g Added Sugars, 33.2 g Protein
Carbohydrate Choices: 2

LAMB

The main market for sheep in Canada is for meat. We produce about 40 percent of the lamb we consume, the rest is imported from Australia, New Zealand, Wales and Iceland.

In recent years, due to the diversity of our population, the demand for Canadian-raised lamb has been growing in leaps and bounds, but the supply has not. With federally funded programs Canada's Lamb industry hopes to grow to meet some of those demands. The Canadian Lamb Producers Cooperative produces commercially sold Canadian lamb that is halal as well as USDA approved, which allows those lamb products to be exported.

For more information check out www.cdnlamb.com.

Lamb Chops Spring/Summer

Rachel Johnstone, OHEA Student Member

"I was 18 years old the first time I tried lamb, and I fell in love. This recipe is so easy, and so very simple, which I think is why it is so good. Less really can be more."—Rachel

METHOD

1. In a small bowl, combine boiling water and sugar; stir to dissolve. Add mint and vinegar and mix well. Set aside.
2. Lightly rub the oil over the lamb, making sure to oil all areas.
3. Sprinkle lamb with the rosemary and salt and pepper, gently pressing the mixture onto the meat. Refrigerate until ready to use.
4. Preheat oven to 350°F (180°C). Line a rimmed baking pan with parchment. Place chops on top.
5. Roast in the oven for about 5 minutes, then turn each chop. Roast for another 3 to 5 minutes (depending on their size) or until you reach an internal temperature of 150°F (65°C) for medium, or 145°F (63°C) for rare. Serve with the mint relish drizzled over the meat.

Makes 8 chops One serving = 2 lamb chops
Per serving: 391 Calories, 26.6 g Total Fat, 6.5 g Saturated Fat, 0.9 g Trans Fat, 268 mg Sodium, 5.5 g Carbohydrate, 2.6 g Fibre, 2.1 g Sugars, 2.1 g Added Sugars, 32.5 g Protein
Carbohydrate Choices: less than 1

INGREDIENTS

Mint Relish

1 Tbsp (15 mL) boiling water
2 tsp (10 mL) granulated sugar
1 1/2 cups (375 mL) finely chopped fresh mint
1/3 cup (80 mL) white wine vinegar

Lamb Chops

1/4 cup (60 mL) canola oil
1 rack of Ontario spring lamb (approx. 1 1/4 lb/590 g) trimmed, Frenched (bones cleaned) and cut into chops
4 sprigs of fresh rosemary, chopped fine
1/4 tsp (1 mL) iodized salt
1/4 tsp (1 mL) black pepper

PHEC TIP:

For a more intense flavour, prepare the lamb chops the day before. Prep the chops according to the method, but let them sit in the refrigerator covered overnight before cooking.

Fish and Seafood from Coast to Coast to Coast

267 Crab Cakes with Garlic Aioli

268 Mussels in Spicy Tomato Sauce

271 Spring Trout Cakes

272 Hot Smoked Salmon and Seaweed Salad

on Asian-Style Spoons

274 Seafood Chowder

276 Bouillabaisse

278 Bruschetta Grilled Pickerel

280 Crispy Oven Baked Pickerel with Greek

Yogurt Tartar Sauce

282 Cod Cakes with Asian-Style Coleslaw

284 Canadian Canned Salmon Cakes with Tartar Sauce

286 Fish Tacos with Red Pepper and Corn Salsa

288 Fresh Shrimp Pasta Salad

290 Salmon with Peach Salsa

292 Aquaculture in Canada

293 Salmon Teriyaki

294 Tandoori Crusted Cod

295 Lobster with Pasta and Cherry Tomatoes

297 Asian-Style Nova Scotia Scallops with Miso Glaze

Canada is unique in more ways than one. We play hockey all year round, know what a double-double is and when it comes to fishing, we have three oceans and four Great Lakes to choose from.

From BC's wild sockeye salmon to the Maritime's lobsters, Canada has one of the most rich and diverse fishing industries in the world. With approximately 85 percent of our wild capture fish and seafood products being exported around the world, this valuable natural resource generated more than $3.9 billion in export revenues in 2013. That's a *whole lotta* fish and seafood.

Crab Cakes with Garlic Aioli Spring/Summer

Rachel Johnstone, OHEA Student Member

"" —Rachel

METHOD

1. To make the Garlic Aioli, whisk together 2 cloves garlic, mayo and 1 to 2 Tbsp (15 to 30 mL) vinegar in a small bowl. Store in the fridge until serving time or up to 2 days in advance.

2. Heat oil in a large skillet over medium heat; add 1 clove garlic and sauté for 1 minute.

3. Add red, white and green onions and the red pepper; cook until slightly soft, about 6 to 8 minutes. Add parsley and 2 Tbsp (30 mL) apple cider vinegar.

4. Remove from heat and place in a sieve over a bowl to drain; let cool. Wipe out pan with a paper towel. Set aside.

5. When the vegetable mixture is completely cooled, whisk the egg white until frothy in a large bowl. Add the vegetable mixture, crabmeat and breadcrumbs. Form into 6 equal cakes.

6. Place skillet back over medium-high heat; add a small amount of oil and fry until browned on both sides. Serve each crab cake with 1 Tbsp (15 mL) Garlic Aioli.

Makes 6 crab cakes One serving = 1 crab cake with 1 Tbsp (15 mL) Garlic Aioli
Per serving: 150 Calories, 8.2 g Total Fat, 1 g Saturated Fat, 0 g Trans Fat, 453 mg Sodium, 6.8 g Carbohydrate, 1 g Fibre, 2 g Sugars, 0 g Added Sugars, 13.8 g Protein
Carbohydrate Choices: 1/2

PHEC TIP:

The flavour of the crab really comes through in this recipe, but if you want to add some zing, add 1/4 tsp (1 mL) cracked black pepper to the ingredients.

INGREDIENTS

Garlic Aioli (makes 1/3 cup/80 mL)
2 cloves garlic, minced
1/4 cup (60 mL) low fat mayonnaise
1–2 Tbsp (15–30 mL) apple cider vinegar

Crab Cakes
1 Tbsp (15 mL) canola oil + extra for frying
1 clove garlic, minced
1/3 cup (75 mL) minced red onion (approx. 1 small onion)
1/4 cup (60 mL) minced white onion (approx. 1/4 of an onion)
4 green onions, sliced
1/2 cup (125 mL) minced red pepper (approx. 1/2 a red pepper)
3 Tbsp (45 mL) finely chopped parsley
2 Tbsp (30 mL) apple cider vinegar
1 large egg white *or* 2 Tbsp (30 mL) pasteurized egg white (see page 54)
2 1/4 cups (560 mL) fresh or frozen, thawed Canadian crabmeat
1/4 cup (60 mL) 100% whole wheat Panko crumbs

INGREDIENTS

2 Tbsp (30 mL) canola oil

1/2 white onion, diced

1 jalapeño, seeded and diced

3 cloves garlic, minced

1/2 cup (125 mL) Canadian VQA
dry white wine

One 19 oz (540 mL) can low
sodium chopped tomatoes

1/3 cup (80 mL) low sodium
chicken or vegetable broth

1 lb (450 g) Canadian mussels,
cleaned and debearded (see
Mussels 101, p. 270)

1 Tbsp (15 mL) chopped fresh
parsley

1 tsp (5 mL) chopped fresh
oregano

Mussels in Spicy Tomato Sauce Multi-seasonal

Rachel Johnstone, OHEA Student Member

Canada is a large producer of farmed mussels. In 2006, 72 percent of all farmed mussels in Canada came from the tiny island of PEI. New Brunswick and Nova Scotia are also large producers, with the British Columbia mussel industry lower in the pack, but growing. Mussel farming is green and sustainable, and farmed mussels help to reduce greenhouse gases by removing carbon dioxide from the ocean for shell formation.

METHOD

1. In a large saucepan or skillet over medium heat, add oil, onion and jalapeño and sauté until soft (onion will turn translucent), about 2 to 3 minutes. Add garlic and sauté for 1 minute.
2. Add wine. When the liquid starts to boil, reduce to simmer, scraping up any bits that are stuck to the pan.
3. Add the chopped tomatoes and broth and bring to a boil. Turn the heat to medium-low and simmer for about 5 minutes.
4. Add the mussels and simmer, covered, until they're all opened, about 5 to 8 minutes; stir occasionally.
5. Add the chopped herbs and mix well. Serve in shallow soup bowls with a crusty whole-grain baguette.

Makes approx. 4 cups (1 L) One serving = 2 cups (500 mL)
Per serving: 441 Calories, 19.3 g Total Fat, 2 g Saturated Fat, 0.3 g Trans Fat, 547 mg Sodium, 23.6 g Carbohydrate, 3.5 g Fibre, 10.8 g Sugars, 0 g Added Sugars, 30 g Protein
Carbohydrate Choices: 1

MUSSELS 101

- Mussels are a very good source of protein, vitamin B-12, iron, manganese and selenium.
- Fresh mussels are best eaten within a day of buying.
- Immediately store in the fridge where they will stay cold. If any have opened and will not close with a light tap, they have died and should be discarded.
- Discard any cracked mussels
- Debearding? Mussels may have long fibres (beards) coming out of the shell; hold the mussel in your hand and sharply pull the beard off. Discard.
- Mussels are sold in vacuum-sealed containers in the fresh fish sections of larger grocery stores; eat on or before the best before date.

Spring Trout Cakes Spring

Erin MacGregor, PHEc, RD

"Fresh farmed Canadian rainbow trout is available year round. It has a permanent place on my weekly grocery list because it's affordable and preparation is quick and easy. These trout cakes work well for a weeknight meal or a dinner party. They can be prepped in advance and pan-fried just before serving. Leftovers also reheat well." —Erin

METHOD

1. Preheat oven to 400°F (200°C). Line a rimmed baking sheet with parchment paper or foil.

2. Place trout on prepared pan and bake for 10 to 12 minutes or until fish flakes when prodded with a fork. Remove from oven and cool for 15 minutes. Remove the skin and discard. Using a fork, flake the fish into small bite-sized flakes and transfer to a medium bowl. Add breadcrumbs, shallot, mustard, mayo, vinegar, dill, egg, salt and pepper and mix until just combined. Make 8 equal trout cakes. Place on a wax paper–lined plate and refrigerate cakes for at least 1 hour.

3. Preheat oven to 200°F (95°C). Line a rimmed baking sheet with parchment paper or foil, set aside.

4. In a large non-stick frying pan over medium-high heat, add oil and pan-fry cakes for 3 minutes per side. Place cooked cakes in oven on prepared pan to keep warm while you cook the remaining cakes.

Makes 8 trout cakes One serving = 2 trout cakes
Per serving: 338 Calories, 15.5 g Total Fat, 3 g Saturated Fat, 0 g Trans Fat, 436 mg Sodium, 15.7 g Carbohydrate, 2 g Fibre, 1 g Sugars, 0 g Added Sugars, 31.6 g Protein
Carbohydrate Choices: 1

INGREDIENTS

1 lb (450 g) rainbow trout fillets (see note)

1 cup (250 mL) 100% whole wheat Panko crumbs

1 medium shallot, minced

2 Tbsp (30 mL) whole-grain mustard

2 Tbsp (30 mL) low fat mayonnaise

2 tsp (10 mL) white wine vinegar

2 Tbsp (30 mL) chopped fresh dill

1 omega-3 egg, lightly beaten

1/4 tsp (1 mL) iodized salt

1/8 tsp (0.5 mL) freshly ground black pepper

1 Tbsp (15 mL) canola oil

INGREDIENT NOTE:

Rainbow Trout—You can find wild and farmed rainbow trout right across Canada. It is an excellent source of omega-3 fatty acids and a good alternative to salmon.

PHEC TIP:

These taste wonderful with a creamy horseradish sauce. Add 1 Tbsp (15 mL) horseradish to 1/4 cup (60 mL) low fat mayo, mix well and serve.

INGREDIENTS

12 porcelain Chinese spoons

1/3 cup (80 mL) seaweed salad (see note)

2.5 oz (75 g) smoked salmon (see note)

2 Tbsp (30 mL) sour cream, regular or low fat

1 1/2 Tbsp (23 mL) black caviar, herring or lumpfish roe

Hot Smoked Salmon and Seaweed Salad on Asian-Style Spoons Multi-seasonal
Margaret Dickenson, PHEc

"One of life's great joys is getting together with family and friends in the warmth and charm of your own home. My secret to easy, relaxed and successful entertaining is to make it personal, memorable and doable, and to never underestimate the power of hors d'oeuvres. I guarantee it will get your event off to a vibrant start, especially if presented in a clever way. I always try to include Asian-styled spoons, petit containers and unique serving tools in my hors d'oeuvres repertoire, and this recipe is one of my favourites." —Margaret

METHOD

1. Place the 12 spoons on a platter or plate. Equally divide the seaweed salad in the bottom of each of the spoons.
2. Thinly slice the smoked salmon. Divide equally between the 12 spoons.
3. When ready to serve—and not any sooner—top with 1/2 tsp (2 mL) sour cream and "crown" with a scant 1/2 tsp (2 mL) caviar. Serve immediately.

Makes 12 "one-bite" hors d'oeuvres One serving = 3 hors d'oeuvres
Per serving: 72 Calories, 4 g Total Fat, 1 g Saturated Fat, 0 g Trans Fat, 531 mg Sodium, 4.2 g Carbohydrate, 0.3 g Fibre, 2.7 g Sugars, 0 g Added Sugars, 5.5 g Protein
Carbohydrate Choices: less than 1

SMOKED SALMON

Smoked Salmon is synonymous with the West Coast. Traditionally the West Coast Aboriginal peoples smoked their salmon to prolong its storage. When the settlers arrived they adopted this method of preservation.

INGREDIENT NOTES:

Seaweed Salad—Seaweed Salad is available at larger grocery stores that have a fresh sushi bar section, in fish stores or at most Japanese and Korean food stores. Margaret suggests adding a touch of sesame oil to balance the flavours.

Smoked Salmon—There are two types of smoked salmon, cold and hot. Either type is delicious in this recipe. Hot smoked salmon should be available at most high-end fish/seafood stores, and it is different from cold smoked salmon. In the production of hot smoked salmon, both smoke and heat are involved with the salmon being either baked or barbecued. Cold smoked salmon is only smoked but not cooked, resulting in a more tender salmon than hot smoked salmon. (Margaret Dickenson, PHEc)

INGREDIENTS

2 lb (900 g) fresh Canadian
   mussels (see note)

2 tsp (10 mL) canola oil, divided

2 onions, diced, divided

1/2 cup (125 mL) Canadian VQA
   dry white wine

2 cups (500 mL) water, divided

2 stalks celery, diced

1 bay leaf

1 sprig of thyme

1 tsp (5 mL) paprika

1/4 tsp (1 mL) cayenne pepper

1/4 cup (60 mL) all-purpose flour

2 medium yellow potatoes,
   peeled and cubed

1/2 lb (250 g) fresh or frozen
   Canadian haddock

12 large Canadian shrimp, peeled
   and deveined

1 cup (250 mL) 1% milk

1 Tbsp (15 mL) dulse (see note)

Pepper to taste

1 sprig parsley or dill for garnish

Seafood Chowder Multi-seasonal

Katie Brunke, OHEA Student Member

*"Although I am not officially an East Coaster, I feel as though
I'm an honorary one. I've had the privilege of spending many summer
vacations over the years among great friends in Nova Scotia. Each visit
is filled with many laughs, gracious East Coast hospitality, and the best
food made from the freshest ingredients from backyard gardens and the
nearby ocean. This seafood chowder is inspired by such experiences
and is sure to warm your heart and stomach."* —Katie

METHOD

1. Scrub mussels and remove any beards (the plant-like structure that clings to the shells). Throw away any mussels that do not close when tapped; it means they have died. For more tips see page 270.

2. In a large saucepan over high heat, add 1 tsp (5 mL) oil and half of the onion; sauté for about 3 minutes. Reduce to medium and add white wine and 1 cup (250 mL) water. Cover, reduce heat to low and simmer mussels until they open, about 3 to 5 minutes. Strain mussels into a bowl, reserving broth to set aside, and discard any mussels that did not open. When mussels are cool enough to handle, remove from their shells and set aside.

3. In large saucepan over medium high heat, add the rest of the oil and onion and the celery and sauté for about 3 minutes or until the onion is translucent. Add the bay leaf, thyme, paprika and cayenne pepper, stirring occasionally until the herbs become fragrant, approx. 1 minute.

4. Add the flour, stirring constantly for 1 minute. Stir in the reserved broth and remaining water, add potatoes and bring to a boil. Reduce heat to medium, cover and gently simmer, stirring occasionally until potatoes are tender, about 15 to 20 minutes.

5. Add haddock and shrimp, and allow to simmer for 5 minutes, or until fish is cooked through. Stir in milk, mussels and dulse.

6. Stir until heated through, about 2 minutes. Season with pepper to taste. Discard bay leaf and thyme sprig before serving. Garnish with fresh parsley and/or dill. Serve.

Makes 9 cups (2.25 L) One serving= 1 1/2 cups (375 mL)
Per serving: 432 Calories, 6.2 g Total Fat, 1 g Saturated Fat, 0 g Trans Fat, 365 mg Sodium, 27.7 g Carbohydrate, 2.2 g Fibre, 5 g Sugars, 0 g Added Sugars, 32 g Protein
Carbohydrate Choices: 2

OUR TOP THREE

The top three species, in terms of value for commercial fishing landings in 2011 were, by region:

Atlantic species—lobster, snow crab and shrimp

Pacific species—wild salmon, halibut and geoduck clams

Freshwater commercial species—yellow pickerel, perch and whitefish

INGREDIENT NOTE:

Mussels—Mussel shells can be rinsed, crushed and added to your garden as compost.

Dulse—Dulse is red or purple seaweed that grows on rocks in the North Atlantic and Northwest Pacific. It is more commonly eaten in Atlantic Canada. You can find dulse in larger grocery stores and in health food stores. It contains vitamins, minerals and trace elements, especially iodine.

TEN REASONS TO EAT CANADIAN FISH AND SEAFOOD TWICE A WEEK:

1. Healthier heart
2. Healthier blood vessels
3. Healthier joints
4. Healthier eyes
5. Healthier brain
6. Healthier nervous system
7. Healthier skin
8. Healthier GI tract
9. Healthier lungs
10. Healthier outlook on life

INGREDIENTS

1 Tbsp (15 mL) canola oil

1 large leek, thinly sliced (see note p. 63)

1 onion, chopped

1 large carrot, scrubbed well and diced

1 small fennel bulb, diced

2 cloves garlic, minced

1 large yellow potato, scrubbed well and diced

1/2 cup (125 mL) Canadian VQA dry white wine

2 medium tomatoes, diced

1 tsp (5 mL) dried thyme leaves

3 whole bay leaves

1 tsp (5 mL) cayenne pepper

Two 8.3 oz (236 mL) bottles clam juice

5 1/4 cups (1.3 L) water, divided

1 Tbsp (15 mL) cornstarch

One 1 lb (454 g) pkg frozen raw Canadian peeled shrimp (16–20 per bag; see note)

Bouillabaisse Multi-seasonal

Astrid Muschalla, PHEc

"This is one of our family's favourite special occasion meals. We often have it as a first course for Christmas dinner. In a traditional bouillabaisse, the fish is cooked whole in water, but the method I chose for this recipe ensures extra flavour development at the start to minimize salt and utilizes the convenience of frozen seafood. It's also gluten free."—Astrid

METHOD

1. Heat oil in a large soup pot over medium heat; add onion and leek and sauté for 5 minutes or until softened, not browned.

2. Add carrot and fennel and sauté 3 more minutes. Stir in garlic and potato and sauté for 1 minute.

3. Add white wine and cook on medium heat for another minute, scraping any browned bits up with a wooden spoon.

4. Add tomatoes, thyme, bay leaves, cayenne pepper, clam juice and 5 cups (1.25 L) water. Bring to a boil, reduce heat to low and cook uncovered for 15 minutes.

5. Dissolve cornstarch in 1/4 cup (60 mL) water. Stir in and bring to boil.

6. Add frozen shrimp, scallops and salmon (or trout, if using) and cook on medium heat until shrimp has started to turn pink and fish is almost cooked.

7. Add the can of clams, including the liquid. Stir in the parsley and dill; bring to a final boil. Remove from heat and let sit for 3 to 5 minutes. Remove bay leaves and season with pepper, if desired; serve.

Makes 16 cups (4 L) One serving = 1 1/2 cups (375 mL)
Per serving: 177 Calories, 4 g Total Fat, 0.8 g Saturated Fat, 0 g Trans Fat, 269 mg Sodium, 13.4 g Carbohydrate, 2 g Fibre, 2.2 g Sugars, 0 g Added Sugars, 21 g Protein
Carbohydrate Choices: 1

HEALTH BITE

All fish and seafood contain high quality protein, as well as vitamins, specifically Vitamins A and D. They also include important minerals like iodine (which helps with thyroid function), as well as selenium, zinc, iron and potassium. Fatty fish like salmon and trout contain omega-3 fatty acids, which are important for heart and brain health

SIZE MATTERS

Know what one serving of protein really looks like? You might be shocked—it's a measly 2 1/2 oz (75 g) or 1/2 cup (125 mL) cooked fish, shellfish, poultry or lean meat. That's approximately the size of a small deck of cards. When was the last time you only ate that?

INGREDIENTS (CONT'D)

One 14 oz (400 g) bag of frozen raw wild Nova Scotia scallops
1/2 lb (250 g) frozen Canadian salmon or trout fillets, thawed and cut into 1-inch (2.5 cm) pieces (see note)
One 5 oz (142 g) can baby clams (including liquid)
3 Tbsp (45 mL) fresh parsley, finely chopped
3 Tbsp (45 mL) finely chopped fresh dill
Extra pepper (optional)

INGREDIENT NOTES:

Shrimp—If using unpeeled raw shrimp, thaw in advance, then peel. Add to the soup in the last 3 minutes of cooking.
Salmon/Trout—Feel free to use Canadian farmed tilapia or halibut instead of the salmon or trout.

INGREDIENTS

1 Tbsp (15 mL) canola oil, divided

2 pickerel fillets (each approx. 12 oz/375 g; see note)

2 cups (500 mL) grape or cherry tomatoes, cut in half (see note)

1 large clove garlic, minced

2 Tbsp (30 mL) chopped fresh basil

1/4 tsp (1 mL) freshly ground black pepper

1/8 tsp (0.5 mL) iodized salt

Bruschetta Grilled Pickerel Summer/Fall

Jennifer MacKenzie, PHEc

"Living in the Kawarthas area of Ontario surrounded by beautiful lakes and rivers means seeing hardy fisher-people out in rain, fog or even out on the ice in the cold of winter. Meanwhile, more fair-weathered types (like me) wait for a bright, sunny day to cast our lines. Fishers in this region weather all sorts of conditions in the hopes of catching a prize pickerel, also known as walleye, and some have travelled from around the world to our plentiful Ontario waters just for our fish.
Pickerel is well regarded as one of the best-tasting fresh water fish in North America and I agree! It's a favourite whether caught from the dock or purchased at the fish market or grocery store." —Jennifer

METHOD

1. Preheat barbecue grill to medium-high.
2. Cut four 12-inch (30 cm) squares of foil. Fold in half to make a double layer. Fold up 1 inch (2.5 cm) along each side and pinch edges to seal to form an open tray. Repeat to make 4 trays. Place trays on a baking sheet. Brush about half of the oil over insides of trays.
3. Lightly rinse fish fillets and pat dry. Remove any bones and belly fat. Cut each fillet in half lengthwise, then cut crosswise where the thicker portion of the fillet starts to taper thinner. You will have 8 pieces. Place 2 fish pieces of equal thickness, skin side down, on each oiled foil tray.

4. In a bowl, combine tomatoes, the remaining oil, garlic, basil, pepper and salt. Spoon evenly over and around fish.

5. Slide foil trays onto the grill, close lid and grill for 8 to 15 minutes, depending on thickness, or until fish is opaque and flakes easily with a fork and tomato topping is lightly browned. Check the thinner portions earlier and remove them as they're cooked. Slide trays back on to the baking sheet to remove from the grill.

6. Slide a thin spatula under fillets to lift from foil. Divide fish and topping equally among serving plates.

PHEC TIP:

Arranging fish fillets on foil trays by pairing up pieces of similar thickness allows you to cook the thinner pieces for less time and remove them when they're done, while allowing the thicker pieces to cook longer, resulting in 8 pieces of perfectly cooked fish.

Makes 4 servings One serving = 1/4 recipe
Per serving: 134 Calories, 4.9 g Total Fat, 0.5 g Saturated Fat, 0 g Trans Fat, 126 mg Sodium, 3.5 g Carbohydrate, 1 g Fibre, 2 g Sugars, 0 g Added Sugars, 18.7 g Protein
Carbohydrate Choices: less than 1

INGREDIENT NOTE:

Pickerel—If using frozen fish, place package in a dish and let thaw overnight in the refrigerator. Or, seal tightly in a bag and immerse in a sink full of cold water, changing the water frequently to keep it cold, until fish is thawed. Never re-freeze thawed fish.

Tomatoes—If you don't have grape or cherry tomatoes, use 2 medium/large tomatoes. Cut each in half crosswise and squeeze out some of the juice and seeds and discard, then dice the tomatoes. This prevents the bruschetta mixture from being too wet.

INGREDIENTS

Tartar Sauce (makes 1 cup/250 mL)

1/2 cup (125 mL) 0% fat Greek yogurt

1 Tbsp (15 mL) low fat mayonnaise

2 Tbsp (15 mL) relish (dill or sweet) *or* low sodium dill pickles, diced

1/2 Tbsp (7 mL) finely chopped dill (optional)

1 Tbsp (15 mL) finely chopped red onion

1 large clove garlic, crushed

Pepper, to taste

Baked Pickerel

1 omega-3 egg

1/2 cup (125 mL) 100% whole wheat Panko crumbs

1/4 cup (60 mL) finely shredded Canadian Parmesan cheese

2 Tbsp (30 mL) minced fresh parsley

1 tsp (5 mL) garlic powder

1 tsp (5 mL) paprika

1/4 tsp (1 mL) iodized salt

1/4 tsp (1 mL) freshly ground black pepper

1 lb (450 g) boneless pickerel fillet, cut into 4 equal pieces

Crispy Oven Baked Pickerel with Greek Yogurt Tartar Sauce
Spring, Summer and Autumn
Anna Shier, PHEc, RD

"This recipe brings back fond childhood memories of fishing for pickerel with my dad on Lake Simcoe, Ontario. Not only did my dad teach me how to fish, but he also taught me the unpleasant jobs of scaling, gutting and filleting a fish. When we arrived home after a long day of fishing, my mom and I would prepare the fish by breading it and frying it in a skillet—nothing compares to that fresh flavour. My father-in-law is also an avid fisherman and greatly enjoys fried fish of any kind. I created this healthier version of my mom's recipe so you too can enjoy all the health benefits of fish with your family and friends, and dedicate it to him." —Anna

METHOD

1. To make the tartar sauce, combine yogurt, mayo, relish (or dill, if using), onion, garlic and pepper in a medium bowl. Cover and store in the refrigerator until ready to use, or up to 1 day in advance.
2. Preheat oven to 450°F (230°C). Line a large rimmed baking sheet with parchment paper.
3. Lightly beat the egg in a bowl and set aside. In a separate bowl, combine bread crumbs, cheese, parsley, garlic powder, paprika, salt and ground pepper.

4. Dip each piece of fish into the egg mixture and then into the bread crumb mixture, making sure both sides are coated. Place on the prepared pan.

5. Bake for 7 to 10 minutes or until fish flakes when prodded with a fork. Do not overcook. Serve each serving with 1/4 cup (60 mL) tartar sauce.

Makes 4 filets One serving = 1 filet with 1/4 cup (60 mL) tartar sauce
Per serving: 246 Calories, 6.4 g Total Fat, 2 g Saturated Fat, 0 g Trans Fat, 422 mg Sodium, 14.3 g Carbohydrate, 1.7 g Fibre, 3.2 g Sugars, 0 g Added Sugars, 32 g Protein
Carbohydrate Choices: 1

PICKEREL ON THE BBQ

"My husband and I do a traditional Northern Ontario shore lunch at home on the barbecue. On thick tin foil, place thinly sliced potatoes in a layer the same size as the fish, top with fresh cleaned pickerel, add a layer of sliced onions, another layer of thinly sliced carrots and 1 Tbsp (15 mL) butter on top. Season with salt and pepper. Tightly seal foil, place on a grill or a campfire and cook through, about 12 to 20 minutes depending on the thickness of the fish and the potatoes." (Jennifer Rennie, PHEc)

INGREDIENTS

Asian-Style Coleslaw (makes 3 cups/750 mL)

2 Tbsp (30 mL) pure maple syrup

2 Tbsp (30 mL) apple cider vinegar

2 tsp (10 mL) cold pressed canola oil

1 Tbsp (15 mL) grated fresh ginger (see note p.134)

1/4 green or Savoy cabbage, thinly sliced or shredded

Cod Cakes

2 large baking potatoes, peeled and cut into chunks

3 Tbsp (45 mL) canola oil, divided

1 small onion, finely chopped

2/3 lb (350 g) fresh or frozen Canadian cod filets cut into 4 equal pieces

1/4 cup (60 mL) finely chopped chives

2 Tbsp (30 mL) plain 0% MF Greek-style yogurt

1 cup (250 mL) 100% whole wheat Panko crumbs

2 tsp (10 mL) coarsely ground black pepper

2 omega-3 eggs, beaten

Pinch of iodized salt

Cod Cakes with Asian-Style Coleslaw Fall/Winter

Spencer Finch-Coursey, PHEc

"When I visited the East Coast provinces with my family, we were introduced to fish cakes. After we had tried many different versions, the type of fish cake that I liked the best was mostly fish with just a small amount of potatoes. Depending on the season or the mood I'm in, I use chives with spices such as turmeric, paprika or chili flakes to create different flavours." —Spencer

METHOD

1. To make Asian-Style Cole Slaw, whisk together maple syrup, vinegar, oil and ginger in a large bowl. Add cabbage and toss to coat. Store in the fridge until serving time. Can be made 1 day ahead.

2. Place potatoes in a medium saucepan, just covering with cold water, bring to the boil Cover, reduce heat to medium and gently boil until tender, about 10 to 15 minutes. Drain, mash and set aside.

3. Meanwhile, in a large skillet over medium-high heat, add 1 Tbsp (15 mL) oil and onion and sauté for 3 to 5 minutes or until transparent. Add cod and cook for 6 to 8 minutes or until fish flakes when prodded with a fork. Using a fork, flake the cod right in the pan, creating small bite-sized flakes. Transfer to a plate and let cool.

4. In a large bowl, combine mashed potatoes, chives and yogurt. Add the cod and mix until just combined. Form into 8 cod cakes. Place on a wax paper–lined plate and refrigerate cakes for at least 1 hour.

5. Preheat oven to 200°F (95°C). Line a rimmed baking sheet with parchment paper or foil and set aside.

6. Place beaten eggs in a shallow dish. In a separate shallow dish, add breadcrumbs and pepper. Place each cod cake into the egg to coat, then into the breadcrumb mixture. Place on a clean plate.

7. In a large non-stick frying pan add oil and pan-fry cakes over medium-high heat 4 minutes per side. Place cooked cakes in oven on prepared pan to keep warm while you cook the remaining cakes.
8. Place 3/4 cup (175 mL) of the Asian-Style Cole slaw on each plate, top with two cod cakes per plate and serve.

Makes 8 cod cakes
One Serving = 2 cod cakes with 3/4 cup (175 mL) Asian-Style Coleslaw
Per serving: 494 Calories, 17 g Total Fat, 1.2 g Saturated Fat, 0.3 g Trans Fat, 206 mg Sodium, 62.2 g Carbohydrate, 7.8 g Fibre, 12.8 g Sugars, 6.1 g Added Sugars, 25.4 g Protein
Carbohydrate Choices: 3 1/2

COD

Canada's cod industry has seen the highest highs and the lowest lows. In 1992 the Canadian Government placed a moratorium on the Northern Cod Fishery to protect the nearly decimated species. The impact this had on Newfoundland, both economically and socially, was devastating, with over 35,000 fishers and plant workers from over 400 coastal communities being affected.

The cod population has still not recovered from over-fishing, although in 2012, according to the Head of the Fisheries Conservation Group, Dr. George Rose, there are clear signs that the cod stocks are in better health with increases in size and numbers. Atlantic Cod is currently being farmed in Newfoundland, Labrador and New Brunswick.

Salmon Cakes

1 clove garlic, minced

Three 7 1/2 oz (213 g) cans red sockeye or pink salmon (see note)

Two omega-3 eggs, beaten

1/2 cup (125 mL) whole grain cracker crumbs (see note)

1 small celery stalk with leaves, minced

1 onion, minced

1 Tbsp (15 mL) chopped fresh parsley

1/4 tsp (1 mL) iodized salt

1/4 tsp (1 mL) freshly ground black pepper

1 Tbsp (15 mL) canola oil

1 Tbsp (15 mL) butter

Canadian Canned Salmon Cakes with Tartar Sauce
Multi-seasonal Janet Butters, PHEc

"These simple salmon cakes are delicious year round and were always a staple at our house when I was growing up." —Janet

METHOD

1. Drain cans of salmon and place (including the bones—a great source of calcium!) in a large bowl; flake well.
2. Add eggs, garlic, crackers, celery, onion, parsley, salt and pepper. Mix well. Shape into 8 salmon cakes, each approx. 3 inches (8 cm) thick.
3. Preheat oven to 325°F (160°C). Line a rimmed baking sheet with parchment paper or foil and set aside.
4. Heat a large skillet over medium heat; add oil and butter. Brown both sides of each salmon cake. Place on the prepared pan and bake for 15 to 20 minutes or until completely heated through.
5. While the salmon cakes are cooking, prepare the tartar sauce: in a small bowl mix together yogurt, mayo, horseradish, green onion and parsley. Store covered in the fridge until serving time.
6. To serve, place 1 salmon cake on a plate and top with 1 Tbsp (15 mL) tartar sauce.

Makes 8 salmon cakes One Serving = 1 salmon cake with 1 Tbsp (15 mL) Homemade Tartar Sauce
Per serving: 235 Calories, 15 g Total Fat, 3.5 g Saturated Fat, 0 g Trans Fat, 536 mg Sodium, 8 g Carbohydrate, 1.2 g Fibre, 2 g Sugars, 0 g Added Sugars, 16.5 g Protein
Carbohydrate Choices: 1/2

ARCTIC CHAR

Arctic Char may look like salmon but is more closely linked to trout. These cold-water-loving fish are found mainly in Atlantic provinces and territories of Canada, mainly in Northern Labrador.

ARCTIC CHAR IN THE CLASSROOM

In one of my classes when we were looking at regional foods of Canada, my students did an awesome recipe with Arctic char. They mixed apple juice with juniper berries, which provided a luxurious poaching liquid. By mashing the berries slightly a kind of wildness resonated throughout the liquid, flavouring the delicate fish flavours. When opaque, they removed the fish from the liquid and kept it warm. They reduced liquid to about half by boiling gently, then stirred in a small amount of whipping cream, simmering gently until somewhat thickened. They strained it and then poured it over the fish. It was worth an A. (Diane O'Shea, PHEc)

INGREDIENTS

Tartar Sauce (makes 1/2 cup/125 mL)
1/4 cup (60 mL) 0% MF Greek-style yogurt
3 Tbsp (45 mL) low-fat mayonnaise
2 Tbsp (30 mL) horseradish
1 green onion, chopped
1 Tbsp (15 mL) fresh parsley

INGREDIENT NOTE:

Canned Salmon—Canned salmon is readily available year round. Remove skin if desired, but don't discard the bones—mash them up, they are a great source of calcium.

Cracker Crumbs—The recipe calls for 1/2 cup (125 mL) whole grain cracker crumbs—we used 5 Rye Vita crackers. Alternately, you can substitute the crackers with 1 large cooked and mashed baking potato.

INGREDIENTS

Salsa

1 tsp (5 mL) canola oil

1/4 small red onion, minced

1 small red bell pepper, diced

1 jalapeño pepper, seeded and
   minced (see note)

1 cup (250 mL) fresh or frozen
   corn

1/8 tsp (0.5 mL) iodized salt

1/8 tsp (0.5 mL) freshly ground
   black pepper

1 Tbsp (15 mL) apple cider
   vinegar

Sauce (make 2/3 cup/160 mL)

1/4 cup (60 mL) low-fat
   mayonnaise

1/4 cup (60 mL) plain 1% yogurt

2 Tbsp (30 mL) apple cider
   vinegar

2 tsp (10 mL) liquid honey

Fish Tacos with Red Pepper and Corn Salsa
Multi-seasonal Erin MacGregor, PHEc, RD

"Fish tacos are all the rage these days and, despite their Mexican roots, we grow all of the ingredients to make our own Canadian version right at home. I love using seasonal vegetables and fruit to experiment with different varieties of salsa."—Erin

METHOD

1. To make the salsa, heat a medium skillet over medium heat and add oil, onion, red pepper and jalapeño pepper; sauté for 3 minutes until the ingredients begin to soften. Add corn and sauté for another minute until heated through. Season with salt, pepper and apple cider vinegar, transfer to a bowl and set aside for serving.

2. To make the sauce, whisk together the mayo, yogurt, vinegar and honey in a small bowl and set aside for serving.

3. Pat and dry fish. Season both sides of the perch fillets with chili powder and salt.

4. Heat a large skillet over medium high heat and add oil. Cook perch in batches, cooking each side for about 2 to 3 minutes, until just firm to the touch at the thickest part. Set aside.

5. To build the tacos, fill each tortilla with a layer of cabbage; add salsa and top with a fillet of perch. Drizzle about 1 Tbsp (15 mL) of sauce over and serve.

Makes 10 tacos One serving = 2 tacos
Per serving: 470 Calories, 15.2 g Total Fat, 2.5 g Saturated Fat, 0 g Trans Fat, 758 mg Sodium, 48.5 g Carbohydrate, 6.5 g Fibre, 6.8 g Sugars, 2.4 g Added Sugars, 35.3 g Protein
Carbohydrate Choices: 3

PERCH

If you're an angler, or you've ever eaten fish at an angler's home, you've probably eaten perch. Abundant and caught in all seasons with a rod and reel, perch is a popular Canadian fresh water fish.

INGREDIENTS

Tacos
1 1/2 lb (700 g) fresh or frozen Canadian perch fillets, thawed (approx. 10–12 fillets)
1 1/2 tsp (7 mL) chili powder
1/4 tsp (1 mL) iodized salt
1 Tbsp (15 mL) canola oil
10 small 100% whole wheat flour *or* 100% corn tortillas
2 cups (500 mL) shredded Napa cabbage
1 cup (250 mL) cilantro leaves, or to taste

INGREDIENT NOTE:
Jalapeño Peppers—Jalapeño peppers are relatively low on the Scoville Scale of heat units, averaging 3,500 to 8,000. To avoid burning eyes, burning cuts or irritating your skin, wear rubber gloves when working with any hot pepper, and NEVER EVER touch your eyes or anything else on your body when you are handling cut jalapeño peppers, gloves or not.

INGREDIENTS

Dressing (makes approximately
   1/2 cup/125 mL)
1/3 cup (80 mL) canola oil
2 1/2 Tbsp (37 mL) red wine
   vinegar
1/2 tsp (2 mL) Dijon mustard (see
   sidebar)
1 clove garlic, minced
1/4 tsp (1 mL) iodized salt
1/4 tsp (1 mL) freshly ground
   black pepper

PHEC TIPS:

• To transport the salad to a
picnic, be sure to pack in an
insulated cooler with an ice pack
and keep the cooler away from
direct sunlight.

• As a first course, serve in
martini or any stemmed glasses
and garnish with fresh sprigs
of dill.

Fresh Shrimp Pasta Salad Summer

Teresa Makarewicz, PHEc

"This salad is bursting with fresh flavours and is so versatile—we have taken it on road trips (in an insulated cooler), picnicking at Niagara-on-the-Lake or anywhere the back roads might take us. Our close friends even served it at their wedding reception."—Teresa

METHOD

1. To make the dressing, whisk together oil, vinegar, mustard, garlic, salt and pepper in a small bowl; set aside.
2. To make the salad, heat a large pot of water over high heat and cook pasta 3 minutes less than the suggested time on the package directions, adding broccoli and carrots to the last 2 minutes of cooking time. Drain well. Place in a serving bowl and add shrimp, tomatoes, onion, dill and parsley. Pour dressing over the salad and toss to coat. Cover and refrigerate for at least 1 hour, but no longer than 8 hours.

Makes approx. 9 cups (2.25 L) One serving = 1 cup (250 mL)
Per serving: 229 Calories, 8.9 g Total Fat, 1 g Saturated Fat, 0.2 g Trans Fat, 257 mg Sodium, 24.7 g Carbohydrate, 4 g Fibre, 3 g Sugars, 0 g Added Sugars, 14 g Protein
Carbohydrate Choices: 1 1/2

MUSTARD SEED

Canada produces superstars in so many areas: hockey, music and science just to name a few. Did you know we are also a superstar in the mustard world? Yes, my fellow Canadians, we are the world's largest producer of mustard seed, grown primarily in Alberta and Saskatchewan with Saskatchewan winning the Walk of Fame as the biggest producer. Canada's oldest mustard mill is located in Hamilton, Ontario.

Although we are the biggest producers of mustard seed we aren't the biggest mustard maker. But there are many artisanal mustards companies right across Canada. Check out Anton Kozlik's Canadian Mustard, Queen Mary Mustards and Brassica Mustard.

SPOT PRAWNS

Wild BC shrimp are caught through trawling, a method in which large nets that are pulled behind the fishing boat. BC spot prawns, on the other hand, are caught using a slightly different method—spot prawn fishermen spread baited traps along the rocky ocean floor, which has less of an impact on the ocean habitat. Both methods are sustainable.

Want to eat your fill? Check out the annual Spot Prawns Festival in Vancouver BC mid-May.

INGREDIENTS

Salad

8 1/2 oz (250 g) short whole wheat or whole grain pasta (fusilli, rotini or penne)

2 cups (500 mL) small broccoli florets

2 carrots, scrubbed well, halved lengthwise and sliced

1 lb (450 g) shelled cooked Canadian shrimp (or spot prawns)

1 cup (250 mL) grape tomatoes, halved

1/2 cup (125 mL) slivered red onion

1/4 cup (60 mL) chopped fresh dill

3 Tbsp (45 mL) chopped fresh flat-leaf parsley

INGREDIENTS

Peach Salsa (makes
approximately 2 cups/500 mL)
1 large ripe juicy peach, peeled
and diced
1/2 red pepper, diced
1 ripe tomato, diced
1/2 cup (125 mL) finely chopped
chives
1 Tbsp (15 mL) liquid honey
1 Tbsp (15 mL) apple cider
vinegar
1/4 tsp (1 mL) iodized salt
Pepper to taste

Salmon
1 lb (450 g) fresh or frozen
farmed Canadian salmon
fillets, cut into 4 equal pieces
1/2 tsp (2 mL) dried basil
1/4 tsp (1 mL) freshly ground
black pepper
1 Tbsp (15 mL) unsalted butter,
melted

PHEC TIP:

Farmed salmon is a richer source
of omega-3 fatty acids than wild
salmon, has a milder flavour and
is readily available year round.

Salmon with Peach Salsa Spring/Summer

Emily Dobrich, SHEA Student Member

*"Growing up in Southwestern Ontario I remember the little peach tree in
my grandparents' back yard. I always looked forward to the sweet and juicy,
fresh-picked fruit from their tree. The fabulous fresh peach flavours, combined
with salmon, make this a very special recipe to me." —Emily*

METHOD

1. To make the salsa, toss together peach in a small bowl with the red
    pepper, tomato, chives, honey, vinegar, salt and pepper. Cover and
    refrigerate for at least 30 minutes to develop the flavours. Salsa can
    be made up to 2 hours before serving.

2. Preheat oven to 450°F (230°C). Line a rimmed baking sheet with
    parchment paper or foil. Place salmon on the baking sheet and set
    aside.

3. Combine basil and pepper in a small bowl. Brush salmon with
    butter and sprinkle with the basil/pepper mixture. Depending on
    thickness of the fish, bake for 10 to 15 minutes or until it flakes
    when prodded with a fork. Do not overcook.

4. When salmon is done, transfer each fillet to a plate and top with 1/2
    cup (125 mL) of the Peach Salsa.

Makes 4 servings One serving = 1 salmon fillet with 1/2 cup (125 mL) Peach Salsa
Per serving: 253 Calories, 11 g Total Fat, 3 g Saturated Fat, 0.2 g Trans Fat, 209 mg Sodium, 12 g
Carbohydrate, 2 g Fibre, 10 g Sugars, 4.4 g Added Sugars, 26 g Protein
Carbohydrate Choices: 1/2

AQUACULTURE IN CANADA

Aquaculture—the cultivation of aquatic species for human consumption—is essential to the production of many types of seafood in Canada, especially salmon, mussels, oysters and trout. British Columbia and New Brunswick are the two top producers, followed by Newfoundland and Labrador. Every province in Canada, including the Yukon, is involved in farming fish.

The Canadian Aquaculture Industry Alliance (CAIA) is a national organization representing the interests of the aquaculture industry in Canada. It includes aquaculture operators, feed companies and suppliers, along with provincial finfish and shellfish aquaculture associations. All Canadian aquaculture facilities are further regulated by Fisheries and Oceans Canada, Environment Canada, the Canadian Food Inspection Agency, the Canadian Environmental Assessment Agency, Transport Canada and Health Canada, making it one of the most strictly regulated industries in the world. (Source www.aquaculture.ca)

"Sustainable fisheries and aquaculture means the harvesting and farming of fish stocks in a manner that meets the needs of the present without compromising the ability of future generations to meet their own needs." (Source: Fisheries and Oceans Canada)

FARMED SALMON

Farmed salmon is the most important farmed fish in Canada. Antibiotics are used in farmed salmon, but only a veterinarian can administer them, and a strictly regulated withdrawal period is followed to ensure the active compounds are gone before the fish are sold to consumers. Wild salmon eat crustaceans that account for the deep pink colour, whereas farmed salmon are fed carotenoids to promote a pinkish flesh colour. Carotenoids are yellow, orange and red pigments synthesized by plants and are responsible for the orange colour in carrots and squash. Carotenoids also provide vitamin A, which helps support a fish's immune system.

Salmon Teriyaki Summer (when fresh, wild BC sockeye are running) Mairlyn Smith, PHEc

"I was born and raised in Vancouver, BC, so it was only wild sockeye salmon for the Smith Household, canned, fresh or frozen. Sockeye's dark colour and full flavour is what salmon should look and taste like to me. When I first moved to Toronto, I had never even heard of Atlantic salmon (the breed more readily available in Toronto, also much less expensive than BC wild sockeye) and it took some getting used to. Now for the sheer economics of it, I eat farmed salmon in Toronto, but the minute I hit Vancouver, it's wild sockeye all the way." —**Mairlyn**

METHOD

1. Line an 8- × 8-inch (20 × 20 cm) pan with parchment paper. Place salmon in the pan, skin side down.

2. In a small bowl, mix together the soy sauce, vinegar, maple syrup, ginger and wasabi (if using) and pour over the fish. Make a bowl with the parchment paper by tightening the four corners of the parchment paper and twisting them into a tight point, so the sauce is mostly on the salmon and not mostly on the bottom of the pan. Place in the fridge for 20 minutes or up to 1 hour to slightly marinate.

3. Preheat oven to 425°F (220°C). Remove fish from fridge and let it sit at room temperature while the oven is preheating. Depending on the thickness of the fish, bake for 15 to 20 minutes or until it flakes when prodded with a fork. Do not overcook. Serve.

Makes 4 fillets One serving = 1 filet
Per serving: 164 Calories, 6 g Total Fat, 1 g Saturated Fat, 0 g Trans Fat, 272 mg Sodium, 7.5 g Carbohydrate, 0 g Fibre, 6.6 g Sugars, 6.1 g Added Sugars, 19 g Protein
Carbohydrate Choices: 1/2

INGREDIENTS

One 13 oz (390 g) fresh wild BC sockeye salmon filet, cut into 4 equal pieces
2 Tbsp (30 mL) sodium-reduced soy sauce
2 Tbsp (30 mL) rice vinegar (with no added sodium or sugar)
2 Tbsp (30 mL) pure maple syrup
2 tsp (10 mL) finely grated fresh ginger (see page 134)
1 tsp (5 mL) wasabi paste (optional)

SOCKEYE SALMON

Wild sockeye salmon has a much stronger salmon flavour than farmed salmon, is lower in fat and is Mairlyn's personal favourite.

INGREDIENTS

3/4 lb (375 g) fresh or frozen Canadian cod filets, cut into 4 equal pieces

3 Tbsp (45 mL) plain 0% MF Greek-style yogurt

2 Tbsp (30 mL) tandoori masala powder (see note)

2 tsp (10 mL) canola oil

½ tsp (2 mL) red chili powder (optional)

3 Tbsp (45 mL) 100% whole wheat Panko crumbs

INGREDIENT NOTE:

Tandoori Masala Powder— You can find Tandoori Masala Powder at any local Indian grocery store or in larger grocery stores in their International section.

Tandoori Crusted Cod Multi-seasonal

Nazima Qureshi, PHEc

"Growing up in Canada as a child of immigrant parents, I was raised eating authentic Indian food. This is one of my favourite fish recipes, combining Canadian fish with the flavours I was raised on." —Nazima

METHOD

1. Preheat oven to 350°F (180°C). Line a 9- × 13-inch (3.5 L) baking pan with parchment paper or foil and set aside.
2. Place cod filets on paper towels and pat dry completely.
3. In a shallow bowl, mix yogurt, tandoori masala powder and canola oil. For added heat, add red chili powder, if desired. Mix until well combined.
4. Dip cod into yogurt-mix bowl and coat fish completely. Place fish in the baking pan. Repeat with all filets.
5. Evenly sprinkle Panko crumbs over filets and lightly press into the fish.
6. Depending on the thickness of the fish, bake for 12 to 15 minutes or until fish flakes when prodded with a fork. Do not overcook. Turn on broiler for 2 to 3 minutes or until top browns slightly, creating a crust. Serve.

Makes 4 filets One serving = 1 filet
Per serving: 122 Calories, 3 g Total Fat, 0.3 g Saturated Fat, 0 g Trans Fat, 60 mg Sodium, 3.8 g Carbohydrate, 1 g Fibre, 0.2 g Sugars, 0 g Added Sugars, 18 g Protein
Carbohydrate Choices: less than 1

Lobster with Pasta and Cherry Tomatoes Multi-seasonal
Mairlyn Smith, PHEc

"My family drove across Canada from Vancouver to PEI in the summer of 1968. Aside from wanting to strangle my little sister, who was 9 years old at the time, it was an awesome road trip. Like most young Canadian girls I had read Anne of Green Gables *and I was so excited to see Green Gables on our trip. I will never forget taking the ferry across to PEI and seeing the red dirt for the very first time, just like Anne had described. The other best memory of PEI was the lobster dinner my family and I attended at a local church where we were camping. One bite of freshly caught lobster and I was hooked for life."*—**Mairlyn**

METHOD
1. Put a large pot of water over high heat and bring to the boil. Cook pasta 2 minutes less than the package directions. Remove 1/2 cup (125 mL) boiling pasta water and set aside.
2. In a large skillet over medium heat, add oil, celery and shallots and sauté for 3 to 5 minutes or until the shallots are golden and very soft.
3. Add garlic, tomatoes and pepper flakes and sauté until tomatoes are beginning to soften, about 1 to 2 minutes.
4. Place fresh or frozen peas in a large colander. When pasta is 2

INGREDIENTS

2 Tbsp (30 mL) cold pressed canola oil

2 stalks celery, diced

4 shallots, diced

6 cloves garlic, sliced thinly

2 cups (500 mL) grape tomatoes, cut in halves

1/2 tsp (2 mL) red pepper or jalapeño flakes

1 lb (450 g) fresh or frozen Canadian lobster meat, thawed and cut into bite-sized pieces (see note)

1 cup (250 mL) fresh or frozen peas

2 cups (500 mL) bow-shaped pasta

INGREDIENT NOTE:
Lobster—You can find Lobster in the freezer section with the frozen seafood. Sold in pieces or in claws, I prefer the pieces, for ease and flavour. Thaw in the fridge and eat or use in a recipe immediately after thawing.

minutes shy of al dente, drain pasta over top of the peas and set aside.

5. Add lobster to the vegetables and sauté until the lobster is heated through. Add pasta and peas. If the dish looks dry, add the reserved water; if not, discard the water and leave as is. Heat the pasta dish through and serve.

Makes 8 cups (2 L) One serving = 2 cups (500 mL)
Per serving: 353 Calories, 9 g Total Fat, 1 g Saturated Fat, 0.2 g Trans Fat, 434 mg Sodium, 36.5 g Carbohydrate, 6.6 g Fibre, 6 g Sugars, 0 g Added Sugars, 31.4 g Protein
Carbohydrate Choices: 2

PHEC TIP:

On a tour of the Barilla pasta plant in Italy, the resident RD explained to the group of food professionals I was traveling with that al dente pasta, cooked but still firm, has a low glycemic index, making it diabetes friendly. Boiling the living daylights out of it, the way most Canadians do, turns that healthy pasta into a high glycemic food. Take away learning: cook it the Italian way, al dente.

LOBSTER

Lobster is often called the King of Seafood in the Maritimes, and its Canada's most valuable seafood export species, with 2013 exports totaling more than $1.17 billion. (Source: Fisheries and Oceans Canada, Economic Analysis and Statistics.). Depending on the area that lobster is being caught in Atlantic Canada, lobster season is anywhere between late April to late July, with some areas around Nova Scotia still being active into October.

Asian Style Nova Scotia Scallops with Miso Glaze Spring

Mairlyn Smith, PHEc

I thought this recipe would be a great flavour combo to fuse my Vancouver roots and the Asian influence that the city has had on my taste buds, with my love of Nova Scotian scallops. It worked the first time I tried it and every time since. I'm calling this my "Bi-Coastal Salute to Canadian Seafood." —Mairlyn

METHOD

1. To make the Miso Glaze, whisk together vinegar in a small bowl with the water, soy sauce, miso paste, red pepper flakes, garlic and cornstarch. Set aside.

2. Remove scallops from package; lightly rinse and lay out on paper towels to dry.

3. Heat a large skillet on medium-high. Add 1 Tbsp (15 mL) oil and scallops. Cook for 4 to 6 minutes or until the scallops are a light golden brown and cooked through. Remove from pan using a slotted spoon and set aside.

4. Add remaining oil and shallots, sauté until shallots are softened and slightly golden coloured. Add asparagus and stir-fry for 3 minutes. Add red pepper and continue stir-frying until the vegetables are your version of tender crisp. Add scallops back to the pan. Whisk the glaze together once more and pour into skillet.

5. Stir until the glaze bubbles and becomes thick. Continue sautéing for 1 more minute, making sure the glaze covers all of the vegetables and scallops. Serve.

Makes 8 cups (2 L) One serving = 2 cups (500 mL)
Per serving: 224 calories, 7 g Fat, 0.7 g Sat. Fat, 0 g Trans Fat, 403 mg Sodium, 19 g Carbohydrates, 6.3 g Fibre, 7 g Sugars, 0 g Added Sugars, 24 g Protein
Carbohydrate Choices: 1

INGREDIENTS

Miso Glaze

3 Tbsp (45 mL) rice vinegar, no added sugar or sodium
2 Tbsp (30 mL) water
1 Tbsp (15 mL) lower sodium soy sauce
1 Tbsp (15 mL) red miso paste
1/4 tsp (1 mL) red pepper flakes
2 cloves garlic, crushed
1 tsp (5 mL) cornstarch

Scallops

One 14 oz (400 g) bag of frozen raw wild Nova Scotia scallops, thawed
1 1/2 Tbsp (22 mL) canola oil, divided
2 large shallots, cut in half and sliced thinly
2 lb (900 g) fresh local asparagus, washed, trimmed and cut into 2-inch (5 cm) pieces
1 large red pepper, sliced thinly

Canadian Poultry

301 GRILLED JERK CHICKEN THIGHS

302 HARVEST APPLE AND THYME ROASTED CHICKEN

(WITH PLANNED LEFTOVERS)

305 POULTRY COOKING CHART

306 WEST INDIAN-STYLE CURRY CHICKEN

309 STUFFED CHICKEN BURGERS

310 CHICKEN CACCIATORE WITH HOT HOUSE PEPPERS

312 TURKEY TOURTIERE

314 GRILLED TURKEY SCALLOPINI SANDWICH WITH

PICKLED VEGETABLE MAYO

316 DUCK PILAF WITH KAMUT AND WILD RICE

318 BRAISED GOOSE IN DARK BEER

POULTRY

Most people think that poultry and chicken are one and the same, but poultry also includes turkey, geese and duck, which are all raised in Canada. In this chapter we've included recipes utilizing all of the Canadian members of the poultry family, though of course we are starting with the most common and familiar family member: chicken.

Chicken is easy to cook, nutrient dense and popular with your entire family at the dinner table. In Canada, there are over 2,700 chicken farmers dedicated to raising and producing fresh, safe and high-quality chicken for consumers. All chicken raised in Canada is hormone and steroid free and has been since the 1960s. When cooked to perfection, chicken offers unsurpassable taste and nutrition. (Source: Chicken Farmers of Canada)

Most chickens are raised on family owned farms in Canada, with the chicken industry contributing $6.5 billion annually to Canada's Gross Domestic Product. The new Canadian chicken label allows you to know that your chicken was raised by a Canadian farmer, so look for "Raised by a Canadian Farmer" the next time you're buying chicken.

Grilled Jerk Chicken Thighs Multi-seasonal (if you're a true Canadian and BBQ all year long)

Rosemarie Superville, PHEc

*"Jerk barbecue originated in Jamaica and is a Caribbean method of cooking in which marinated meats are smoked in a charcoal pit over pimento wood. I have adopted it as one of my tropical family favourites. Definitely a crowd pleaser for summer barbecues, there are lots of jerk marinades on the market, though making your own spice mix allows you to control the 'heat' and salt."—*Rosemarie

METHOD

1. In a large bowl, combine onion, garlic, allspice, pepper, thyme, brown sugar, salt, cayenne, cinnamon, cloves, oil, vinegar and soy sauce. Mix well.

2. Add chicken pieces and toss until well coated. Cover and marinate in refrigerator for at least 4 hours or overnight, turning occasionally. Tip: the longer the marinating time the stronger the flavour, though you shouldn't marinate longer than 24 hours.

3. Preheat grill pan or barbecue on high. Place chicken on hot grill, reduce heat and grill over medium-high for 6 minutes, turning to cook on the other side for 6 to 8 minutes or until chicken is cooked through (check with a food thermometer inserted sideways through the thickest part of the thigh for an internal temperature of 165°F/74°C). Place on a clean plate and serve.

Makes 8 pieces One serving = 2 thighs
Per serving: 325 Calories, 21.3 g Total Fat, 5.3 g Saturated Fat, 0 g Trans Fat, 727 mg Sodium, 8 g Carbohydrate, 1.5 g Fibre, 3.6 g Sugars, 1.7 g Added Sugars, 48.5 g Protein
Carbohydrate Choices: 1/2

INGREDIENTS

1 small onion, minced

3 cloves garlic, minced

2 tsp (10 mL) ground allspice

1 1/2 tsp (7 mL) ground black pepper

1 1/2 tsp (7 mL) dried thyme leaves

1 1/2 tsp (7 mL) packed dark brown sugar

3/4 tsp (4 mL) iodized salt

1/2 tsp (2 mL) cayenne pepper

1/2 tsp (2 mL) cinnamon

1/4 tsp (1 mL) ground cloves

1 Tbsp (15 mL) canola oil

1 Tbsp (15 mL) white vinegar

1 Tbsp (15 mL) sodium-reduced soy sauce

8 boneless skinless chicken thighs (approx. 2 lb/900 g; see note)

INGREDIENT NOTE:

Chicken—Rinsing chicken can splatter and spread bacteria around your kitchen, putting you or your family at risk of developing a food-borne illness. Pat chicken dry using a paper towel. (Source: Chicken Farmers of Canada)

PHEC TIP:

Serve with potato salad and coleslaw. Also delicious with the Lentil and Roasted Sweet Potato Salad on page 200.

INGREDIENTS

1 whole chicken (3 lb/1.4 kg)
1 bunch fresh thyme, divided
1 medium Royal Gala apple,
    scrubbed, peel left on, cut into
    8 wedges
3 Tbsp (45 mL) canola oil
1/2 tsp (2 mL) iodized salt
1 tsp (5 mL) freshly ground black
    pepper

Harvest Apple and Thyme Roasted Chicken (with Planned Leftovers) Fall/Winter

Michele McAdoo, PHEc

Saving time in the kitchen is all about planning ahead. Roast the chicken and serve *as is* on day one, then two days later you can transform the leftovers into one of the four recipes suggested on the next page.

METHOD

1. Preheat oven to 425°F (220°C). Get a shallow roasting pan with a rack ready and waiting.
2. Remove chicken giblets and neck. Remove any excess fat and pat to dry with a paper towel. Stuff the cavity of the chicken with 10 sprigs thyme and the apple wedges.
3. Remove leaves from remaining thyme stems and chop to make 1 Tbsp (15 mL) thyme.
4. In a small bowl mix together chopped thyme, oil, salt and pepper.
5. Brush bottom of chicken with the mixture. Tuck wings under the chicken and place it breast-side-up on rack in the roasting pan. Brush remaining mixture under the breast skin and on the outside surface of the chicken.

6. Roast the chicken for 1 1/2 hours or until cooked through (chicken should reach an internal temperature of 185°F/85°C when a food thermometer is inserted into the breast or the deep thigh). Remove from roasting pan, cover with foil and let stand for 10 minutes. Carve. Serve. Remove and refrigerate any leftovers from the carcass within 1 hour.

Makes 1 whole chicken One serving = 1/8 chicken
Per serving: 320 Calories, 15.6 g Total Fat, 3.2 g Saturated Fat, 0 g Trans Fat, 267 mg Sodium, 3 g Carbohydrate, 0.6 g Fibre, 1.8 g Sugars, 0 g Added Sugars, 40 g Protein
Carbohydrate Choices: less than 1

FOUR GREAT WAYS TO USE LEFTOVER CHICKEN:
- Chicken Quesadillas: add cooked leftover chicken to your favourite cheese quesadilla recipe.
- Chicken Salad Sandwiches: finely chop leftover chicken and stir in low-fat mayonnaise, Dijon mustard, diced celery and green onion for a great chicken salad sandwich.
- Chicken Fried Rice: add cooked leftover chicken to your favourite Fried Rice recipe.
- Chicken Noodle Casserole: instead of canned tuna, add cooked leftover chicken to your favourite noodle casserole recipe.

PHEC TIP

Among the many nutrients a chicken provides, its major claim to fame is being a lean source of protein. A good way to keep chicken moist and still low in fat is by cooking it with the skin on and then removing the skin prior to serving. You'll have a tender piece of meat without the fat. Chicken has a mild flavor, allowing you to get creative with some fabulous recipes for bold sauces, marinades and stews that will take your healthy meals to a whole new level. (Kelly Atyeo, PHEc, who has worked with Chicken Farmers of Canada)

POULTRY COOKING CHART

Cut	Internal Temperature	Average Cooking Time*	Maximum Grilling Time*
Boneless, skinless breast			
Small piece (5 oz/140 g raw)	165°F (74°C)	35 minutes	9 minutes per side
Large piece (7 oz/200 g raw)		45 minutes	12 minutes per side
Boneless, skinless thigh			
Small piece (2 oz/60 g raw)	165°F (74°C)	20 minutes	5 minutes per side
Large piece (4 oz/115 g raw)		30 minutes	8 minutes per side
Bone-in, skinless thigh/drumstick			
Small piece (3 oz/80 g raw)	165°F (74°C)	35 minutes	7 minutes per side
Large piece (4 1/2 oz/130 g raw)		45 minutes	10 minutes per side
Bone-in breast			
Small piece (1/3 lb/170 g raw)	165°F (74°C)	40 minutes	14 minutes per side
Large piece (1/2 lb/250 g raw)		50 minutes	17 minutes per side
Bone-in legs			
Small piece (7 oz/200 g raw)	165°F (74°C)	40 minutes	15 minutes per side
Large piece (10 oz/300 g raw)		55 minutes	18 minutes per side
Ground chicken patties			
(4 oz/120 g raw)	165°F (74°C)	30 minutes	6 minutes per side
Whole chicken (stuffed)			
(3 lb/1.5 kg raw)	185°F (85°C)	2 hours 10 minutes	1 hour 25 minutes
Whole chicken (unstuffed)			
(3 lb/1.5 kg raw)	185°F (85°C)	1 hour 40 minutes	8 minutes per side
Wings			
(3 oz/90 g raw)	165°F (74°C)	25 minutes	

*Average cooking time is based on the internal temperature of the chicken when roasted, uncovered, in a 350°F (190°C) oven.

*Maximum time is based on a medium heat grill with the lid down.

(With permission from Chicken Farmers of Canada)

INGREDIENTS

2 tsp (10 mL) ground cumin

1 1/2 tsp (7 mL) ground coriander

1 tsp (5 mL) ground black pepper

1/2 tsp (2 mL) turmeric

1/2 tsp (2 mL) iodized salt

1/2 tsp (2 mL) ground ginger

1/4 tsp (1 mL) cayenne pepper (or
to taste)

1 lb (450 g) boneless skinless
chicken breasts, cut into 1-inch
(2.5 cm) chunks

1 Tbsp (15 mL) canola oil

1 onion, chopped

2 cloves garlic, minced

1 medium potato, peeled and
cubed (approx. 1/2 inch/1 cm)

2 small tomatoes, chopped

1 medium carrot, scrubbed well
and thinly sliced

1 1/4 cups (310 mL) sodium-
reduced chicken broth

PHEC TIP:

Serve over cooked hulless oats
(see page 120 for directions) or
with a whole-wheat roti.

West Indian–Style Curry Chicken Fall/Winter

Rosemarie Superville, PHEc

*"This is one of my 'go to' recipes when I feel like an island dinner.
It's definitely one of my favourite comfort foods. My Mom would
have used her favourite curry powder in this recipe, but I have created my
own spice mix. You can control the degree of 'heat' by the
amount of cayenne used."* —Rosemarie

METHOD

1. In large bowl, stir together the cumin, coriander, black pepper,
    turmeric, salt, ginger and cayenne; toss with chicken pieces and let
    stand 15 minutes or longer in the refrigerator.

2. In a large deep non-stick skillet over medium heat, add the oil and
    onion, sautéing for 8 to 10 minutes or until lightly browned.

3. Add chicken pieces and garlic and cook until lightly browned, about
    3 to 5 minutes

4. Add potato, tomatoes, carrot and broth and bring to a boil; cover
    and simmer for 15 to 20 minutes, stirring occasionally or until the
    chicken and vegetables are tender. Any leftovers can be covered and
    stored in the fridge for up to 3 days.

Makes 4 cups (1 L) One serving = 1 cup (250 mL)
Per serving: 242 Calories, 5.4 g Total Fat, 0.7 g Saturated Fat, 0 g Trans Fat, 564 mg Sodium,
18.3 g Carbohydrate, 3 g Fibre, 4.6 g Sugars, 0 g Added Sugars, 32.2 g Protein
Carbohydrate Choices: 1

HEALTH BITE

The nutrient content of chicken breast differs only slightly compared to dark meat; breast meat has more niacin (vitamin B-3) and less fat (including saturated fat) than dark meat, but dark meat also contains higher amounts of zinc. Dark meat also contains more vitamin B-12 than white; almost threefold more, or about 47 percent of the daily value. The content of the other vitamins and minerals analyzed doesn't differ in a meaningful way between breast and dark meat, so feel free to choose your favourite cut. (Source: Chicken Farmers of Canada)

Stuffed Chicken Burgers Spring/summer

Emily Richards, PHEc (with permission from Dairy Farmers of Canada)

Don't skip the yogurt sauce; it adds a great twist to these barbecued burgers.

METHOD

1. To make the Yogurt Cucumber Sauce, stir together yogurt, cucumber, garlic and vinegar in a small bowl. Add iodized salt to taste. Cover and refrigerate until ready to use. Can be made up to 2 days in advance.
2. For the burgers, use your hands to combine chicken, parsley, rosemary, garlic and pepper in a large bowl. Shape into 8 patties. Equally divide cheese among half of the patties. Top with remaining patties and press gently to seal and enclose the cheese. Chill up to 4 hours, if desired.
3. Preheat barbecue on high. Place burgers on the grill, reduce heat to medium heat, close lid and grill, turning once until a food thermometer inserted sideways reads 170°F (75°C), about 14 minutes. Serve with approx. 1/4 cup (40 mL) Yogurt Cucumber Sauce.

Makes 4 burgers
One serving = 1 burger (without bun) with 1/4 cup (60 mL) Yogurt Cucumber Sauce
Per serving: 388 Calories, 28.2 g Total Fat, 12.5 g Saturated Fat, 0.4 g Trans Fat, 292 mg Sodium, 4.3 g Carbohydrate, 0.6 g Fibre, 2.1 g Sugars, 0 g Added Sugars, 29.2 g Protein
Carbohydrate Choices: less than 1

INGREDIENTS

Yogurt Cucumber Sauce
(makes approximately 1 1/4 cups/310 mL)
3/4 cup (185 mL) plain Balkan-style 1% MF yogurt
1/2 cup (125 mL) grated English cucumber, squeezed dry
2 garlic cloves, minced
1 Tbsp (15 mL) apple cider vinegar
Iodized salt to taste

Stuffed Chicken Burgers
1 lb (450 g) extra-lean ground chicken
3 Tbsp (45 mL) chopped flat leaf Italian parsley
2 tsp (10 mL) chopped fresh rosemary
3 garlic cloves, minced
1/4 tsp (1 mL) fresh ground pepper
4 oz (125 g) Canadian jalapeño havarti cheese, diced

INGREDIENTS

1 tsp (5 mL) canola oil

3 lb (1.4 g) bone-in chicken thighs (approx. 8 thighs)

1 onion, chopped

2 hot house peppers, chopped

4 garlic cloves, minced

5 tsp (25 mL) whole wheat flour

1 cup (250 mL) Canadian VQA dry red wine

1 cup (250 mL) no salt added chicken broth

One 19 oz (540 mL) can no salt added diced tomatoes, drained

2 tsp (10 mL) minced fresh thyme leaves

2 tsp (10 mL) minced fresh sage leaves

1/2 tsp (2 mL) iodized salt

PHEC TIP:

Serve over cooked wild rice, barley or hulless oats.

Chicken Cacciatore with Hot House Peppers Fall/Winter

Cathy Ireland, PHEc

"This is one of my favourite fall camping recipes. I make it over a campfire, transferring the browned chicken and deglazed veggies to an aluminum foil pan, covered with foil. Simmer as you would on the stove top."—Cathy

METHOD

1. Heat oil in a large deep skillet over medium-high heat. Add thighs, skin side down. Cook without moving until skin is crispy and well browned, about 5 minutes. Flip thighs over and brown another 5 minutes. Remove from skillet and set aside.

2. Drain all but 1 Tbsp (15 mL) fat from skillet. Add onion and peppers and sauté until softened, about 5 minutes. Add garlic and stir just until fragrant. Stir in flour; cook and stir for 1 minute.

3. Add wine, scraping bottom of the skillet to loosen browned bits. Stir in broth, tomatoes and thyme. Add chicken and bring to boil; cover, reduce heat to low and continue to cook for about 35 minutes. Remove lid and cook another 10 minutes or until chicken is cooked through (it should reach an internal temperature of 165°F/74°C with a food thermometer inserted sidewise through the thickest part of the thigh—avoid hitting the bone as it will give you a false reading).

4. Stir in sage and salt. Serve.

Makes 16 cups (4 L) One serving = 2 chicken thighs
Per serving: 512 Calories, 17.2 g Total Fat, 4.5 g Saturated Fat, 0 g Trans Fat, 521 mg Sodium, 13.7 g Carbohydrate, 2.5 g Fibre, 6.2 g Sugars, 0 g Added Sugars, 58.6 g Protein
Carbohydrates Choices: 1

INGREDIENTS

Top Crust

1 cup (250 mL) all-purpose flour

1/2 tsp (2 mL) iodized salt

1/2 cup (125 mL) non-
hydrogenated margarine

1–2 Tbsp (15–30 mL) ice water

Filling

1 1/2 tsp (7 mL) canola oil

1/2 cup (125 mL) diced onion

1/2 cup (125 mL) diced celery

1 lb (450 g) extra lean ground
turkey

1 1/4 cups (310 mL) no salt
added chicken broth

1 1/2 tsp (7 mL) dried thyme
leaves

1 1/2 tsp (7 mL) ground sage

1 1/2 tsp (7 mL) crushed dried
rosemary leaves

1/2 tsp (2 mL) iodized salt

1/2 tsp (2 mL) ground black
pepper

1/3 cup (75 mL) steel-cut oats

2 Tbsp (30 mL) chopped fresh
parsley (optional)

Turkey Tourtiere Fall/Winter

Spencer Finch-Coursey, PHEc with Olga Kaminskyj, PHEc and Susanne Stark, PHEc

A spin on the Christmas Eve classic. We've switched the pork to turkey.

METHOD

1. To make the top crust, combine flour and salt in a medium mixing bowl. Using a pastry cutter or 2 knives, cut margarine into flour mixture, until crumbly. Sprinkle 1 Tbsp (15 mL) ice water at a time into mixture. Using a fork, toss just until dough starts sticking together. Do not over-mix. Transfer on to a sheet of plastic wrap and form into a ball. Wrap dough, flatten slightly into a disc, and refrigerate for at least 30 minutes.

2. Meanwhile, make the filling. In a large saucepan over medium heat, add oil, onion and celery and sauté for 5 minutes or until onion is soft. Add turkey, breaking up with a fork. Stir in broth, herbs, salt and pepper. Bring to boil. Cook for 5 minutes or until meat is cooked, stirring frequently.

3. Stir in oats. Cover and reduce heat to low. Simmer for 30 minutes or until oats are tender and most of the liquid has been absorbed. Remove from heat and let cool. Stir in parsley, if using. Transfer meat mixture to 9-inch (23 cm) Pyrex or oven safe glass pie plate.

4. Preheat oven to 425°F (220°C).

5. Take the dough from the refrigerator and place on a lightly floured sheet of parchment paper. Using a floured rolling pin, gently roll out into a circle, approximately 10 1/2 inches (26 cm) in diameter. Carefully invert crust over pie plate; remove and discard parchment paper. Fold any excess dough under crust. Using fingers or a fork, crimp and seal edge. Cut vents in top.

6. Bake for 30 to 40 minutes, or until golden. Let stand 5 minutes before serving. Slice into 6 equal slices and scoop out the tourtière.

Makes one 9-inch (23 cm) tourtiere One serving = 1/6 pie
Per serving: 354 Calories, 24.6 g Total Fat, 4.3 g Saturated Fat, 0.2 g Trans Fat, 693 mg Sodium,
23.7 g Carbohydrate, 2.2 g Fibre, 1.2 g Sugars, 0 g Added Sugars, 20.6 g Protein
Carbohydrate Choices: 1 1/2

TURKEY FARMERS OF CANADA

The Turkey Farmers of Canada was created in 1974 under the federal *Farm Products Agencies Act*. The organization works to encourage cooperation throughout the Canadian turkey industry and to promote the consumption of turkey in Canada, while acting as the voice for Canadian turkey farmers both domestically and internationally. (Source: Turkey Farmers of Canada)

INGREDIENTS

Pickled Vegetable Mayo

(makes 1 cup/250 mL)

1 cup (250 mL) chopped drained
  pickled mixed vegetables (mild
  or hot) (see note)

3 Tbsp (45 mL) 0% MF plain
  Greek yogurt

3 Tbsp (45 mL) light mayonnaise

1 Tbsp (15 mL) chopped fresh
  parsley

1 clove garlic, minced

Pinch freshly ground black pepper

Turkey Scallopini Sandwich

3/4 lb (375 g) turkey scaloppini,
  cut into 4 equal portions

1 Tbsp (15 mL) canola oil

1 tsp (5 mL) dried oregano

1 tsp (5 mL) dried basil leaves

Pinch of freshly ground black
  pepper

4 small whole wheat sub buns,
  halved

2 cups (500 mL) shredded lettuce

1 tomato, chopped

Grilled Turkey Scallopini Sandwich with Pickled Vegetable Mayo Summer

Emily Richards, PHEc (with permission from Turkey Farmers of Ontario)

"Growing up part of an Italian family influenced my love of food and desire to share it with others. It helped me tune into what I was eating and why it tasted so good. It was seasonal, local food. Creating recipes using delicious, easy to find Canadian ingredients helps me share my love of food with so many people. It is so cool to go into a local market, farm stand or grocery store and see an abundance of great local products created close to home. Being able to speak to the producers and vendors gives me the opportunity to find out more about them, and it's great to bring out those the awesome attributes of their ingredients in recipes that showcase delicious Canadian products."—Emily

METHOD

1. To make the Pickled Vegetable Mayo, stir together the mixed vegetables in a medium bowl with the yogurt, mayonnaise, parsley, garlic and pepper. Stir until combined. Set aside or store in the fridge for up to 2 days.

2. Place turkey on a plate. In a small bowl, whisk together the oil, oregano, basil and pepper. Using a pastry brush or a spoon, brush or spread each scaloppini with the oil herb mixture on both sides.

3. Preheat barbecue to high. Place turkey on grill, reduce heat to medium and close lid. Grill for about 5 to 8 minutes or until no longer pink inside, turning once. Place cooked turkey on a clean plate. Toast buns if desired.

4. Spread 2 Tbsp (30 mL) vegetable mayo on each side of the open bun. Place turkey on top and add lettuce and tomato. Serve.

Makes 4 servings
One serving = approx. 2 1/2 oz (75 g) turkey scaloppini, 1/4 cup (60 mL) vegetable mayo, 1 slice of tomato, 1/2 cup (125 mL) shredded lettuce and 1 small whole wheat sub bun
Per serving: 322 calories, 10.5 g Total Fat, 1.8 g Sat. Fat, 0 g Trans Fat, 777 mg Sodium, 34.4 g Carbohydrate, 5.7 g Fibre, 4.6 Sugars, 0 g Added Sugars, 36 g Protein
Carbohydrate Choices: 2

INGREDIENT NOTE:
Pickled Vegetables—You can find pickled vegetables in the grocery aisle where pickles and olives are sold or at your local Italian grocery store.

PHEC TIP:
Skillet Option: You can cook the scaloppini in a non-stick skillet over medium-high heat for about 8 minutes, turning once until no longer pink inside

INGREDIENTS

One 14 g pkg dried porcini
  mushrooms (see note)
1 Tbsp (15 mL) unsalted butter
1 Tbsp (15 mL) canola oil
1 1/2 lb (700 g) skinless duck
  meat
2 stalks celery, finely chopped
1 large carrot, scrubbed well,
  finely chopped
3 cups (750 mL) duck stock or
  lower sodium beef broth
  (approx.), divided
1/4 cup (60 mL) Canadian VQA
  dry red wine
1 1/2 cups (375 mL) diced red
  onion (approx. 1 large red
  onion)
2 cloves garlic, minced
1 tsp (5 mL) mixed herbs or
  Herbes de Provence
1 tsp (5 mL) iodized salt
1 tsp (5 mL) freshly ground black
  pepper
1 1/2 cups (375 mL) kamut,
  rinsed
1/4 cup (60 mL) wild rice, rinsed
1/2 cup (125 mL) dried
  cranberries
1 Tbsp (15 mL) chopped fresh
  summer savoury or sweet
  marjoram

Duck Pilaf with Kamut and Wild Rice Fall/Winter

Joan Ttooulias, PHEc

Got a duck in your freezer? Do we have a recipe for you. No duck in the freezer? No worries, duck can be bought in some larger grocery stores or at specialty butcher stores. Don't love duck? This delicious pilaf will turn you into a card-carrying duck lover. This is coming out to you, Saskatchewan, you duck loving province, you!

METHOD

1. Soak mushrooms in 1 cup (250 mL) hot water for 20 to 25 minutes. Drain, reserving liquid and set both aside.
2. Heat butter and oil in a large straight-sided skillet over medium heat. Add duck meat and sauté for 3 to 4 minutes until lightly browned. Stir in celery and carrot, cover with parchment paper and pan lid. Reduce heat to low and cook for 15 minutes.
3. Stir in 1/4 cup (60 mL) duck stock or beef broth and wine, re-cover with parchment and lid and simmer for 45 minutes or until duck is tender.
4. Remove duck from pan; add onion, garlic, Herbes de Provence, salt, pepper, drained mushrooms, kamut and wild rice. Increase heat and sauté for 5 minutes, stirring occasionally.

5. Add enough duck stock or beef broth to reserved mushroom liquid to make 3 1/2 cups (875 mL). Pour into the skillet, bring to a boil, reduce heat and simmer for 50 to 60 minutes or until liquid is absorbed and grains are cooked.
6. Cut the duck meat into thin slices and stir into the grain mixture; add cranberries and fresh herbs. Heat until duck meat is heated through and serve to applause.

Makes 12 cups (3 L) One serving = 1 1/2 cups (375 mL)
Per serving: 310 Calories, 9.1 g Total Fat, 3.3 g Saturated Fat, 0 g Trans Fat, 402 mg Sodium, 34.4 g Carbohydrate, 4.6 g Fibre, 6.9 g Sugars, 4 g Added Sugars, 22.2 g Protein
Carbohydrate Choices: 2

INGREDIENT NOTE:

Porcini Mushrooms—Dried porcini mushrooms add a smoky meaty flavour to any dish. You can find them in larger grocery stores in the produce department sold in packages which, depending on the brand and the store, can fluctuate in size. If you don't have any luck finding them, check out an Italian grocery store, and if that seems like way too much work (or you don't live anywhere close to an Italian grocery store) then substitute dried shiitake mushrooms, which are becoming more readily available.

KAMUT

Kamut is an ancient grain grown in Canada that is brown in colour with a slightly nutty flavour and related to the wheat family.

INGREDIENTS

2 lb (900 g) skinless goose breast
and legs (see note)

1/4 cup (60 mL) all-purpose flour

1 tsp (5 mL) iodized salt

1 tsp (5 mL) freshly ground black
pepper

1 Tbsp (15 mL) unsalted butter

1 Tbsp (15 mL) canola oil

3 shallots, finely chopped

2 stalks celery, finely chopped

3 medium parsnips, scrubbed and
chopped

1 cup (250 mL) baby carrots

1/2 lb (250 g) assorted
mushrooms

One 6 oz (175 g) pkg smoked
back bacon, diced

2 cloves garlic, minced

2 tsp (10 mL) dried thyme leaves

2 cups (500 mL) dark beer (local
craft beer preferred!)

One 14 oz (398 mL) can no salt
added diced tomato

INGREDIENT NOTE:

Goose—If goose portions are
not available, buy a 57 lb
(26 kg) goose and ask your
butcher to joint it.

Braised Goose in Dark Beer Fall/Winter

Joan Ttooulias, PHEc

*"This is a delicious winter casserole, which can be served for weekends or
holiday feasting. Serve with sweet potatoes or potato mash,
as well as freshly steamed broccoli or Swiss chard. For festive
occasions serve with spiced red cabbage."* —Joan

METHOD

1. Pat goose pieces dry using a paper towel. Set aside.
2. In a plastic or paper bag, toss together flour, salt and pepper. Place goose pieces into flour mixture and shake gently until evenly coated.
3. Melt butter in a large straight-sided skillet over medium heat. Add oil, goose pieces and sauté until lightly browned. Remove from pan with tongs.

4. Add shallots, celery, parsnips, carrots, mushrooms, bacon, garlic and thyme. Cook over medium to low heat for 15 minutes until vegetables are slightly softened. Add remaining seasoned flour and stir until no trace of dry flour remains.

5. Add beer, stirring continuously until mixture comes to a boil. Return goose to pan and add diced tomatoes. Cover pan with lid and simmer for 1 to 1 1/2 hours or until goose is tender. Serve.

Makes 10 cups (2.5 L) One serving = 1 1/4 cups (310 mL)
Per serving: 315 Calories, 9.6 g Total Fat, 2.6 g Saturated Fat, 0 g Trans Fat, 696 mg Sodium, 16.5 g Carbohydrate, 3 g Fibre, 4.5 g Sugars, 0 g Added Sugars, 35.6 g Protein
Carbohydrate Choices: 1

PHEC TIP:

Use the legs and breast meat in this recipe and use remainder to make a delicious game stock. Roast the goose bones with an onion, carrot and celery stalk, and toss in a little canola oil for about 1 hour. Add water to cover, simmer for a few hours, strain and discard bones and vegetables. Refrigerate overnight. Remove fat layer and freeze stock until required.

CRAFT BEER

It started with the spruce beer brewed by Aboriginal peoples in the 1500s, progressed to the Jesuit Brother Ambroise in Quebec being named the first brewer in Canada in 1668, and eventually included such names as Molson, when John Molson established the first Canadian brewery in 1786. Yes, we Canadians know our beer.

Craft beers began springing up across Canada in the 1990s thanks to a group of vigilant small beer brewery cheerleaders who lobbied the government to allow for new licences for small breweries.

Canadian craft beer harkens back to a time when small local businesses were creating small batches of beer that were from their community, for their community, embracing the true sense of local.

With names like Holy Smoke Scotch Ale from the Church-Key Brewing Company in Campbellford, Ontario (www.churchkeybrewing. com), Fighting Irish Red from the Yellow Belly Brewery in St. John's, Newfoundland (www.yellowbellybrewery.com), Sasquatch Stout from the Old Yale Brewery in Chilliwack, BC (www.oldyalebrewing.com), Brewhouse Pilsner from the Great Western Brewing Co in Saskatoon, Saskatchewan (www.gwbc.com) and Pothole Porter from the Half Pints Brewing Co in Winnipeg, Manitoba (www.halfpintsbrewing.com), craft breweries or microbreweries are springing up right across Canada and creating beers for every taste and event.

Check out the *Canadian Craft Beer Cookbook* (Whitecap 2013) by David Ort for recipes and more information on craft beers.

Ode to Canadian Beef

325 Beef Nutrition 101

328 "Kick-Ass" Barbecued Burgers

331 Beef Steak and Lentil Salad

332 Steak Grilling Chart

334 Grilled Flank Steak on Roasted Kale Salad

336 Slow Cooker Beef and Barley Stew

337 Slow Cooker Bistro Beef and Beer Simmering Steak

338 Gluten-Free PEI Potato Lasagna

340 Shepherd's Pie with Beef and Mushrooms

341 Beef and Mushroom Stew

342 Cracked Pepper and Horseradish–Crusted Oven
Roast with Easy Pan Gravy

344 Roasting Guide

345 Yorkshire Pudding

346 Bison Meat Loaf

Canadians love their beef, with the average Canadian eating 43.5 (19.8 kg) annually. Even more impressive, there are 68,500 beef farms and ranches with beef cattle in Canada, raising a total of 3.82 million beef cows. Raised in every province, the average herd size for beef cattle is 63, and beef production contributed $13 billion to Canada's GDP in 2013 with over $35 billion in sales of goods and services. (Source: Ag Census information 2013)

Canadian beef is renowned worldwide for its rigorous and progressive grading, inspection and food safety standards. Canada's beef farmers and ranchers have the only mandatory cattle identification system in North America, and as part of food safety efforts, Canadian cattle are each identified with individualized radio frequency identification (RFID) tags through the Canadian Cattle Identification Agency. These electronic tags link to a database that stores information about each animal such as date of birth and farm of origin. The tags help maintain and promote food safety and traceability.

If the label says Canadian beef it means the beef comes from cattle raised and processed right here in Canada. To ensure that you are buying Canadian beef, look for the Canadian Beef logo on packages of beef in grocery stores.

For more information check out www.beefinfo.org

BEEF NUTRITION 101

Beef is an excellent source of high-quality protein, plus it is packed with B vitamins and those two all-important and often neglected minerals, iron and zinc.

Iron is a key factor in ensuring that enough oxygen is carried to every cell, and without enough iron your cells don't function correctly. Without enough iron in your diet you can become anemic.

Iron is also important in forming red blood cells, which helps in fighting infections. Without this vital mineral you can feel tired, irritable, depressed, headache-y and have a reduced resistance to infections. Beef contains heme iron, an easily absorbed form of iron.

The iron found in vegetables and beans is called non-heme iron, which isn't as easily absorbed as the iron found in beef. Because of this decreased absorption of non-heme iron, vegetarians must pay close attention to their iron sources. It is advised that they eat twice as

RECOMMENDED DIETARY ALLOWANCE (RDA) (mg/d - total iron intake)		
Ages	Males	Females
7–12 months	11	11
1–3 years	7	7
4–8 years	10	10
9–13 years	8	8
14–18 years	11	15
19–50 years	8	18
> 50 years	8	8
Pregnancy		27

Note: The requisite iron intake for vegetarians is 1.8 times higher due to the lower bioavailability of iron in a vegetarian diet.
(Reference: Institute of Medicine: Dietary Reference Intakes for Vitamin A, Vitamin K, Arsenic, Boron, Chromium, Copper, Iodine, Iron, Manganese, Molybdenum, Nickel, Silicon, Vanadium and Zinc [2001]. National Academy Press, Washington, 2001.)

much iron from vegetarian sources to maintain healthy levels. Eating food that contains vitamin C along with non-heme iron foods helps in absorption, though coffee and tea have the opposite effect. You should avoid drinking tea or coffee with meals, and up to one hour after, to maximize iron absorption.

One serving of beef, according to Canada's Food guide, is 2 1/2 oz (75 g) cooked, which has 6.11 mg iron (68 percent of your required **D**aily **V**alue). (Reference: Health Canada, Canadian Nutrient File, 2010. Value for food code beef, roast composite [#6166])

BREAST FEEDING?

Health Canada has set up new guidelines for babies—by about six months your baby needs more iron than breast milk alone can provide, and adding iron-rich foods while continuing to breastfeed is vital for brain development and growth. Too little iron can affect a baby's development, and iron deficiency can have severe and irreversible effects.

ZINC

Zinc's biggest claim to fame is that it helps strengthen your immune system. It also supports normal growth and development in all ages while helping your body use the carbohydrates, proteins and fat it consumes. Aside from oysters, beef leads the way as a source of zinc. A 3 1/2 oz(100 g) serving of beef provides at least 50 percent of your daily zinc requirement.

WHAT DO BEEF CATTLE EAT?

For the majority of their lives, beef cattle eat a diet comprised of pasture grasses and other plants in the summer, and hay (dried grasses and plants) in the winter months. These grasses and plants are referred to as forages. Salt and other minerals are often made available to cattle on pasture in the form of a free-choice salt lick. These minerals are required for optimum cattle health and growth.

At 9 to 11 months of age, when they reach approximately 900 pounds, cattle typically are placed in a feedlot where they are brought to a finished weight of around 1,300 pounds. Beef production on a feedlot begins with a diet made up of forages and progressively moves to about 90 percent grain. The diet is changed progressively because a sudden change could cause digestive upset in the cattle.

The main reason grain is fed to cattle is to produce tender, marbled beef. In Canada, barley and corn are the grains usually used for beef finishing. Additional protein in the form of soybean or canola meal may also be added to cattle feed. Plant-based proteins are virtually the only source of protein used in beef cattle feed in Canada. Since 1997 Canada has banned the feeding of ruminant-based meat-and-bone meal to other ruminants such as cattle. This feed ingredient is believed to have caused the spread of Bovine Spongiform Encephalopathy in Europe. Use of this feed ingredient was never common in beef cattle rations in Canada due to our abundant cropland available for growing high-protein crops. (Source: Prepared by the Canadian Cattlemen's Association and Beef Information Centre 2010 www.cattle.ca)

GETTING THE GRADE

Canada's top beef grades are Canada Prime, Canada AAA, Canada AA and Canada A. The difference between the four grades is the degree of marbling, with Canada Prime having the most marbling. The three A grades account for over 75 percent of beef produced in Canada. Canada Prime is mostly sold to restaurants or exported. Look for these grades in your retail flyer and at the beef counter, or ask your meat department manager or local butcher. (Source: Canada Beef)

INGREDIENTS

2 lb (900 g) medium ground beef
(see note)

1 onion, grated or finely diced
(see note)

2 cloves garlic, minced

1 omega-3 egg

1/4 cup (60 mL) 100% whole
wheat breadcrumbs or Panko
crumbs

1 Tbsp (15 mL) Worcestershire
sauce

1/4 tsp (1 mL) iodized salt

1/4–1/2 tsp (1–2 mL) freshly
ground pepper

INGREDIENT NOTES:

Medium Ground Beef—If
you are wondering what makes
this Kick-Ass Burger worthy of
its name, *taste* the difference
that medium ground makes
vs lean beef. With only a 6
percent difference in fat content
compared to lean ground beef,
the difference is well worth it.

Onion—Grating the onion on a
box grater helps to incorporate it
better into the patty so there are
no 'alien bits' that young picky
eaters might take offense to.

"Kick-Ass" Barbecued Burgers Summer

(For Pickled Red Onions see recipe on page 226)
Joyce Parslow, PHEc (with permission from Canada Beef)

*"Medium ground beef makes a juicy burger for the barbecue.
Grilling will reduce the total fat in a burger patty by about a third,
leaving you with a tender juicy burger full of flavour. You can't tell if a
burger is done by cooking to colour, so use a digital instant-read thermometer
inserted sideways into each patty to confirm. Using
a food thermometer is how chefs do it—it's not a geek tool!
Cook burgers to 160°F (71°C)—just remember, 'Your burger's
done at 71.'"*—Joyce

METHOD

1. Crumble beef in a large bowl. Add onion, garlic, egg, breadcrumbs
   (or Panko crumbs, if using), Worcestershire sauce, salt and pepper.
   Combine gently but thoroughly. Divide meat mixture into 8 equal-
   sized balls and gently shape into 3/4-inch (2 cm) thick patties.
   Make a shallow depression in the centre of each patty to keep
   patties from puffing up during cooking.

2. Preheat barbecue on high. Place patties on and reduce heat to
   medium-high (400°F/200°C). Cook for 5 to 7 minutes per side,
   testing doneness with a digital rapid-read food thermometer
   inserted sideways into centre of each patty; burgers are completely
   cooked when thermometer reads 160°F (71°C).

Makes 8 patties One serving = 1 burger patty (without bun or condiments)
Per serving: 344 Calories, 13 g Total Fat, 5 g Saturated Fat, 0.4 g Trans Fat, 198 mg Sodium,
4.3 g Carbohydrate, 0.6 g Fibre, 1 g Sugars, 0 g Added Sugars, 36.4 g Protein
Carbohydrate Choices: less than 1

PHEC TIP:

Skip the cheese and bacon on this burger, you won't need any more bells and whistles. The burger stands on its own, just add condiments.

BEST BURGERS 101

- Manage the meat gently when forming the patty to make patties more tender—compressing the patty makes it more dense, which makes it seem tougher.
- Don't press on your patty while grilling, this presses juices out.
- The patty is ready to flip on the grill when you see meat juices rising to the surface.
- Making patties ahead and refrigerating them helps them hold together better on the grill and makes for a better flavour.
- Keep your tools and hands clean between handling raw and cooked meat—soap and water does the trick.

Beef Steak and Lentil Salad Summer

Joyce Parslow, PHEc (with permission from Canada Beef)

"More than just a salad, this celebration of summer's farmers' market bounty is a full-fledged dinner! This is a great way to extend your steak: slice cooked steak and serve with grilled veggies such as asparagus, red pepper, garlic and zucchini, all tossed together with lentils and a tangy dressing."—Joyce

METHOD

1. To prepare the spice rub, combine the Italian seasoning, pepper, garlic powder and salt in a small bowl. Rub mixture over steak and let stand for 15 minutes.
2. In a large bowl, whisk together oil, red onion, garlic, vinegar, basil, salt and oregano; set aside.
3. Preheat barbecue on high. Place summer vegetables on grill (or place in a grill basket) and reduce heat to medium-high; grill until lightly charred, about 5 minutes, flipping often. When done, remove and place in a large bowl or a platter, allowing vegetables to cool slightly.

INGREDIENTS

Spice rub

1 tsp (5 mL) Italian seasoning

1 tsp (5 mL) coarsely ground black pepper or cracked black pepper

1/2 tsp (2 mL) garlic powder

1/2 tsp (2 mL) coarse salt

Salad

1 lb (450 g) beef grilling steak (either striploin or top sirloin; see note)

1/4 cup (60 mL) cold pressed or regular canola oil

1/2 cup (125 mL) red onion, minced

2 cloves garlic, minced fresh *or* roasted and mashed

2 Tbsp (30 mL) red wine vinegar

1/4 cup (60 mL) chopped fresh basil

1/4 tsp (1 mL) iodized salt

1/2 tsp (2 mL) dried oregano leaves

2 cups (500 mL) summer vegetables, cut into chunks (try zucchini, red peppers or asparagus)

2 plum tomatoes, seeded and cut into chunks

One 19 oz (540 mL) can lentils, well rinsed and drained

Pepper to taste

4. When cool enough to handle, add grilled vegetables, tomatoes and lentils to the salad dressing. Gently toss together; set aside.

5. Grill steak over medium-high heat for 4 to 7 minutes per side for medium doneness. Let rest for 5 minutes. Carve steak into thin slices; toss lightly with salad veggies and serve.

Makes approximately 8 cups (2 L) One serving = 1 cup (250 mL)
Per serving: 222 Calories, 10.7 g Total Fat, 2.1 g Saturated Fat, 0.3 g Trans Fat, 178 mg Sodium, 10.6 g Carbohydrate, 2.6 g Fibre, 1.7 g Sugars, 0 g Added Sugars, 19.4 g Protein
Carbohydrate Choices: 1/2

STEAK GRILLING CHART			
THICKNESS	**TOTAL COOKING TIME** (Using medium-high heat)		
	MED RARE 145°F/63°C	MEDIUM 160°F/71°C	WELL-DONE 170°F/77°C
1/2–3/4 inch (12 cm)	6-8	8-10	10-12
1 inch (2.5 cm)	10-12	12-14	14-18
1 1/2 inches (4 cm)	18-20	20-28	30-36
2 inches (5 cm)	22-28	28-36	36-44
(with permission from Canada Beef [www.canadabeef.ca])			

INGREDIENTS

Marinade

1/2 cup (125 mL) red wine
   vinegar

1 Tbsp (15 mL) canola oil

2 Tbsp (30 mL) lower sodium soy
   sauce

1 tsp (5 mL) Dijon mustard

2 sprigs fresh rosemary (optional)

2 cloves garlic, minced

Salad

1–1 1/2 lb (450–700 g) flank
   marinating steak

2 bunches of kale, rinsed and
   stem removed, patted dry

1 Tbsp (15 mL) canola oil

Pinch of salt

Crusty bread for serving

Tomato wedges for serving

1 Tbsp (15 mL) chopped fresh
   rosemary (optional)

Grilled Flank Steak on Roasted Kale Salad Fall/Winter

Diane O'Shea, PHEc

"Our farm raised great beef and as a Professional Home Economist I promoted beef for Ontario producers at fairs and trade shows. Flank steak is a lean cut that conveniently comes in cuts approx. 1 to 1 1/2 lb (450 to 700 g). It has no waste, which makes it highly economical. Since it is considered a less tender cut, marinating for at least 30 minutes or more is required to break down the muscle tissue. Roast the kale while grilling the steak on the barbecue, and be sure to let the steak sit for five to ten minutes after cooking. This makes the steak juicier and the slicing easier."—Diane

METHOD

1. To make the marinade, combine vinegar, 1 Tbsp (15 mL) oil, soy sauce, mustard, rosemary (if using) and garlic in a large re-sealable plastic bag. Add steak, seal the bag and *gently* toss the marinade about to coat the meat. Refrigerate for at least 30 minutes, but no longer than 6 hours.

2. 30 minutes before you start the dinner, preheat oven to 350°F (175°C). Line a rimmed baking sheet with parchment paper. Tear or chop kale into small mouth-sized pieces.

3. In a large bowl, toss kale with 1 Tbsp (15 mL) oil to coat well. This takes a bit of time, but it's well worth it. Spread kale out on to the

prepared baking sheet. Roast for about 15 to 20 minutes, or until the leaves are a little crispy on the edges. Stir occasionally. This is the perfect time to grill the steak, if you can multi-task…

4. Preheat barbecue on high. Remove steak from the marinade, discarding marinade. Place meat on the grill and reduce heat to medium-high. Close lid and allow meat to cook for about 4 to 5 minutes or until browned. Turn and continue for another 4 to 5 minutes, or until browned. Test for doneness with a digital rapid-read food thermometer inserted sideways into the centre of the steak. The internal temperature should be 160°F (71°C).

5. Transfer steak to a cutting board and cover loosely with a piece of tin foil.

6. To assemble, dust the roasted kale with a pinch of salt and place on a serving platter. Slice the steak as thinly as possible on the diagonal and pile on top of the roasted kale. Add any meat juices.

7. Garnish with chopped rosemary, if desired. Serve with crusty bread and tomato wedges.

PHEC TIPS:
- Look for the "packaged on" date or the "best before" date when buying meat. This is the best indicator of freshness.
- Canada Beef has made it easier for the consumer by labeling cuts of beef with the method required for cooking. Check out the packaging for "grilling steak," "marinating steak," "simmering steak," "fast fry steak," "oven roast," "pot roast," "rotisserie roast" and "stew beef."

Makes 4 servings One serving = 1/4 recipe (without bread or tomato wedges)
Per serving: 443 Calories, 20 g Total Fat, 6 g Saturated Fat, 0.5 g Trans Fat, 461 mg Sodium, 14.4 g Carbohydrate, 3.5 g Fibre, 0.3 g Sugars, 0 g Added Sugars, 48 g Protein
Carbohydrate Choices: 1

1 lb (450 g) lean stewing beef

2 Tbsp (30 mL) canola oil, divided

1 onion, chopped

2 carrots, scrubbed well and
   chopped into 1/2-inch (1 cm)
   chunks

1 clove garlic, minced

1/3 cup (80 mL) pot or pearl
   barley, rinsed

2 1/2 cups (625 mL) no salt
   added beef broth

2 Tbsp (30 mL) tomato paste
   (see note)

1 Tbsp (15 mL) packed brown
   sugar

1 Tbsp (15 mL) red wine vinegar

1/2 tsp (2 mL) iodized salt

1/2 tsp (2 mL) dried thyme leaves

1/4 tsp (1 mL) fresh ground black
   pepper

1 cup (250 mL) frozen peas,
   thawed

Slow Cooker Beef and Barley Stew Fall/Winter

Barb Holland, PHEc

*"On cold snowy Sunday afternoons, we enjoy a walk or
snowshoe in the valley behind our house. Even better is to come
in from the cold, light a fire and enjoy warm comfort food. This
stew is ideal, as it cooks away ever so gently and efficiently in the
slow cooker while you are outside having fun."*—Barb

METHOD

1. Trim any excess fat from beef and cut any large pieces into smaller pieces.

2. Heat 1 Tbsp (15 mL) oil in a large skillet over medium-high heat. Cook beef until browned (in 2 batches if necessary) and transfer to slow cooker.

3. Add remaining oil to skillet and add onion, carrots and garlic; cook a few minutes until lightly softened.

4. Stir in barley, broth, tomato paste, brown sugar, vinegar, salt, thyme and pepper. Bring to a simmer, then pour into the slow cooker.

5. Cover and cook on low heat for 8 to 10 hours (or on high for 4 to 5 hours), or until the beef and barley are tender.

6. Turn off slow cooker, stir in peas and let stand 10 minutes to heat peas. Serve.

Makes 9 cups (2.12 L) One serving = 1 1/2 cups (375 mL)
Per serving: 271 Calories, 10.6 g Total Fat, 2.7 g Saturated Fat, 0.6 g Trans Fat, 326 mg Sodium, 21.2 g Carbohydrate, 4.2 g Fibre, 6.5 g Sugars, 2.3 g Added Sugars, 21.8 g Protein
Carbohydrate Choices: 1

INGREDIENT NOTE:

Tomato Paste—Tomato paste is now sold in squeezable tubes and is perfect for when you only need a small amount. You can find it on the shelf with the other tomato products or in the refrigerated section of your local grocery store. Otherwise, freeze the remaining contents of a small can of tomato paste in 1 Tbsp (15 mL) amounts: wrap well and freeze.

Slow Cooker Bistro Beef and Beer Simmering Steak Fall/ winter Donna-Marie PHEc (adapted from *The Best Family Slow Cooker Recipes* [Robert Rose Publishing 2003])

"Simmering steak gives you the same experience as a pot roast, but is a better size for a small family. It's also much like a stew, without the effort of cutting and browning all the beef cubes. And with the use of a slow cooker, dinner is ready when you are." —Donna-Marie

METHOD

1. For the spice rub, combine thyme, marjoram, salt and pepper in a small bowl. Rub all over steak to season.

2. In a large non-stick skillet, heat oil over medium-high heat. Add beef and brown all over, then transfer to slow cooker.

3. Add beer and broth to skillet and bring to a boil, stirring to scrape up any brown bits from the pan. Transfer to slow cooker. Add tomato paste, mustard, vinegar, Worcestershire sauce, onion, garlic, carrots and mushrooms; mix well.

4. Cook, covered on low heat, for 8 to 10 hours until beef and vegetables are fork-tender and sauce is bubbling. Serve.

Makes 4 1/2 cups (1.12 L) One serving = 3/4 cup (175 mL)
Per serving: 332 Calories, 14.2 g Total Fat, 4.8 g Saturated Fat, 0.4 g Trans Fat, 423 mg Sodium, 10.5 g Carbohydrate, 2.5 g Fibre, 4.3 g Sugars, 0 g Added Sugars, 36.8 g Protein
Carbohydrate Choices: 1/2

PHEC TIP:

Don't have a slow cooker? Brown steaks in a heavy Dutch oven (enameled cast iron ideally). Add beer and stock and continue with the recipe, cooking everything together in the Dutch oven—covered with a tight fitting lid— in a 325°F (160°C) oven for 2 hours, or until beef and vegetables are fork-tender.

INGREDIENTS

Spice Rub

1/2 tsp (2 mL) dried thyme leaves
1/2 tsp (2 mL) dried marjoram leaves
1/2 tsp (2 mL) iodized salt
1/2 tsp (2 mL) fresh ground black pepper

Simmering Steak

2 lb (900 g) beef simmering steak (blade, cross rib or boneless short ribs)
1 Tbsp (15 mL) canola oil
1 cup (250 mL) beer (your choice of Canada's best)
1 cup (250 mL) no salt added beef broth
2 Tbsp (30 mL) tomato paste
1 Tbsp (15 mL) Dijon mustard
1 Tbsp (15 mL) red wine vinegar
2 tsp (10 mL) Worcestershire sauce
1 large onion, diced
4 garlic cloves, minced
2 cups (500 mL) baby carrots
8 1/2 oz (250 g) small button mushrooms

INGREDIENTS

1/2 lb (250 g) extra-lean ground beef

1/2 onion, chopped

1 cup (250 mL) sliced fresh mushrooms

1/2 green pepper, chopped

1 stalk celery, chopped

2 cloves garlic, minced

One 24 oz (640 mL) jar gluten-free tomato pasta sauce

One 19 oz (540 mL) can no salt added kidney beans, well rinsed and drained

1 tsp (5 mL) dried thyme leaves

1/2 tsp (2 mL) ground cumin

1 tsp (5 mL) chili powder

4 small baking potatoes, scrubbed and very thinly sliced

1/2 cup (125 mL) packed shredded cheddar cheese

Gluten-Free PEI Potato Lasagna Fall/Winter

Janet Buis, PHEc

"Nothing warms up the hockey crowd like potato lasagna when they come home hungry after the game. It's also a perfect choice to serve to friends and relatives who follow a gluten-free diet." —Janet

METHOD

1. Preheat oven to 375°F (190°C). Line a 9- × 13-inch (23 × 33 cm) baking dish with wet parchment paper and set aside.

2. Brown beef in a large frying pan over medium heat. Add onion, mushrooms, green pepper, celery and garlic and sauté for 5 minutes or until softened.

3. Stir in pasta sauce, kidney beans, thyme, cumin, chili powder and cook until heated through.

4. Arrange half of the potato slices over bottom of prepared dish, overlapping if necessary. Top with half of the beef mixture. Layer the remaining potato slices and cover with the rest of the beef mixture.
5. Cover with foil. Bake for 50 minutes or until the potatoes are tender.
6. Uncover and sprinkle with cheddar cheese. Bake until cheese melts, about 10 minutes. Let stand for 10 minutes before serving.

Makes 10 cups (2.5 L) One serving = 1 1/2 cups (375 mL)
Per serving: 298 Calories, 5.7 g Total Fat, 2.7 g Saturated Fat, 0.1 g Trans Fat, 349 mg Sodium, 43.8 g Carbohydrate, 9 g Fibre, 11 g Sugars, 0 g Added Sugars, 18.5 g Protein
Carbohydrate Choices: 2

PEI POTATOES

Who hasn't heard of a PEI potato? Islanders have been growing potatoes since the late 1700s. The island's red, sandy soil is rich in iron, and is the perfect medium for growing tubers.

INGREDIENTS

2 large Yukon gold potatoes, scrubbed well and cut into quarters

3 Tbsp (45 mL) canola oil + extra for the pan

1 large onion, chopped

1/2 lb (250 g) portobello mushrooms, sliced

1/2 lb (250 g) medium ground beef

3/4–1 cup (175–250 mL) water *or* no salt added beef or mushroom broth

3 Tbsp (45 mL) all-purpose flour

1/2 tsp (2 mL) iodized salt

1/2 tsp (2 mL) fresh ground black pepper

Shepherd's Pie with Beef and Mushrooms Fall/Winter

Maria Depenweiller, PHEc

"This is a wonderful example of comfort food, perfect for a family dinner on a fresh fall evening or as something to bring along to a potluck."—Maria

METHOD

1. Place potatoes in a medium saucepan. Just cover with water, bring to a boil and cook until tender. Drain and mash. Season if desired and set aside.

2. To make the filling, heat a large frying pan over medium heat. Add oil and onion and sauté for about 5 minutes or until the onion is transparent.

3. Preheat oven to 400°F (200°C) and lightly oil an 8- × 8-inch (20 × 20 cm) baking pan. Set aside.

4. Add mushrooms to the onion, increase heat to medium high and sauté until they become golden brown on the edges, about 5 to 7 minutes.

5. Add ground beef and continue sautéing until meat is cooked through. Add water or broth. Sprinkle in flour, stirring until the mixture thickens. Season with salt and black pepper.

6. Spoon meat mixture into prepared pan. Spoon the mashed potatoes over top and bake for about 30 minutes until golden crust appears on the potato layer. Serve.

Makes one 8- × 8-inch (20 × 20 cm) pie One serving = 1/6 shepherd's pie
Per serving: 277 Calories, 14.2 g Total Fat, 3.4 g Saturated Fat, 0.4 g Trans Fat, 229 mg Sodium, 10.7 g Carbohydrate, 1.6 g Fibre, 2.4 g Sugars, 0 g Added Sugars, 10 g Protein
Carbohydrate Choices: 1/2

Beef and Mushroom Stew Fall/Winter

Jan Main, PHEc

Easy to make, with a rich and hearty flavour, this is one delicious family friendly stew.

METHOD

1. Stir together flour, 1/2 tsp (2 mL) salt and pepper in a large mixing bowl. Toss beef in flour mixture, coating evenly.
2. Heat 1 Tbsp (15 mL) oil in a large saucepan or Dutch oven over medium-high heat; add beef in batches and brown. Remove beef from saucepan and set aside.
3. Add remaining 1 Tbsp (15 mL) oil, onion, leek, garlic and mushrooms; stir well and cover. Cook for about 5 minutes or until onions are softened.
4. Return beef to saucepan. Stir in beef stock, red wine, bay leaves, thyme, 1/2 tsp (2 mL) salt and pepper, scraping up any browned bits on bottom of pan. Cover, reduce heat and simmer 2 to 3 hours or until beef is really tender. (Time will vary according to the size of the beef stew chunks and saucepan.)
5. When tender, discard bay leaves. Stir in parsley and serve (with horseradish, if desired).

Makes 6 cups (1.5 L) One serving = 1 cup (250 mL)
Per serving: 372 Calories, 16 g Total Fat, 5 g Saturated Fat, 1 g Trans Fat, 536 mg Sodium, 12 g Carbohydrate, 1.7 g Fibre, 3 g Sugars, 0 g Added Sugars, 38.7 g Protein
Carbohydrate Choices: 1

PHEC TIP:

Store leftovers in the fridge for up to 2 days. To reheat beef, place in a 350°F (175°C) oven for about 40 to 45 minutes.

INGREDIENTS

1/4 cup (60 mL) all-purpose flour
1 tsp (5 mL) iodized salt, divided
1/4 tsp (1 mL) fresh ground black pepper
2 lb (900 g) stewing beef (see note)
2 Tbsp (30 mL) canola oil, divided
1 large onion, chopped
1 leek, sliced (see note p. 63)
2 cloves garlic, minced
8 1/2 oz (250 g) pkg cremini mushrooms, cleaned and sliced
1 1/2 cups (375 mL) sodium-reduced beef stock
1/2 cup (125 mL) Canadian VQA dry red wine
2 bay leaves
1 tsp (5 mL) dried leaf thyme
1/4 tsp (1 mL) freshly ground black pepper
1/2 cup (125 mL) freshly chopped parsley
Dash of horseradish (optional)

INGREDIENT NOTE:

Stewing Beef—Choose precut stewing beef or cut it yourself for savings from Blade or Cross Rib Simmering Steak or Pot Roast.

INGREDIENTS

Oven Roast

1/3 cup (80 mL) prepared
   horseradish

3 Tbsp (45 mL) cracked
   multicoloured peppercorns

1 tsp (5 mL) coarse salt

3 lb (1.5 kg) beef oven roast (any
   variety)

Gravy (makes 2 cups/500 mL)

1/2 cup (125 mL) Canadian VQA
   dry red wine

2 cups (500 mL) low sodium beef
   broth

4 sprigs fresh thyme

1–2 Tbsp (15–30 mL) heavy
   cream

1 Tbsp (15 mL) cornstarch
   (optional)

1 Tbsp (15 mL) cold water
   (optional)

Salt and pepper to taste

Cracked Pepper and Horseradish–Crusted Oven Roast with Easy Pan Gravy Fall/Winter

(Yorkshire pudding recipe on page 345 in the background)

Joyce Parslow, PHEc (with permission from Canada Beef)

"The horseradish and cracked pepper crust makes something simple seem special. Use any roast labelled an 'oven roast' by Canada Beef, such as tenderloin, prime rib, strip loin, top sirloin or outside round. To crack the peppercorns, place them in a sturdy plastic freezer bag and crush with the back of a heavy skillet or hammer." —Joyce

METHOD

1. Preheat oven to 450°F (230°C).

2. Combine horseradish, peppercorns and coarse salt; rub all over roast. Place fat side up on a rack in a shallow roasting pan. Insert oven-safe meat thermometer into centre of roast (try a programmable thermometer).

3. Oven-sear for 10 minutes. Reduce heat to 275°F (140°C) and cook uncovered. For medium doneness, cook until thermometer reads 145°F (63°C), about 1 1/2 hours. Remove roast and place on cutting board; cover loosely with foil for 20 to 30 minutes.

• A programmable thermometer is just what you need for roasting success. So simple: program in what doneness you want (medium-rare at about 140°F to 145°F/60°C to 63°C for example) and the alarm will sound when your roast reaches that temperature.

• Always let a roast rest for at least 15 minutes before you carve it.

• Cook times are guidelines only and vary with ovens, roast shape and type. Roasts may be done up to 30 minutes sooner or later than estimated times.

4. To make the gravy, place roasting pan over medium-high heat and pour in red wine; bring to a boil, stirring and scraping up any brown bits from bottom of pan. Cook until reduced by half. Stir in broth and add thyme; simmer for 5 minutes. Strain out bits and return liquid to pan. Heat through and finish with cream, to taste. If desired, thicken by stirring in a mixture of cornstarch mixed with 1 Tbsp (15 mL) cold water; cook, stirring until thickened slightly, about 5 minutes. Season with salt and pepper to taste. Makes 2 cups (500 mL). If desired, serve with Yorkshire Pudding (see page 345).

Serves 10 to 12 One serving = 1/12 roast (approx. 3 oz/84 g) with 3 Tbsp (45 mL) gravy
Per serving: 197 Calories, 6.2 g Total Fat, 2.5 g Saturated Fat, 0.2 g Trans Fat, 289 mg Sodium, 2.7 g Carbohydrate, 0.8 g Fibre, 0.9 g Sugars, 0 g Added Sugars, 29.3 g Protein
Carbohydrate Choices: less than 1

ROASTING GUIDE: AVERAGE ROASTING TIMES			
Weight (kg)	**Medium-Rare** 145°F (63°C)	**Medium to Well-Done** 160°F (71°C) or greater	**Weight (lb)**
1	1 h 45 min– 2 h 15 min	2 h–2 h 30 min	2
1.5	2 h–2 h 30 min	2 h 15 min–2 h 45 min	3
2	2 h 15 min– 2 h 45 min	2 h 30 min–3 h	4
2.5	2 h 30 min– 3 h	2 h 45 min–3 h 15 min	5 1/2
(with permission from Canada Beef [www.canadabeef.ca])			

Yorkshire Pudding [pictured on page 343] Fall/Winter
Mairlyn Smith, PHEc

*My Granny may have cooked the living daylights out of
her Brussels sprouts but she made the best Yorkshire puddings.
I have tried other recipes but when I found this recipe in a small
yellow recipe box at my mom's house, I threw my other recipe out.
This is a winner!* —Mairlyn

METHOD
1. Whisk the eggs in a large bowl until fluffy. Whisk in milk. Add flour and salt and whisk until very smooth, with no lumps. Let rest on the counter for 30 minutes.
2. While roast is resting, preheat oven to 450°F (230°C).
3. Divide the oil (or fat from the roast) evenly between 12 muffin tins, pouring approx. 1/2 tsp (2 mL) into each tin. Place in oven until the oil is hot, about 1 to 2 minutes. Remove from oven and quickly pour approximately 1/4 cup (60 mL) of the batter into each muffin tin. Bake for 10 minutes then reduce temperature to 350°F (175°C) and continue baking for 30 to 35 minutes, or until the Yorkshires are puffy and cooked through. Serve right away.

Makes 12 One serving = 1 Yorkshire pudding
106 Calories, 6 g Total fat, 1 g Sat Fat, 0 g Trans Fat, 81 mg Sodium, 9 g Carbohydrate, 0.3 g Fibre, 1.3 g Sugars, 0 g Added Sugars, 4 g Protein
Carbohydrate Choices: 1/2

INGREDIENTS

4 omega-3 eggs
1 cup (250 mL) 1% milk (see note)
1 cup (250 mL) all-purpose flour, spoon into a dry measuring cup and level off
1/4 tsp (1 mL) iodized salt
2–3 Tbsp (30–45 mL) fat from the roast or high-stability canola oil

INGREDIENT NOTE:
Milk—1% milk has just the right amount of fat to help encapsulate the air bubbles that make the Yorkshires puff up in the oven. Do not substitute.

PHEC TIP:
Don't even think about opening the oven during the first 10 minutes—those gorgeous puffy Yorkshires will end up a soggy mess if you do (just warning you).

INGREDIENTS

2 lb (900 g) ground bison or extra
lean ground beef

3/4 cup (175 mL) large flake
rolled oats

1/2 cup (125 mL) 1% milk

1 onion, chopped

1 clove garlic, minced

2 omega-3 eggs, lightly beaten

2 tsp (10 mL) Worcestershire
sauce

1/2 cup (125 mL) low sodium
ketchup

3 Tbsp (45 mL) packed brown
sugar

1 1/2 tsp (7 mL) dry mustard

Meatloaf Multi-seasonal

Michele McAdoo, PHEc

The history of Canadian bison is really a conservation success story.
With nearly a complete loss of bison in North America, ranchers in
both Canada and the USA kept herds in National Parks as well as
private smaller herds. By the 1990s the industry started to gain public
awareness, and today there are almost 2000 bison producers in Canada
with approximately 250,000 bison.

METHOD

1. Preheat oven to 325°F (160°C). Lightly oil a 9- × 13-inch (23 × 33
   cm) baking pan or line with parchment paper.
2. Crumble bison in a large bowl; add oats, milk, onion, garlic, eggs
   and Worcestershire sauce. Gently mix until combined.
3. Shape meat mixture in a free form shape resembling a loaf of bread
   and place onto the prepared pan.
4. In a small bowl, mix together ketchup, sugar and mustard and set
   aside.
5. Bake meat loaf for 40 to 45 minutes.
6. Spread ketchup mixture over top of loaf. Bake for an additional 10
   to 15 minutes. Test for doneness with a food thermometer inserted
   sideways into the centre of the meatloaf until you reach 160°F
   (71°C). Do not cook beyond this temperature or the meatloaf will
   become dry. Let stand for 10 minutes before cutting into slices.

Makes 1 loaf with 10 slices One serving = 1 slice or 1/10 meatloaf
Per serving: 309 Calories, 17.5 g Total Fat, 7.3 g Saturated Fat, 0 g Trans Fat, 124 mg Sodium,
14.7 g Carbohydrate, 1 g Fibre, 9.6 g Sugars, 8.2 g Added Sugars, 21.6 g Protein
Carbohydrate Choices: 1

BISON

Bison is a very lean and intensly flavoured red meat, having 2.5 g of total fat per 100 g cooked serving. For more information about bison go to www.canadianbison.com You can also check out *Buffalo Girl Cooks Bison* (Touchwood 2014) by Jennifer Bain, food editor at the *Toronto Star* for an entire cookbook on bison.

Fruity Treats and Fresh-Picked Indulgences

351 Treats—A Cautionary Tale

352 Four Classic Canadian Crisps

352 Ginger Rhubarb Crisp

353 Blueberry Pear and Hazelnut Crisp

354 Cranberry Apple Crisp

355 Saskatoon Berry Crisp

356 Apple and Dried Cherry Bread Pudding

357 Saskatoon Maple Bread Pudding

358 Cranberry Maple Butter Tarts

360 Garden Carrot Cake

362 Beautiful Beetday Cake

364 Apple Fruitcake with Whisky Glaze

366 Saskatoon Cheesecake Swirl

368 Apple Blackberry Crumble Pie

371 Sour Cherry Pie Filling (or Topping)

372 Pumpkin Pie

374 Grilled Peaches

376 Yogurt Berry Pops

378 Double Cranberry Blondies

379 Pumpkin Muffin-Top Cookies

We grow fabulous fruits and berries right across Canada. Blueberries from BC and the Maritimes, apples predominately from Ontario and BC and rhubarb in our own backyards. Whether it's fresh-picked strawberries in a bowl or peaches baked into a dessert, every province has you covered in the dessert world.

TREATS—A CAUTIONARY TALE

Treats! We all love'em, and an occasional treat is *okay* to fit into your eating plan—*occasional* being the operative word, as in once in a while, once in a blue moon, not very often, when someone in your immediate family gets The Order of Canada…

Knowledge is power, and the more you know the better choices you can make. So go ahead and indulge, *occasionally*, just check out the serving size, calories and grams of fat and added sugars that go into each and every treat before you dive head first into your second piece of Garden Carrot Cake (page 360). That foray into indulgence is going to cost you 513 calories, 23.8 g of total fat, 59.2 g of carbohydrates and 39 g of added sugars, which is still far less than some commercial cakes. Oh, yes, treats come with a price.

Having said that, I believe you can make *room* for treats in your diet; it just has to be a really little tiny *room* in a really special house/occasion.

Merriam Webster definition:
Treat *noun*
: something that tastes good and that is not eaten often

INGREDIENTS

Filling

4 cups (1 L) fresh or frozen
   chopped rhubarb, cut into
   1-inch (2.5 cm) pieces
3/4 cup (185 mL) granulated
   sugar
1 tsp (5 mL) pure vanilla extract
2 Tbsp (30 mL) finely grated fresh
   ginger (see note p.134)
2 Tbsp (30 mL) all-purpose flour

Topping

1 cup (250 mL) large flake rolled
   oats
1/2 cup (125 mL) whole wheat
   flour
1 Tbsp (15 mL) natural wheat
   germ
1/3 cup (75 mL) packed golden
   brown sugar
1/2 cup (125 mL) unsalted butter,
   softened

Four Classic Canadian Crisps

Crisps are easier to make than pie, which means they're quicker to prepare and also have less calories. But—crisps do *have* calories, and some have more than you'd think. Fortunately there are a couple of redeeming qualities when it comes to crisps: they're made with fruit, and the ones we feature in this chapter all have whole grains in the crisp part.

Ginger Rhubarb Crisp Michele McAdoo, PHEc

When spring finally arrives in Canada somewhere between March and May, this is one of those desserts you start craving.

METHOD

Preheat oven to 350°F (175°C) and have a 9-inch (23 cm) baking dish ready. In a large bowl, combine the filling ingredients together, then place into the prepared pan. In a separate large bowl, mix all of the dry topping ingredients together. Cut the butter in with a pastry blender or 2 knives, until mixture resembles coarse crumbs, then tip over the prepared filling, gently patting it down. Bake for 1 hour, or until topping is golden and filling is tender and bubbling. Serve warm or cooled to room temperature.

Makes 4 1/2 cups (1.12 L) One serving = 1/2 cup (125 mL) and a wee bit
Per serving: 278 Calories, 12 g Total Fat, 7 g Saturated Fat, 0.6 g Trans Fat, 6 mg Sodium, 40 g Carbohydrate, 2.8 g Fibre, 24.7 g Sugars, 23.9 g Added Sugars, 3.4 g Protein
Carbohydrate Choices: 2 1/2

Blueberry Pear & Hazelnut Crisp Bridget Wilson, PHEc

Hazelnuts, sometimes called filberts, are the only nut crop produced commercially in BC. They are grown in the eastern part of the Fraser Valley, mainly around Chilliwack and Agassiz.

METHOD

Preheat oven to 350°F (175°C). Line a 6-cup (1.5 L) baking dish with wet parchment paper (see page 388). In a large bowl, combine all of the filling ingredients together and place into the prepared pan. In a separate large bowl, mix together all of the dry topping ingredients, including hazelnuts. Add the oil and stir in until the mixture is crumbly, then tip over the prepared filling, gently patting it down. Bake for 40 to 45 minutes or until fruit is tender and bubbly and topping is golden brown. Serve warm or cooled to room temperature.

Makes 6 cups (1.5 L). One serving = 1/2 cup (125 mL)
Per serving: 147 Calories, 7 g Total Fat, 0.6 g Saturated Fat, 0.1 g Trans Fat, 2 mg Sodium, 20.8 g Carbohydrate, 3 g Fibre, 11.3 g Sugars, 4.5 g Added Sugars, 2 g Protein
Carbohydrate Choices: 1

INGREDIENTS

Filling

3 cups (750 mL) fresh or frozen blueberries or honeyberries

2 cups (500 mL) ripe pears, peeled, cored and chopped (approx. 2 large pears)

1 Tbsp (15 mL) cornstarch

1/2 tsp (2 mL) cinnamon

Topping

1/2 cup (125 mL) quick cooking oatmeal, not instant

1/4 cup (60 mL) whole wheat flour

1 Tbsp (15 mL) natural wheat germ

1/4 cup (60 mL) packed golden brown sugar

1 tsp (5 mL) cinnamon

1/4 cup (60 mL) hazelnuts, toasted and chopped

1/4 cup (60 mL) canola oil

INGREDIENTS

Filling

8 cups (2 L) Macintosh apples, peeled, cored and sliced thinly (about 6 large apples)

1 cup (250 mL) fresh or frozen cranberries

1/2 cup (125 mL) dried cranberries

1/4 cup (60 mL) pure maple syrup

1 tsp (5 mL) cinnamon

Topping

1 1/2 cup (375 mL) large flake rolled oats

1/2 cup (125 mL) whole-wheat flour

1 Tbsp (15 mL) natural wheat germ

1/2 cup (125 mL) packed dark brown sugar

1 Tbsp. (15 mL) cinnamon

1/2 cup (125 mL) canola oil

Cranberry Apple Crisp Amy Whitson, PHEc

Every McIntosh apple is a direct descendant of the original apple trees that United Empire Loyalist John McIntosh discovered in 1811 growing on his newly purchased farm in Dundas County, Ontario.

METHOD

Preheat oven to 350°F (180°C). Have an 11- × 7-inch (28 × 18 cm) baking pan ready. In a large bowl, combine all of the filling ingredients together and place into the prepared pan. In a separate large bowl, mix together all of the dry topping ingredients. Add the oil and stir in until the mixture is crumbly, then tip over the prepared filling, gently patting it down. Bake for 45–50 minutes or until the fruit is bubbly and the topping is golden brown. Serve warm or cooled to room temperature.

Makes 7 cups (1.75 L). One serving = 1/2 cup (125 mL)
Per Serving: 231 Calories, 9.2 g Total Fat, 0.8 g Saturated Fat, 0.2 g Trans Fat, 3 mg Sodium, 36 g Carbohydrate, 3.4 g Fibre, 21.3 g Sugars, 2.5 g Protein
Carbohydrate Choices: 2

Saskatoon Berry Crisp Linda Reasbeck, PHEc

*"My home was on a farm in rural Alberta, near Paradise Valley.
One of my fondest memories of summer holidays was picking and
eating wild Saskatoon berries. Our river pasture had many tall Saskatoon
bushes so we often picked them on horseback. When I moved to Ontario,
my special Aunt Millie would pick Saskatoons and have a frozen
Saskatoon pie ready for me whenever I visited her in Calgary. It was
a true labour of love and a wonderful gift to me."*—Linda

METHOD

Preheat oven to 350°F (175°C). Lightly oil an 8-inch (20 cm) baking
pan. In a large bowl, combine all of the filling ingredients together and
place into the prepared pan. In a separate large bowl, mix together all of
the dry topping ingredients, including nuts. Add the oil and stir in until
the mixture is crumbly, then tip over the prepared filling, gently patting
it down. Bake for 40–45 minutes or until the berries are cooked and the
topping is golden brown. Serve warm or cooled to room temperature.

Makes approximately 3 cups (750 mL). One serving = 1/2 cup (125 mL)
Per Serving: 243 Calories, 8 g Total Fat, 0.7 g Saturated Fat, 0.2 g Trans Fat, 5 mg Sodium, 41 g
Carbohydrate, 6.7 g Fibre, 26 g Sugars, 2.7 g Protein
Carbohydrate Choices: 2

INGREDIENTS

Filling

1/4 cup (60 mL) packed golden
brown sugar

1 Tbsp (15 mL) all-purpose flour

1 tsp (5 mL) cinnamon

4 cups (1L) Saskatoons or
blueberries

Topping

1/2 cup (125 mL) whole-wheat
flour

3 Tbsp (45 mL) packed golden
brown sugar

3 Tbsp (45 mL) canola oil

INGREDIENTS

1/2 cup (125 mL) dried cherries

1/4 cup (60 mL) natural apple juice

One 12 oz (370 mL) can fat-free evaporated milk

4 omega-3 eggs

1 tsp (5 mL) pure vanilla extract

3/4 cup (185 mL) pure maple syrup + extra for serving (optional)

8 cups (2 L) day-old 100% whole wheat bread, cut into 3/4-inch (2 cm) cubes (approx. 8 bread slices)

2 medium apples, scrubbed well, cored and chopped

1 tsp (5 mL) ground cinnamon

1/2 tsp (2 mL) ground nutmeg

NATURAL APPLE JUICE

Natural apple juice is made from whole apples, including the peel, making it a more nutrient dense choice. Usually found where fresh cold juice is sold.

Apple and Dried Cherry Bread Pudding Fall/Winter

Rosemarie Superville, PHEc

"My Mom made bread pudding for dessert when I was a child. In Trinidad, it's often made with raisins or currants—I've Canadianized it by adding apples and dried cherries. Want to jazz this recipe up even more? Soak the cherries in Trinidadian rum!"—**Rosemarie**

METHOD

1. Preheat oven to 350°F (180°C) and line a 9- × 13-inch (23 × 33 cm) baking dish with wet parchment paper (see page 388). Set aside.

2. In a small bowl, toss cherries with apple juice. Set aside.

3. In a large bowl, whisk together milk, eggs, vanilla and maple syrup. Stir in bread cubes and let stand for about 15 minutes, stirring occasionally.

4. In a medium bowl, toss apples with cinnamon and nutmeg.

5. Add cherry and apple mixtures to softened bread, mixing well. Pour into the prepared pan. Gently press down to redistribute cherries, if necessary. Bake for about 40 to 45 minutes or until browned and set. Serve warm with additional maple syrup, if desired.

Makes one 9- × 13-inch (23 × 33 cm) pudding One serving = 1/2 cup (125 mL)
Per serving: 202 Calories, 3 g Total Fat, 0.8 g Saturated Fat, 0 g Trans Fat, 223 mg Sodium, 51.6 g Carbohydrate, 3 g Fibre, 21.3 g Sugars, 13.4 g Added Sugars, 8.8 g Protein
Carbohydrate Choices: 3

Saskatoon Maple Bread Pudding Multi-seasonal

Elaine Silverthorn, PHEc

"I remember picking berries as a child in the pasture of my family farm at Moosomin, near the Qu'Appelle valley, on hot July days. Berry pails tied round the neck with string were all the style, and we could hardly wait to enjoy a Saskatoon dessert later in the day."—Elaine

METHOD

1. Preheat oven to 350°F (175°C). Lightly oil an 8- × 8-inch (20 × 20 cm) Pyrex or glass baking pan.
2. Put the bread cubes into the prepared pan and evenly spread the Saskatoons over the bread. Set aside.
3. In a medium bowl, beat the eggs until thick. Add the sugar, maple syrup, melted butter, vanilla and mix well. Gently mix milk into the egg mixture.
4. Slowly pour milk mixture over the prepared bread and Saskatoons. Using the back of a spoon press the bread down into the milk mixture to ensure even saturation. Bake for 40 to 45 minutes or until the centre of the pudding is set. Serve warm or spoon into dessert bowls with vanilla ice cream or vanilla frozen yogurt.

Makes one 8- × 8-inch (20 × 20 cm) pudding
One serving = 1/2 cup (125 mL) without vanilla ice cream or vanilla frozen yogurt
Per serving: 206 Calories, 5 g Total Fat, 2 g Saturated Fat, 0.1 g Trans Fat, 168 mg Sodium, 32.2 g Carbohydrate, 2.5 g Fibre, 22.4 g Sugars, 15.8 g Added Sugars, 8 g Protein
Carbohydrate Choices: 2

INGREDIENTS

4 cups (1 L) whole wheat bread (approx. 4–6 slices), cut into 1-inch (2.5 cm) cubes
1 cup (250 mL) fresh or thawed Saskatoons or blueberries (see note)
4 omega-3 eggs
1/2 cup (125 mL) granulated sugar
3 Tbsp (45 mL) pure maple syrup
1 Tbsp (15 mL) unsalted butter, melted
1 tsp (5 mL) pure vanilla extract
2 1/2 cups (560 mL) 1% milk
Vanilla ice cream or vanilla frozen yogurt (optional)

INGREDIENT NOTE:

Saskatoons—If Saskatoons are unavailable, substitute blueberries. The flavour of Saskatoons is similar to blueberries but with a distinct hint of almond. The biggest difference between a blueberry and a Saskatoon is that Saskatoons have many tiny seeds inside.

INGREDIENTS

Pastry

1 1/2 cups (375 mL) all-purpose
flour

1/2 cup (125 mL) unsalted butter,
softened

1/2 cup (125 mL) light cream
cheese, softened

Tart Filling

1/2 cup (125 mL) chopped dried
cranberries

1/4 cup (60 mL) unsalted butter,
softened

1/4 tsp (1 mL) iodized salt

1/2 cup (125 mL) lightly packed
brown sugar

1 omega-3 egg

1/4 cup (60 mL) pure maple syrup

1/2 tsp (2 mL) pure vanilla extract

Makes 12 tarts
One serving = 1 tart
Per serving: 264 Calories,
14.6 g Total Fat, 8.8 g
Saturated Fat, 0.7 g Trans
Fat, 110 mg Sodium, 30.7 g
Carbohydrate, 0.7 g Fibre,
17.3 g Sugars, 15.8 g Added
Sugars, 3.5 g Protein
Carbohydrate Choices: 2

Cranberry Maple Butter Tarts Fall/winter

Sue Soderman, PHEc with Pat Moynihan Morris, PHEc and Olga Kaminskyj, PHEc

"Butter tarts always bring back memories of holidays at our family cottage on Lake Huron in Grand Bend, Ontario. We could not arrive without a dozen gooey butter tarts that we bought on our way up. It didn't matter if they got a little mushed during the trip, they still tasted just as good. This recipe is a tribute to that food memory, without the mushed up part."—Sue

METHOD

A new spin on the quintessential Canadian tart renowned throughout the colonies.

1. Pulse together flour, butter and cream cheese in a food processor until mixture is well blended and starts to form a ball. Shape into ball with hands, then wrap tightly with plastic wrap. Refrigerate 1 hour or until chilled.

2. When the pastry is ready to roll out, preheat oven to 375°F (190°C).

3. Place pastry on a lightly floured surface and roll out to 1/4-inch (6 mm) thickness. Cut into 12 rounds with a 4-inch (10 cm) cutter. Place rounds into a 12-muffin-cup pan and gently press into each muffin cup to line. Evenly divide the cranberries and place in the muffin cups.

4. In a large bowl, cream butter, add brown sugar and salt and beat in until smooth. Add egg and lightly beat until mixture is well blended and smooth.

5. Gently stir in maple syrup and vanilla until well incorporated.

6. Fill pastry cups three-quarters full with filling mixture.

7. Bake for 15 to 18 minutes until the filling is set and the pastry golden brown. Remove from oven and allow to cool in the pan before transferring tarts to a wire cooling rack.

INGREDIENTS

Carrot Cake

4 omega-3 eggs

1 cup (250 mL) liquid honey

1/2 cup (125 mL) lightly packed golden brown sugar

1 cup (250 mL) canola oil

1 cup (250 mL) all-purpose flour

1 1/4 cups (310 mL) whole wheat flour

1/2 tsp (2 mL) iodized salt

2 tsp (10 mL) baking powder

1/2 tsp (2 mL) baking soda

1 tsp (5 mL) cinnamon

1/2 tsp (2 mL) freshly ground nutmeg

3 cups (750 mL) grated raw carrots (approx. 2–3 large carrots)

1 cup (250 mL) dried currants

1 cup (250 mL) chopped walnuts

Cream Cheese Icing (optional)

4 oz (125 g) light cream cheese, softened

2 Tbsp (30 mL) unsalted butter, at room temperature

1 tsp (5 mL) pure vanilla extract

1 1/2–2 cups (375 mL–500 mL) icing sugar

Garden Carrot Cake **Multi-seasonal** Patricia Moynihan Morris, PHEc

"My Mom used carrots from her garden and fresh honey from a local beekeeper in Grey County, Chatsworth, Ontario to bake this family favourite. Just after I was married, I gave this recipe to my mother-in-law who loved carrot cake and she added chopped black walnuts. I like to call this a 'cake ingredient marriage.'"—Patricia

METHOD

1. Preheat oven to 325°F (160°C). Line a 13- × 9-inch (33 × 23 cm) baking pan with parchment paper or lightly oil. Set aside.
2. Using an electric mixer, beat eggs in a large bowl until frothy. Gradually add honey and brown sugar, beating until light. Beat in oil until mixture is smooth and a light brown.
3. In a separate bowl, mix together all-purpose and whole wheat flours, salt, baking powder, baking soda, cinnamon, nutmeg, carrots, currants and walnuts; stir into batter and mix until well combined.
4. Pour mixture into prepared pan, spreading out the top so it's even. Bake for 50 to 60 minutes or until a cake tester or a toothpick inserted in the middle of the cake comes out clean. Remove from oven and cool on a cooling rack.
5. When cool, dust with icing sugar, or frost with cream cheese icing. If making the icing, blend together cream cheese, butter and vanilla using an electric mixer. Gradually beat in icing sugar, with just enough to make a smooth, spreadable consistency. Drizzle over carrot cake and serve.

Makes 16 servings One serving = 1/16 cake (without icing)
Per serving: 395 Calories, 21.1 g Total Fat, 2 g Saturated Fat, 0.3 g Trans Fat, 189 mg Sodium, 48.6 g Carbohydrate, 2.7 g Fibre, 33.6 g Sugars, 29.4 g Added Sugars, 5.7 g Protein
Carbohydrate Choices: 3

One serving = 1/16 cake (with icing)
Per serving: 513 Calories, 23.8 g Total Fat, 3.7 g Saturated Fat, 0.4 g Trans Fat, 226 mg Sodium, 59.2 g Carbohydrate, 2.7 g Fibre, 43.8 g Sugars, 39 g Added Sugars, 6.3 g Protein
Carbohydrate Choices: 4

ADDED SUGARS

Added sugars are the unnatural sugars added to a food item by the manufacturer, producer or cook. The list of possible added sugars is long and can can include barley malt, dextrose, maltose, molasses, rice syrup, corn syrup, honey and maple syrup just to name a few. Only total sugar is shown on nutrition labels, which makes it difficult for consumers to figure out the naturally occurring sugars from the added.

Consuming too much added sugar has been associated with heart disease, stroke, obesity, diabetes, high blood pressure and dental cavities. In 2015 the World Health Organization (WHO), concerned about long-term health, set out guidelines for a healthy amount of added sugars to the diet, recommending that only 10 percent of total caloric intake—and ideally that less than five percent—come from added sugars or from honey, syrups or 100% fruit juice. Consumer translation: Limit your daily added sugars to 2 Tbsp (30 mL/25 g) for women and 3 Tbsp (45 mL/38 g) for men.

TRUST THE SCIENTISTS

SugarScience.org, a team of health scientists from the University of California, San Francisco, have created a website to help consumers navigate through the true science behind the current sugar research. Check out their website.

INGREDIENTS

Beetday Cake

2/3 cup (160 mL) granulated
sugar

2/3 cup (160 mL) packed dark
brown sugar

1/2 cup (125 mL) canola oil

2 omega-3 eggs

3 cups (750 mL) grated peeled
beets (approx. 2 medium to
large beets)

1/2 cup (125 mL) buttermilk

1 1/4 cups (310 mL) whole wheat
flour

1 cup (250 mL) all-purpose flour

1/4 cup (60 mL) wheat germ

2 tsp (10 mL) baking powder

1 tsp (5 mL) baking soda

2 tsp (10 mL) ground ginger

2 tsp (10 mL) ground cinnamon

1/4 tsp (1 mL) freshly ground
nutmeg

1/4 tsp (1 mL) ground cloves

Icing (optional)

4 oz (125 g) light cream cheese

1/4 cup (60 mL) unsalted butter,
at room temperature

2 1/2 cups (625 mL) icing sugar,
sifted if lumpy

Beautiful Beetday Cake Multi-seasonal Cristina Fernandes, PHEc, RD

*"This cake is very dense and delicious, plus it packs in the
benefits of potassium, magnesium, fibre, phosphorus, iron,
beta-carotene, beta-cyanine, folic acid and vitamins A, B and C.
Beets are special; they contain betaine, the same substance that is
used to ward off depression, and the tryptophan that it houses
relaxes the mind and creates a sense of well-being, similar
to chocolate!"* —Cristina

METHOD

1. Position rack in the middle of the oven. Preheat to 350°F (175°C).
    Lightly oil two 8-inch (20 cm) cake pans. Line bottom of each pan
    with parchment paper to prevent sticking. Set aside.

2. Using an electric hand-held mixer on medium speed, beat together
    granulated sugar, brown sugar, oil and eggs in a large mixing bowl,
    until the batter is a light golden brown.

3. Add beets and continue to beat on low speed until well blended.
    Add buttermilk and blend in well.

4. In a medium bowl, whisk together the whole wheat and all-
    purpose flours with the wheat germ, baking powder, baking soda,
    ginger, cinnamon, nutmeg and cloves. Add beet mixture and mix
    in slowly until well incorporated. Evenly divide batter between the
    two prepared pans and spread out the tops so they are even.

5. Bake for 30 to 35 minutes or until a cake tester or a toothpick inserted in the centre of the cake comes out clean.

6. Cool in pans 10 minutes on wire racks; remove from pans. Carefully peel off parchment paper and cool cakes completely on wire rack.

7. If making the icing, beat together the cream cheese and butter in a medium mixing bowl, using an electric hand-held mixer on medium speed, until fluffy. Reduce the speed to low and slowly add the icing sugar until well blended and creamy looking. If it's too dry, add a few drops of pure vanilla extract.

8. To apply the icing, place first layer of the cake on a cake stand and spread a small amount of icing on top. Stack the second layer on top. Spoon the remaining icing on top of the cake and then gently spread the icing thinly over the top and down the sides until the cake is covered with the icing.

Makes one 8-inch (20 cm) double layer cake with icing One serving = 1/16 cake (without icing)
Per serving: 229 Calories, 8.6 g Total Fat, 0.9 g Saturated Fat, 0.2 g Trans Fat, 163 mg Sodium, 34.3 g Carbohydrate, 2.2 g Fibre, 19.6 g Sugars, 16.4 g Added Sugars, 4.5 g Protein
Carbohydrate Choices: 2
One serving = 1/16 cake (with icing)
Per serving: 335 Calories, 13 g Total Fat, 3.5 g Saturated Fat, 0.3 g Trans Fat, 201 mg Sodium, 51.4 g Carbohydrate, 2.2 g Fibre, 36.3 g Sugars, 32.5 g Added Sugars, 5.2 g Protein
Carbohydrate Choices: 3

INGREDIENTS

1 cup (250 mL) toasted walnuts
  or hazelnuts (see note)
1 1/2 cups (375 mL) liquid honey,
  divided
3/4 cup (185 mL) canola oil
1/2 cup (125 mL) Canadian
  whisky, divided
1/2 cup (125 mL) packed golden
  brown sugar
3 omega-3 eggs
2 cups (500 mL) all-purpose flour
1 cup (250 mL) whole wheat flour
1 Tbsp (15 mL) natural wheat
  germ
2 tsp (10 mL) ground cinnamon
1 tsp (5 mL) ground ginger
1 tsp (5 mL) freshly grated
  nutmeg
1 tsp (5 mL) baking soda
1/2 tsp (2 mL) iodized salt
1 1/2 cups (375 mL) peeled,
  cored and diced apples
  (approx. 3 apples)
1 cup (250 mL) dried cranberries

Apple Fruitcake with Whisky Glaze Fall/ Winter
Jan Main, PHEc

*"This is one of my favourite cakes; it's perfect for a celebration
or as a substitute for a Christmas fruitcake. For the best flavour,
make it at least one day ahead of serving and, bonus—it freezes
beautifully. If well wrapped, it will keep in the freezer for
up to 3 months."* —Jan

METHOD

1. Preheat oven to 350°F (175°C). Lightly oil 9-inch (23 cm) Bundt or tube pan. Set aside.

2. Spread walnuts (or hazelnuts) out on a rimmed baking sheet and roast for 5 minutes. Remove from oven and let cool; chop and set aside. (For hazelnuts, roll to remove brown papery outer layer and discard, then chop nuts.)

3. In a large mixing bowl, beat 1 cup (250 mL) honey, oil, 1/4 cup (60 mL) whisky and brown sugar together with an electric mixer on medium-high until thick and creamy. Beat in eggs one at a time until well combined.

4. In separate large bowl, stir together both flours, the wheat germ, cinnamon, ginger, nutmeg, baking soda and salt until well combined. Reserve 2 Tbsp (30 mL) of the mixture and place in a small bowl.

5. In a medium bowl, mix together chopped walnuts (or hazelnuts), apples and cranberries. Sprinkle with reserved flour mixture.

6. Gradually beat dry ingredients into creamed ingredients. Stir in floured apples, walnuts and cranberries until well blended.

7. Spoon batter into the prepared pan. Bake 50 to 60 minutes until firm to the touch or until a toothpick inserted into the centre of the cake comes out clean. Cool on cooling rack for about 10 minutes and unmould cake onto serving plate.

8. In a saucepan, bring the rest of the honey and the whisky to a boil and simmer for 1 minute. Drizzle over cake while still warm. Slice with a serrated knife and serve.

Makes one 9-inch (23 cm) Bundt cake One serving = 1/20 cake with glaze
Per serving: 342 Calories, 13.6 g Total Fat, 1.3 g Saturated Fat, 0.2 g Trans Fat, 137 mg Sodium, 50.5 g Carbohydrate, 2.2 g Fibre, 34 g Sugars, 30.7 g Added Sugars, 4.6 g Protein
Carbohydrate Choices: 3

CROWN ROYAL WHISKY

We love our Royals so much that in 1939, when King George VI and Queen Elizabeth visited our shores for their first grand tour of Canada, a new blend of 50 select whiskies was used to create a commemorative bottle of Canada's finest whisky and Crown Royal® was born. Made from milled corn, rye and malted barley, Crown Royal® is aged in both seasoned and new white oak barrels. It is produced solely at their distillery at Gimli, on the shores of Lake Winnipeg.

To celebrate the 75th Anniversary of the original blend and the Royal visit, Canada created their Crown Royal 75th Anniversary whiskey limited edition called Monarch.

PHEC TIPS:

• To glam it up, serve with a dollop of yogurt sweetened with brown sugar and flavoured with a splash of whisky.

• All nuts can go rancid because of the fat they contain. Store them in the freezer in a container or resealable bag for up to 6 months.

INGREDIENTS

Base

18 squares honey graham cracker crumbs

3 Tbsp (45 mL) natural wheat germ

1/4 cup (60 mL) canola oil

Puree

1 cup (250 mL) fresh or thawed blueberries, honeyberries or Saskatoons (see note)

1/2 cup (125 mL) water

3 Tbsp (45 mL) granulated sugar

1 Tbsp (15 mL) 100% cranberry juice blend

Filling

One 8 1/2 oz (250 g) pkg light cream cheese

1/4 cup (60 mL) granulated sugar

1 tsp (5 mL) pure vanilla extract

3/4 cup (185 mL) 0% MF plain Greek yogurt

1 omega-3 egg

1 large egg white

1 Tbsp (15 mL) 100% cranberry juice blend

1 Tbsp (15 mL) all-purpose flour

Saskatoon Cheesecake Swirl Multi-seasonal

Elaine Silverthorn, PHEc

Professional Home Economists are amazing people. When we were going to test the recipes for this book requiring Saskatoons (those amazing berries that only grow in the Prairies), I could not find a Saskatoon anywhere in Toronto to save my soul. I put out a *Twitter Call to Action* asking for help and Jennifer Dyke, PHEc, from Manitoba, stepped up to the plate. She offered to test all the recipes for the cookbook using Saskatoons. That's what I call teamwork.

If you aren't so lucky as to have your own crop of Saskatoons, blueberries are a perfect substitute.

METHOD

1. Preheat oven to 350°F (175°C). Insert a round piece of parchment in the bottom of a 9-inch (23 cm) spring form pan. Set aside.
2. To make the base, pulse the graham crackers and wheat germ in a food processor until the mixture looks like sand. With the processor running, pour in the canola oil and continue to mix until well blended. Pour the mixture, spread out evenly into prepared pan and press firmly to form the base. Bake in the centre of the oven for 7 minutes, or until golden brown. Remove from oven and cool.
3. To make the puree, combine the berries, water, sugar and cranberry juice in a small saucepan over medium heat. Bring to a boil and reduce heat to low. Simmer for 10 minutes, then remove from heat and cool. Puree using an immersion blender or pour into a blender and puree until smooth. Set aside.
4. For the filling, use an electric mixer to beat the cream cheese, sugar and vanilla in a medium bowl, until fluffy. Beat in the yogurt, egg and egg white until fluffy. In a small bowl, whisk together the cranberry juice and flour to form a paste. Add the paste to the

cheese mixture and beat until smooth and combined. Spread the filling over the cooled base.

5. Using a teaspoon, drop 1/2 cup (125 mL) of the puree mixture evenly on to the filling, 1 tsp (5 mL) at a time, leaving spaces between your drops. Reserve the remaining puree in the refrigerator. Using a toothpick, swirl the puree drops around to get a desired swirl pattern.

6. Bake in the centre of the oven for 35 minutes or until the centre is soft and wobbly. Over-baking will cause the cheesecake surface to crack. Cool cake on a wire rack to room temperature.

7. To serve, run a small knife along the outside of the pan edge to loosen. Remove spring form, slice and serve, or chill cake for up to 2 days in an airtight container. Use the remaining chilled puree as a garnish.

Makes one 9-inch (23 cm) spring form pan One serving = 1/12 cheesecake
Per serving: 202 Calories, 9.7 g Total Fat, 2.6 g Saturated Fat, 0.1 g Trans Fat, 178 mg Sodium, 24 g Carbohydrate, 1.4 g Fibre, 15.6 g Sugars, 12.8 g Added Sugars, 5 g Protein
Carbohydrate Choices: 1 1/2

HONEYBERRIES

Haskap or honeyberries are in season in parts of Canada in July. The flavour is a cross between blueberry, raspberry and black current. Known by the ancient Japanese as "The Fruit of Life and Longevity," you'd be on the right track if you guessed that these tiny berries are good for you. You can substitute them into recipes that call for blueberries. Grown in BC, Alberta, Saskatchewan, Manitoba, Ontario, Quebec and the Maritimes, this little nutrient-dense berry is sure to be named the next Canadian superfood.

INGREDIENTS

Pastry

1 cup (250 mL) all-purpose flour

1/2 tsp (2 mL) iodized salt

1/2 cup (125 mL) soft non-hydrogenated margarine

2 Tbsp (30 mL) ice water

Filling

3 medium apples, peeled, cored and sliced

4 cups (1 L) blackberries (see note)

3/4 cup (185 mL) granulated sugar

3 Tbsp (45 mL) all-purpose flour

Streusel topping

1/2 cup (125 mL) all-purpose flour

1/4 cup (60 mL) packed golden brown sugar

1/4 tsp (1 mL) cinnamon

1/4 cup (60 mL) non-hydrogenated margarine

Apple Blackberry Crumble Pie Summer/ Early Fall

Susanne Stark, PHEc

"Blackberries grow wild all over BC and if they don't grow in the backyard, they are usually available to pick in some green space nearby. I'm from Vancouver Island and when the blackberries ripen mid-August, we always make jams, jellies and pies from these sweet and juicy berries." —Susanne

METHOD

1. Heat oven to 425°F (220°C).
2. To make the pastry, mix 1 cup (250 mL) flour with salt in a medium bowl. Cut in 1/2 cup (125 mL) margarine using a pastry cutter or 2 knives. Stir in water with a fork just until slightly moistened. Don't over-mix. Form into a ball. Wrap in plastic wrap and let it chill while you make the filling.
3. To make the filling, toss the apples, blackberries, sugar and 2 Tbsp (45 mL) flour in a large bowl. Set aside.
4. To make the streusel topping, combine 1/2 cup (250 mL) flour, brown sugar and cinnamon in a small bowl. Cut in 1/4 cup (60 mL) margarine using a pastry cutter or 2 knives. Set aside.
5. Remove pastry from the fridge. Gently roll out dough on a large piece of parchment paper sprinkled with flour, forming a 10-inch (25 cm) circle. Place pie plate upside down over the dough, then flip right side up so that the pastry in now in the pie plate. Crimp edges.

6. Transfer filling into the pie crust and sprinkle with the streusel. Bake at 425°F (220°C) for 15 minutes; reduce heat to 350°F (175°C) and bake for 40 to 45 minutes longer or until fruit juices are bubbling. Let cool for 20 minutes before serving.

Makes one 9-inch (23 cm) pie One serving = 1/8 pie
Per serving: 421 Calories,19.2 g Total Fat, 2.6 g Saturated Fat, 0.1 g Trans Fat, 394 mg Sodium, 60 g Carbohydrate, 5.5 g Fibre, 35.2 g Sugars, 26.5 g Added Sugars, 4.7 g Protein
Carbohydrate Choices: 3 1/2

APPLES

One of the great joys of Canadian apples is the variety. Whether it's an apple grown in BC, Ontario or Quebec, Canadian apples are delicious, nutritious and readily available. Apples are especially ubiquitous in BC, where they are the most valuable edible horticulture crop. About 75 percent of all BC orchard land is planted in apples.

These are some of the most popular apple varieties grown from Canadian soil:

- Ambrosia: sweet and crispy; best eaten fresh
- Braeburn: mildly sweet; best eaten fresh, in desserts or juiced
- Cortland: sweet and crisp and resists browning; best eaten fresh or used for baking, salads, pies or in cider
- Crispin (Mutsu): moderately sweet and firm; best eaten fresh, in pies or in chunky sauces
- Empire: crisp, sweet and slighty tart; best eaten fresh or as applesauce
- Fuji: sweet and tart; best eaten fresh

INGREDIENT NOTE:
Blackberries—Blackberries freeze well. Gently rinse and let them air dry. Place berries on a cookie sheet and freeze them; when frozen, transfer to a freezer bag. To use frozen berries in this pie recipe, let them thaw on the counter for an hour. This will take the chill off of them but not enough to allow the juices to seep out.

- Gala: very sweet; best eaten fresh
- Golden Delicious: sweet, firm and juicy; best eaten fresh or in applesauce
- Granny Smith: sweet and tart; best eaten fresh
- Honeycrisp: sweet and very crisp; best eaten fresh
- Idared: tangy, tart and slightly sweet; best eaten fresh or baked
- Jonagold: honeyed; best eaten fresh or cooked in a dessert
- McIntosh: sweet and mildly tart; best eaten fresh, in pies or in sauces
- Nicola: sweet, firm and juicy; best eaten fresh or in salads, pies and sauces
- Northern Spy: mildly sweet and tart, crisp and firm; best eaten fresh and great in pies, cooking and desserts
- Pink Lady: sweet and slightly tart; best eaten fresh or in salads
- Red Delicious: mildly sweet and firm; best eaten fresh
- Red Prince: tangy, sweet and crisp; best eaten fresh, in salads or baked
- Russet: sweet and tangy; best eaten fresh, in pies or as applesauce
- Spartan: fairly sweet; best eaten fresh or in pies
- Sunrise: sweet and tart; best eaten fresh or in salads, pies and sauces

(Source: Agriculture and Agri-Foods Canada)

Sour Cherry Pie Filling (or Topping) Summer

Mary Carver, PHEc

*"Our family farm had a pick-your-own cherry orchard west
of Trenton, Ontario. While my mother's cherry pie recipe was
famous, my Dad believed that in order to have enough fruit to
meet demand, he had to plant one tree for the birds for every
tree planted for human harvest. Sour cherry topping is a lovely
treat to pull from your freezer at Christmas to top waffles with,
or to use in a trifle or on a cheesecake."* —Mary

METHOD

1. In a large saucepan over medium heat, place pitted cherries, plum and sugar; cover and heat fruit until juices are released. Simmer for 10 to 15 minutes, stirring often. Remove from heat, stir in almond or vanilla extract.

2. In a small bowl, whisk together sugar and cornstarch until smooth. Pour this mixture into the hot fruit and combine thoroughly with a wooden spoon.

3. Return to heat, bring to a simmer and cook filling till thickened, about 23 minutes. Remove from heat and let cool. Store in a glass jar in the fridge for up to 1 week, or freeze for that *cherry pie attack* in December.

Makes approx. 4 cups (1 L) of filling One serving = 2 Tbsp (30 mL) as a topping
Per serving: 40 Calories, 0.1 g Total Fat, 0 g Saturated Fat, 0 g Trans Fat, 1 mg Sodium, 10 g Carbohydrate, 0.4 g Fibre, 8.5 g Sugars, 6.3 g Added Sugars, 0.2 g Protein
Carbohydrate Choices: 1/2

INGREDIENTS

4 cups (1 L) packed and pitted sour red Ontario cherries (do not use sweet cherries—see note)

1 ripe red or black plum, rinsed, pitted and chopped (approx. 1 cup/250 mL—see note)

1/2 tsp (2 mL) pure almond or vanilla extract

1 cup (250 mL) granulated sugar

1/4 cup (60 mL) cornstarch

INGREDIENT NOTES:

Sour Cherries—Sour cherries are not the same as Bing or other sweet varieties of cherries. Not only are the flavours different, but sour cherries contain more melatonin, a natural sleep enhancer, than sweet cherries.

Plum—Mary uses a plum to add a natural red colour to her cherry filling, so please leave red skin on so you get that great cherry red colour.

PHEC TIP:

To make into a pie, use your favourite pastry recipe or try the OHEA's recipe for pastry on page 368.

One 9-inch (23 cm) unbaked pie shell with fluted edges (use the pastry recipe for Apple Blackberry Crumble Pie on page 368)

1 cup (250 mL) evaporated 2% milk

2 omega-3 eggs

1 1/2 cups (375 mL) pureed pumpkin (fresh or canned)

1 cup (250 mL) packed dark brown sugar

2 tsp (10 mL) cinnamon

1 tsp (5 mL) ground ginger

1/4 tsp (1 mL) freshly ground nutmeg

1/4 tsp (1 mL) ground cloves

PHEC TIPS:

• For a leafy garnish, roll out extra pastry to 1/8-inch (3 mm) thickness and cut into leaf shapes. While the pie is baking at 425°F (220°C), bake the pastry garnish for 8 to 10 minutes on a small baking sheet. Remove from oven, cool and set aside. Arrange on top of cooled pie. We used a Maple Leaf in the picture.

• Not a pastry fan? Turn the recipe into baked custard: Divide the filling into six 4-inch (10 cm) ramekins or custard cups and bake at 325°F (160°C) for 25 to 30 minutes, or until set.

Pumpkin Pie Fall/Winter

Jennifer Goodwin, PHEc and Mairlyn Smith, PHEc

Canadians may have adopted the traditional pumpkin pie recipe from our southern neighbours, but Canadian Thanksgiving in October just wouldn't seem right without it. Jennifer and I amalgamated our recipes to produce this winner.

METHOD

1. Place oven rack to its lowest position. Preheat oven to 425°F (220°C).

2. Make pie shell according to the recipe on page 368. Roll out according to directions and place in pie plate; crimp edges.

3. In a large bowl, whisk together the evaporated milk, eggs, pumpkin puree, brown sugar, cinnamon, ginger, nutmeg and cloves, until completely combined. Tip: don't over-blend as this can cause the pie to crack.

4. Pour filling into the unbaked pie shell and bake for 20 minutes; reduce heat to 325°F (160°C) and bake 35 to 45 minutes longer, or until the pie is set. Cool to room temperature and chill in fridge until serving. Refrigerate any leftovers (as if…).

Makes one 9-inch (23 cm) pie One serving = 1/6 pie
Per serving: 301 Calories, 9.6 g Total Fat, 4 g Saturated Fat, 0 g Trans Fat, 194 mg Sodium, 48.6 g Carbohydrate, 2.3 g Fibre, 31.7 g Sugars, 22.6 g Added Sugars, 7.5 g Protein
Carbohydrate Choices: 3

INGREDIENTS

6 ripe juicy local peaches (see
   note)
2 Tbsp (30 mL) canola oil *or*
   melted unsalted butter
1 tsp (5 mL) cinnamon
1/2 tsp (2 mL) nutmeg
3/4 cup (185 mL) ricotta cheese
1/3 cup (80 mL) liquid honey

INGREDIENT NOTE:

Peaches—If your peaches
are still firm, place them on the
counter at room temperature and
they should ripen within a few
days. Refrigerate ripe peaches
and eat them within a week of
purchase. Not a fan of peaches?
Use nectarines.

Grilled Peaches Summer

Trevor Arsenault, PHEc

"Peaches are one of my two favourite summertime fruits
(watermelon is the other). When peaches are in their peak
season and I can buy a basket of them that have the perfect
amount of sweetness and juiciness, I eat them all day long—diced
in my oatmeal at breakfast, sliced on a toasted sandwich at lunch,
tossed in a salad for dinner and grilled on the
barbecue for dessert."—Trevor

METHOD

1. Preheat barbecue to high. If you forgot to do so the last time you
   barbecued, clean the grill with a wire brush.
2. Rinse peaches and pat dry. Slice in half from top to bottom
   following the natural crease. Twist apart to reveal 2 halves and use
   a paring knife or soup spoon to remove pits.
3. Stir together oil (or melted butter), cinnamon and nutmeg in a
   small bowl. Brush peach halves with mixture.
4. Cook cut-side down until grill marks appear, about 5 minutes. Flip

over and grill skin-side for another 3 to 5 minutes until slightly charred.

5. Remove peaches from the grill and serve immediately in individual bowls with 1 Tbsp (30 mL) of ricotta cheese and approx. 1 tsp (5 mL) of honey drizzled on each.

Makes 12 halves One serving = 2 halves made with canola oil
Per serving: 84 Calories, 3 g Total Fat, 0.6 g Saturated Fat, 0.1 g Trans Fat, 30 mg Sodium, 13 g Carbohydrate, 1 g Fibre, 12 g Sugars, 7.4 g Added Sugars, 1.5 g Protein
Carbohydrate Choices: 1

PEACHES

Considered a tender-crop stone fruit, peaches are primarily grown in Ontario, Quebec and BC. There is even a town named after this juicy fruit, Peachland, BC, in the Okanagan Valley.

Clingstone peaches, as the name suggests, cling to the stone, whereas freestone peaches don't, making them easier for slicing. Allow peaches to ripen at room temperature, which depending on size can take 3 to 6 days. Store ripe peaches in a single layer in the fridge and eat within 3 to 5 days.

3 cups (750 mL) berries, fresh
  or semi-frozen (strawberries,
  blueberries, blackberries or
  raspberries)

1 cup (250 mL) plain 2% MF
  yogurt

3 Tbsp (45 mL) liquid honey
  (adjust to taste, depending
  on the ripeness of the berries
  or fruit)

PHEC TIPS:

• For easy handling, place filled
cups into a muffin pan. Once the
pops are frozen solid, transfer to
an airtight container and freeze
for up to 2 weeks.

• Change it up and try different
flavoured yogurt and fruit
combinations. If using flavoured
yogurt, eliminate the honey.

Yogurt Berry Pops Spring/Summer

Teresa Makarewicz, PHEc

"These berry pops are great to have on hand when a snacking urge attacks. Create your signature 'pop' by trying different combinations of ripe, juicy local fruits. The difficult step will be waiting for them to freeze!" —Teresa

METHOD

1. Puree berries, yogurt and honey in a blender until smooth. Pour into 1/3 cup (80 mL) paper cups or plastic frozen treat molds.
2. Freeze until partially firm, about 30 minutes, then insert sticks or plastic spoons (skip this step of you are using plastic treat molds). Freeze until solid, about 2 hours.

Makes 8 berry pops One serving = 1 berry pop
Per serving: 75 Calories, 0.7 g Total Fat, 0.3 g Saturated Fat, 0 g Trans Fat, 23 mg Sodium, 15.3 g Carbohydrate, 1 g Fibre, 13 g Sugars, 6.6 g Added Sugars, 2 g Protein
Carbohydrate Choices: 1

INGREDIENTS

1 cup (250 mL) whole wheat flour

1/3 cup (80 mL) flaxseed meal

1/2 cup (125 mL) butter, softened

1 cup (250 mL) packed golden brown sugar

1 omega-3 egg

1 tsp (5 mL) pure vanilla extract

1/2 cup (125 mL) dried cranberries

1 cup (250 mL) fresh or frozen cranberries

PHEC TIP:

Change it up and make Double Cranberry & Nut Blondies: Stir in 1/2 cup (125 mL) chopped walnuts when you add the dried cranberries.

Double Cranberry Blondies Multi-seasonal

Bridget Wilson, PHEc

"Fresh and dried cranberries add a wonderful contrast of sweet and tangy flavour to these squares. I don't use baking powder or baking soda when I make blondies; I like them to be dense."—Bridget

METHOD

1. Position rack in the middle of the oven. Heat oven to 350°F (175°C). Line an 8- × 8-inch (20 × 20 cm) baking pan with foil, ends extending over sides; lightly oil.

2. In a medium bowl, mix flour and flaxseed meal until blended.

3. In a separate medium bowl, beat butter and sugar with a wooden spoon until blended. Add egg and vanilla and mix well. Add flour mixture and stir until combined. Stir in dried cranberries.

4. Spread batter evenly on the bottom of a prepared pan. Sprinkle fresh cranberries evenly over top and press down into batter.

5. Bake 30 to 35 minutes or until a toothpick inserted into the centre comes out clean. Cool completely. Use foil handles to lift blondies from the pan and cut into 16 equal bars. Store in a covered container for up to 1 week or freeze for up to 3 months.

Makes 16 squares One serving = 1 square
Per serving: 169 calories, 7.7 g Fat, 4 g Sat. Fat, 0.4 g Trans Fat, 52 mg Sodium, 24 g Carbohydrates, 2 g Fibre, 16.6 g Sugars, 15.5 g Added Sugars, 2 g Protein
Carbohydrate Choices: 1 1/2

Pumpkin Muffin-Top Cookies Fall/winter

Teresa Makarewicz, PHEc

"These yummy, big pumpkin cookies look and taste like the best part of a muffin—the top. They are wholesome, moist and easy to make." —Teresa

METHOD

1. Position rack in the middle of the oven. Preheat oven to 350°F (175°C). Line 2 baking sheets with parchment paper.

2. In a large bowl, whisk flour, 1/2 cup (125 mL) pumpkin seeds, wheat germ, cinnamon, baking powder, baking soda, nutmeg and salt.

3. In a separate bowl, whisk eggs, pumpkin puree, sugar, oil and vanilla; stir into flour mixture until blended.

4. Drop batter onto prepared baking sheets in 1/4-cup (60 mL) portions, with each portion approx. 2 inches (5 cm) apart. Flatten portions slightly and sprinkle tops with remaining pumpkin seeds.

5. Bake cookies in batches for 15 minutes, or until a toothpick inserted into the centre of a cookie comes out clean. Remove from the oven and let cool on baking sheet for 3 minutes, then transfer to a wire rack to cool completely. Store in a covered container for up to 5 days or freeze for up to 2 months.

Makes 14 very large soft cookies One serving = 1 large cookie
Per serving: 203 calories, 8.8 g Fat, 1.3 g Sat. Fat, 0.1 g Trans Fat, 170 mg Sodium, 26 g Carbohydrates, 3 g Fibre, 10.8 g Sugars, 9.7 g Added Sugars, 6 g Protein
Carbohydrate Choices: 1 1/2

PHEC TIP:

If you only have one baking sheet, let it cool between batches. A hot baking sheet will cause cookie batter to spread, resulting in a change in texture and shape.

INGREDIENTS

2 cups (500 mL) whole wheat flour
1/2 cup + 2 Tbsp (155 mL) unsalted green pumpkin seeds, divided
3 Tbsp (45 mL) natural wheat germ
1 1/2 tsp (7 mL) ground cinnamon
1 tsp (5 mL) baking powder
1 tsp (5 mL) baking soda
1/2 tsp (2 mL) ground nutmeg
1/4 tsp (1 mL) iodized salt
2 omega-3 eggs
1 1/4 cups (310 mL) pure pumpkin puree (see note)
2/3 cup (160 mL) packed dark brown sugar (see note)
1/4 cup (60 mL) canola oil
1 tsp (5 mL) pure vanilla extract

INGREDIENT NOTES:

Pumpkin Puree—For optimum flavour use pure pumpkin puree and not a pumpkin and squash combination. Leftover pumpkin puree can be frozen in an airtight container for another batch of cookies.

Brown Sugar—If your brown sugar is lumpy, pass through a sieve or crumble with fingertips.

HOMEGROWN

Want to wow your company with a menu created for a special occasion? The OHEA are here to help.

SUMMER:

Your friends from Alberta are coming over and they have never had lobster. You decide to introduce them to this amazing shellfish with a pasta dish:

- a mixed green salad with Birch Syrup Salad Dressing (page 208), served in large salad bowls or plates
- Lobster with Pasta and Cherry Tomatoes (page 295), served on large plates

A family reunion barbecue with all of your cousins, aunts, uncles, parents and grandparents coming to your house (you may have to more than double the recipes):

- Grilled Jerk Chicken Thighs (page 301), made ahead and stored in the fridge to eat cold
- Asian-Style Edamame and Corn Salad (page 240), for the vegetarians in the crowd
- Festive Fruit and Nut Coleslaw (page 192)
- a large green salad with Ice Syrup Salad Dressing (page 210)
- Grilled Peaches (page 374)

You've decided to host a Canada Day celebration (depending on the crowd, you may have to double or triple the recipes):

- "Kick-Ass" Barbecued Burgers (page 328) with all the fix'ns
- New Potatoes with Shallots and Mint (page 183)
- a massive green salad with Honey Mustard Salad Dressing (page 211)
- Cranberry Maple Butter Tarts (page 358)
- Yogurt Berry Pops (page 376) using raspberries to create that great Canadian red colour, for all the kids

FALL:

A hunter is coming to dinner (or someone who loves to try new exciting foods):

- Braised Goose in Dark Beer (page 318)
- Easy Rutabaga (or Turnip) and Sweet Potato Casserole (page 172)
- frozen Canadian green peas, lightly steamed

You want to impress the socks off your fish-loving friends:

- a mixed green salad with Ice Syrup Salad Dressing (page 210)
- Seafood Chowder (page 274) served with crusty whole-grain artisanal bread

Your team made it to the Grey Cup, and you are hosting a Grey Cup dinner to eat during the game:

- Maple Pulled Pork (page 251)
- Gourmet Poutine, Eh!? (page 180)
- a vegetable platter with fresh Canadian veggies (try peppers, carrots and cucumbers) and your favourite dip

WINTER:

You are throwing a Downton Abbey dinner, because you are a huge fan and love using the good dishes:

- VQA sparkling white wine (page 71)
- Cracked Pepper and Horseradish–Crusted Oven Roast with Easy Pan Gravy (page 342)
- Yorkshire Pudding (page 345)
- fresh local green peas, lightly steamed
- your family recipe for mashed potatoes
- Ginger Rhubarb Crisp (page 352), served in the small bowls from your china set that you probably have never used before

Professional home economists work in all areas of the public and private sectors. We use our specialized education and training to assist people in enhancing their daily lives. A provincial act respecting the Ontario Home Economics Association (OHEA) recognizes the right of individuals who have met the membership qualifications to use the designation Professional Home Economist (PHEc). As professionals we are committed to empowering individuals and families with the knowledge and skills to achieve and maintain a desirable quality of life. We are educated and knowledgeable in such areas as nutrition, food production and preparation, clothing, child development, resources and development, housing, consumer issues and family relationships. Home economists work in fields that include education, journalism, recipe development, food styling, international development, consumer consulting and more. Visit ohea.on.ca to learn more about what it means to be a professional home economist, and if you are looking for a new career, join the team!

PROFESSIONAL HOME ECONOMIST (PHEC) TIPS

If you can't have a PHEc in your kitchen to help alongside, the next best thing is to have our advice on the page. Throughout the cookbook keep your eye out for PHEc tips—these are recipe notes that we have added to help you have success when you make the recipe.

NUTRIENT BREAKDOWNS AND CARBOHYDRATE CHOICES

I believe knowledge is power. If you know the amount of calories, grams of fat or carbohydrates your meal contains, you can make better dietary decisions. Throughout the book we have included Nutrient Breakdowns that detail the nutritional components of each recipe, as well as Carbohydrate Choices for anyone living with diabetes.

NUTRIENT BREAKDOWNS (compiled by Katie Brunke)

For each recipe in this cookbook I have taken on the task of preparing a complete nutritional analysis. This allows the reader to make informed decisions when preparing meals, with suggested portion sizes and complete nutrient profiles. We have also included the total amount of sugar for each recipe, singling out the added sugars from the natural ones. Having this information available helps the reader distinguish when some recipes are best as a treat, and others as an everyday go-to. Analysis is based primarily on information gathered from the Canadian Nutrient File database and trips to the grocery store to scope out nutrition fact labels.

From start to finish the experience was a great one, though I must confess, for a couple months every time I closed my eyes I saw excel spreadsheets! When I'm not crunching numbers I enjoy spending time in the kitchen cooking with friends and family. I am currently completing the Bachelor of Science, Food and Nutrition degree at Ryerson University, and working towards becoming a Registered Dietitian. I am particularly interested in recipe development for the endless creative possibilities it offers me, and I find great satisfaction in sharing great food and health ideas with others. (Katie Brunke)

CARBOHYDRATE CHOICES (compiled by Cristina Fernandes)

The desire to coach others on how to adopt a healthy lifestyle came at a young age and deepened over the years. I became a Certified Diabetes Educator (CDE) early in my Dietetic career to aid in this feat.

The Carbohydrate feature in this cookbook allows for accuracy and ease of carb counting. It is consistent with standardized carb counting, such as that used by the Canadian Diabetes Association, where one 'Carb Choice' is equivalent to 15 grams of available (ie., "useable") carbohydrates. A carb is composed of sugar and/or starch and/or fibre. However, fibre does not contribute to your sugar intake, nor does it contribute to your calorie intake—fibre is the best F word ever! So a

"Carb Choice" represents the starch and sugar, minus the fibre, from the original carb source.

With the exception of individualized nutritional requirements, most people require two to four carb choices at each meal, with a minimum of eight carb choices per day. Having an adequate carb intake is crucial to health goals—it's the main fuel for our very means of being! If you ever feel unsatisfied, start evaluating whether or not you are getting enough of the other important nutrients with your meal (such as lean proteins and healthy fats); balance has a lot to do with it! Also, think about where your carbohydrates are coming from. Are they sugar-laden products that have very few vitamins and minerals? These are low quality carbs that won't keep you satisfied for long and pack a lot of carb in a small serving. Stick to the high quality choices that contain fibre and loads of vitamins and minerals, yet are humble on the overall calorie count—these will keep you fueled and satisfied while leaving your waistband at a neutral position. (Cristina Fernandes, RD, PHEc, CDE)

CREATING SUCCESS FROM THE INGREDIENTS UP

Below are some general recipe tips on ingredients that are used throughout the cookbook:

APPLE CIDER VINEGAR

Throughout the cookbook we have used apple cider vinegar instead of lemon juice for our Canadian version of that citrus zing. Buy authentic apple cider vinegar at farmer's markets or health food stores. This type of apple cider vinegar was made using natural fermentation, is usually cloudy and may have the word "mother" on the label.

BUTTER

If the recipe calls for butter it means salted butter. It will specifically state unsalted when required.

1. If you want success in the kitchen you need to make parchment paper your friend. Using wet or dry parchment paper is a wonderful way to reduce cleanup time.

2. We use dry to line cookie sheets, but using wet parchment paper will have you singing its praises. Tear off a piece of parchment paper that is approx. 6 inches (15 cm) bigger than the pan you are going to line. Scrunch paper up under cold running water, ring out, shake off excess water and line pan. You're most welcome.

BUTTERMILK

In Canada buttermilk is made using 1% MF milk. If you don't have any buttermilk, substitute with the same amount of 1% MF milk plus 1 Tbsp (15 mL) plain or apple cider vinegar

COLD PRESSED CANOLA OIL

Canada has its own equivalent to extra virgin olive oil: cold pressed canola oil. Flavourful, with grassy notes and slightly acidic bite (depending on where it was grown), cold pressed canola oil adds flavour to a recipe. Regular canola oil has a neutral flavour and is used in baking, roasting and high-temperature cooking. Use cold pressed canola oil when you want the flavour of the oil to shine through. We have used it in most of the salad dressings.

HIGH STABILITY CANOLA OIL

Canola oil has a high smoke point, making it ideal for roasting, BBQing or stir frying. High stability canola oil is used in deep-frying and is a great choice for high-heat applications like the recipe for Yorkshire Pudding on page 345. If you don't have any, feel free to use regular canola oil.

GARLIC

Some antioxidants are more available to your body cooked, some raw. When it comes to garlic, letting the garlic oxidize helps your body absorb these antioxidants better; they call it bioavailability. Mince or crush your garlic and set it aside to allow this to happen. Let garlic breathe for 5 to 15 minutes before adding it to a recipe for maximum oxidization. Note: Crushed garlic has a stronger garlic flavour than minced.

IODIZED SALT

Canadians are getting too much salt/sodium on a daily basis. But whether or not we are getting enough iodine is another matter. It was my decision to use as many *no salt added* products in the book as possible because most of the sodium in packaged foods has not been iodized.

Recipes ask instead for the addition of iodized salt. This way you add your own iodized table salt, adding traces of iodine back into your diet. For more information on iodine, see page 46. Kosher salt does not contain iodine.

MAPLE SYRUP

Don't substitute pancake syrup for the real deal in any recipe that calls for pure maple syrup. We used amber for all these recipes.

ONIONS

When we call for an onion we mean a medium onion. If a large or a small onion is required it will be mentioned specifically in the recipe.

PURE PUMPKIN PUREE

Pure pumpkin puree and pumpkin pie filling are two totally different things. All the recipes in this cookbook using canned pumpkin call for *pure pumpkin puree,* which is made from squash and pumpkin or from pumpkin and nothing else. Pumpkin pie filling has added sugars and spices and will ruin any recipe that calls for the *pure* stuff.

Thank you to Nick Rundall at Whitecap who asked, "Would the OHEA like to write another award winner?" and greenlit this project. Without him this would never have happened. I'd wanted to write a Canadian ingredient cookbook for many years; once he said yes, we were off to the races. I sent out the call for recipes and PHEcs from across Ontario sent in their creations.

Over three weekends in January 2014 at the Kraft Kitchens in Toronto, Ontario, 187 recipes were tested to find the ones that fit the cookbook. One hundred and sixty made the cut.

Thank you to Eileen Stanbury, PHEc, for organizing the list of volunteers—a logistical nightmare, but she did it.

Thanks to Michele McAdoo for facilitating the Kraft connection. Kraft generously allowed us to *invade* their four complete test kitchens. We could not have created this amazing collection of recipes without Kraft or Michele. Bless their generosity and their stainless steel dishwashers.

And of course, thank you to all the PHEcs and students who worked their collective butts off testing and tasting recipes:

PHECS

Gerry Anthony, Mary Ann Binnie, Katie Brunke, Janet Butters, Lucy Chesney-Abbensetts, Joyce De Decker, Alessandra DiMattia, Marlene Dyer, Spencer Finch-Coursey, Jennifer Goodwin, Barb Holland, Gabriele Hossbach, Diana Huey, Cathy Ireland, Mary Johnston, Olga Kaminskyj, Jan Main, Erin MacGregor, Michele McAdoo, Bonnie McBain, Maria McLellan, Marinoush Megardichian, Pat Moynihan-Morris, Astrid Muschalla, Donna Naylor, Camille Naranjit, Christine Petruszkiewicz, Diane O'Shea, Joyce Parslow, Diana Rodel, Suzanne Stark, Charlene Summerfield, Joan Ttooulias, Amy Snider-Whitson, Bridget Wilson and Catherine Long (non-member who offered help when we had cancellations)

STUDENTS

Rand Alrajie, Nadia Anjum, Stephanie Aresta, Katie Brunke, Nouran El Sayed, Raneem Kansura, Emily Kichler, Jennifer Lam, Martina Luketich, Pooja Mansukhani, Kerry Miller, Courtney South

When it came time to photograph our creations, many hands responded to the "we need help" email that was sent out. Donna Naylor drove in from Barrie, Sandra Venneri made her way from London and so did Corrine Kamphius. Professional Home Economists and students all made the long trek to my house in Toronto for the photo shoot. Crammed into my newly renovated kitchen, the PHEcs and helpers gave my kitchen the christening it deserved, cooking with love and laughter. Thanks to Eileen Stanbury, PHEc, again for organizing the list of volunteers.

Thank you to the volunteers themselves: Andrea Villneff, Rosemary Superville, Lauren Baker, Sandra Venneri, Judy Coveney, Katrine Gahol, Mara Alexanian-Farr, Gloria Ho, Antonia Morganti, Catherine Chong and Simone Quenville.

Thank you to the Dream Team, Mike McColl and Joan Ttooulias, PHEc, for the fabulous pictures that were taken. Mike has an amazing eye and a kind heart and Joan, aside from being a fabulous food stylist, is a joy to work with who kept me laughing each and every day. I had a definite vision for the look and feel of the book; thank you both for making that come true, even if I did ask you to reshoot numerous times because a spoon was in the wrong place….

A special photo shoot shout out to Brittany Pettigrew, for not only coming in on the GO Train, but for the loan of her red apron in the picture with Rosemarie, which we literally snapped right off her. Thanks to Michelle Ng for scrubbing the Maple Leaf for the cover shot! It has never been so clean. And thank you Cathy Ireland, PHEc extraordinaire, who kept coming back to help and brought treats for us to sample.

Thanks to my partner, Scott, who made numerous trips to the grocery store to pick up a missing ingredient and thanks to Pierre Gautreau for my author picture.

Thanks to my neighbours Evelyne and Tom Carter for the loan of their backyard for the shoot days in June and their rhubarb for the Ginger Rhubarb Crisp we used in the photo shoot. It's always great to have neighbours who have a brilliant garden and rhubarb!

Thanks to Olaf Mertens who lent us the Maple Leaf for the cover, to Mike's photo assistant Lee (even if he did eat his weight in Yorkshire puddings) and to Michale Brode, my dear friend, who offered to help but wasn't a PHEc so I had to say no. The next book, I promise…

A huge thank you to Nancy Greiter who acted as my right-hand woman when I couldn't find a recipe, a thank you or a fill in the blank here! If anyone is ever looking for an executive secretary or a personal assistant, she's your pick. She acted as my personal wrangler throughout the cookbook process.

And last but not least, thank you to Patrick Geraghty who sent me so many questions and suggestions that I had to answer, and even though I cursed him as I researched and rewrote, his inquiring mind made this book the most important book I have written to date. Thank you to Kerry Plumley, who put up with all my changes and additions with great patience, and the rest of the Whitecap design team for making this book as beautiful to look at as to cook from.

For more information on the following topics, please see the links provided.

APPLES
BC Tree www.bctree.com
Ontario Apple Growers onapples.com

BEEF
Canadian Beef www.beefinfo.org
Canadian Bison www.canadianbison.ca

CANOLA OIL
Canola Eat Well www.canolaeatwell.com
Canola Info.org www.canolainfo.org/

DAIRY
Dairy Farmers of Canada www.dairyfarmers.ca
Cheeselover.ca cheeseloverca.wordpress.com
Canadian Dairy Information Centre cheese-fromage.agr.gc.ca

EGGS
Egg Farmers of Canada www.eggfarmers.ca

FLAXSEED
Flax Council of Canada flaxcouncil.ca
Healthy Flax HealthyFlax.org

GRAINS
Canadian Grain Commission www.grainscanada.gc.ca
Canadian National Millers www.canadianmillers.ca
Whole Grains Council wholegrainscouncil.org

Naked Oats canadiannakedoats.com
GoBarley www.gobarley.com

LIVESTOCK
Ontario Ministry of Agriculture, Food and Rural Affairs (Livestock)
www.omafra.gov.on.ca/english/livestock/index.html
Put Pork on Your Fork putporkonyourfork.com

MUSHROOMS
Mushrooms Canada www.mushrooms.ca

NUTRITION
Resistant Starch www.resistantstarch.com
Health Canada (Food and Nutrition)
www.hc-sc.gc.ca/fn-an/index-eng.php
Healthy Canadians (Food and Nutrition) healthycanadians.gc.ca/
eating-nutrition/index-eng.php
The Nutrition Source www.hsph.harvard.edu/nutritionsource
Food Digestive Health Foundation www.cdhf.ca

POULTRY
Chicken.ca www.chicken.ca
Turkey Farmers of Canada www.turkeyfarmersofcanada.ca

PRODUCE
BC Greenhouse Growers' Association bcgreenhouse.ca
Canadian Produce Marketing Association www.cpma.ca/en/home.aspx

PULSES
Pulse Canada www.pulsecanada.com
Lentils.ca www.lentils.ca

REGIONALIZED FOOD AND AGRICULTURE

Agriculture and Agri-Food Canada www.agr.gc.ca

Foodland Ontario www.ontario.ca/foodland/foodland-ontario

Buy BC Food http://www.buybcfood.ca

Taste Alberta tastealberta.ca

Great Tastes of Manitoba greattastesmb.ca

Taste of Nova Scotia tasteofnovascotia.com

PEI Flavours peiflavours.ca

Foods of Quebec www.foodsofquebec.com/products

SEAFOOD

Canadian Aquaculture Industry Alliance www.aquaculture.ca

Fisheries Conservation Group fishcons.mi.mun.ca

A

al dente pasta, 296
Apple and Dried Cherry Bread
    Pudding, 356
Apple Blackberry Crumble Pie,
    368–69
apple cider vinegar, 238–39, 387
Apple Fruitcake with Whisky
    Glaze, 364–65
Apple Hemp Heart Salad, 198
Apple Maple Cheddar Spread, 73
Apple Sage Cheddar Bread, 42
apples, 199, 369–70
Apple and Dried Cherry Bread
    Pudding, 356
Apple Blackberry Crumble Pie,
    368–69
apple cider vinegar, 238–39, 387
Apple Fruitcake with Whisky
    Glaze, 364–65
Apple Hemp Heart Salad, 198
Apple Maple Cheddar Spread, 73
Apple Sage Cheddar Bread, 42
    Beet Apple Coleslaw, 190
    Cranberry Apple Crisp, 354
    Harvest Apple and Thyme
        Roasted Chicken, 302
aquaculture, 292
Asian-Style Coleslaw, 282
Asian-Style Edamame and Corn
    Salad, 240
Asian Style Eggplant, 178
Asian Style Nova Scotia Scallops
    with Miso Glaze, 297
asparagus, 137
    Canadian Aged Cheddar and
    Asparagus Soup, 136

B

bacon, 143
Baked Goat Cheese with Cranberry
    or Plum Compote, 96–97
Baked Tomato Spinach Spaghetti
    Squash, 165
balsamic vinegar, 250
barley, 106–08
Barley Stuffed Acorn Squash,
    112–14
Basic Barley Pancake Batter, 20
Easy Family-Friendly Barley Pilaf,
    109
Greek Barley Salad, 115
Grilled Vegetable, Barley and
    Feta Salad, 207
Pearl Barley and Butternut
    Squash Risotto, 110–11
Slow Cooker Beef and Barley
    Stew, 336
barley flour, 11
Barley Stuffed Acorn Squash,
    112–14
Basic Barley Pancake Batter, 20
basil, 201
bean sprouts, 257
Beautiful Beetday Cake, 362–63
beef, 324
Beef and Mushroom Stew, 341
beef cattle diet, 327
beef grades, 327
Beef Steak and Lentil Salad,
    331–32
bison, 347
Bison Meat Loaf, 346
burger tips, 330
    Cracked Pepper and
    Horseradish–Crusted Oven Roast
    with Easy Pan Gravy, 342–44

Gluten-Free PEI Potato Lasagna,
    338–39
Grilled Flank Steak on Roasted
    Kale Salad, 334–35
"Kick-Ass" Barbecued Burgers,
    328
labeling cuts of beef, 335
nutrition, 325–26
roasting guide, 344
Shepherd's Pie with Beef and
    Mushrooms, 340
Slow Cooker Beef and Barley
    Stew, 336
Slow Cooker Bistro Beef and Beer
    Simmering Steak, 337
Yorkshire Pudding, 345
Beef and Mushroom Stew, 341
Beef Steak and Lentil Salad,
    331–32
beer, craft, 320
    Braised Goose in Dark Beer, 318
    Slow Cooker Bistro Beef and Beer
    Simmering Steak, 337
Beet Apple Coleslaw, 190
beets, 191
    Beautiful Beetday Cake, 362–63
Beet Apple Coleslaw, 190
berries see fruits and berries
bison, 347
Bison Meat Loaf, 346
Bison Meat Loaf, 346
Blue Cheese and Pear Phyllo Tarts,
    76–79
blueberries, 125
Borscht, 154–56
Bouillabaisse, 276–77
Braised Goose in Dark Beer,
    318–19
breads, 8

Apple Sage Cheddar Bread, 42
Autumn Pumpkin Seed Bread, 48
Caramelized Onion and Cheddar
    Scones, 43
Whole Wheat Seed Bread, 44,
    46
Bruschetta Grilled Pickerel,
    278–79
Brussels sprouts, 164, 194
    Maple Brussels Sprout Slaw, 194
    Roasted Brussels Sprouts with
    Cranberries, 162
Buckwheat Buttermilk Pancake
    Batter, 18
buckwheat flour, 12
butter, 387
buttermilk, 388
    Buckwheat Buttermilk Pancake
    Batter, 18
    Oatmeal Buttermilk Pancake
    Batter, 19

C

Canadian Aged Cheddar and
    Asparagus Soup, 136
Canadian Canned Salmon Cakes
    with Tartar Sauce, 284–85
Canadian Cassoulet, 254–55
canola oil, 388
Caramelized Onion and Cheddar
    Scones, 43
carbohydrates, 386–87
carrots, 138
    Curried Carrot Soup, 138
    Garden Carrot Cake, 360
    Roasted Red Pepper, Pear, Corn
    and Carrot Soup, 150–51
    Zucchini & Carrot Breakfast
    Muffin, 34

cereals, 122
  oats, 119–20
  Overnight Blueberry Irish
  Oatmeal for Two, 124
cheese, 68–69, 93
  Apple Maple Cheddar Spread, 73
  Baked Goat Cheese with
  Cranberry or Plum Compote,
  96–97
  Blue Cheese and Pear Phyllo
  Tarts, 76–79
  Canadian Aged Cheddar and
  Asparagus Soup, 136
  Caramelized Onion and Cheddar
  Scones, 43
  cheddar cheese, 74
cheese platters, 70
  Great Canadian Cheese Fondue,
  72
  Grilled Cheese Sandwiches, 82
  Grilled Vegetable, Barley and
  Feta Salad, 207
  Mac and Cheese, 92–93
  Mushroom and Spinach
  Cannelloni with Italian Cheese
  Blend Sauce, 94–95
  Parmesan cheese, 167
  Savoury Cheddar Shortbread
  Diamonds, 80–81
  Traditional French Onion Soup,
  139
  see also pizza
chicken see poultry
Chicken Cacciatore with Hot House
  Peppers, 310
Chickpea and Cauliflower Curry,
  237
Chickpea Burgers, 232–33
Chipotle Black Bean Chili, 234–36

Cod Cakes with Asian-Style
  Coleslaw, 282–83
cookies
  Oat Barley Cookies, 127
  Pumpkin Muffin-Top Cookies, 379
  Toasted Oatmeal Cookies, 126
corn, 176
  Asian-Style Edamame and Corn
  Salad, 240
  Corn Chowder, 142
  Grilled Corn, 174
  Red Pepper and Corn Salsa, 286
  Roasted Red Pepper, Pear, Corn
  and Carrot Soup, 150–51
  Silky Summer Corn Bisque, 144
  see also cornmeal
Corn Chowder, 142
cornmeal, 12
  Cornmeal Pancake Batter, 17
  Creamy Herbed Polenta, 104
  Cornmeal Pancake Batter, 17
Crab Cakes with Garlic Aioli, 267
Cracked Pepper and Horseradish–
  Crusted Oven Roast with Easy
  Pan Gravy, 342–44
craft beer, 320
cranberries, 253
  Baked Goat Cheese with
  Cranberry or Plum Compote,
  96–97
  Cranberry Apple Crisp, 354
  Cranberry Maple Butter Tarts, 358
  Festive Fruit and Nut Coleslaw,
  192
  Roasted Brussels Sprouts with
  Cranberries, 162
  Roasted Sweet Potatoes and
  Cranberries, 170
  Cranberry Apple Crisp, 354

Cranberry Maple Butter Tarts, 358
Creamy Herbed Polenta, 104
crisps, 352
  Blueberry Pear & Hazelnut Crisp,
  353
  Cranberry Apple Crisp, 354
  Ginger Rhubarb Crisp, 352
  Saskatoon Berry Crisp, 355
Crispy Oven Baked Pickerel with
  Greek Yogurt Tartar Sauce,
  280–81
Crown Royal whisky, 365
Crustless Kohlrabi Quiche, 62
Curried Carrot Soup, 138
Curried Lamb Stew with Fall
  Vegetables, 261–62
curry and curry powders, 134
  Chickpea and Cauliflower Curry,
  237
  Curried Lamb Stew with Fall
  Vegetables, 261–62
  Tandoori Crusted Cod, 294
  West Indian–Style Curry Chicken,
  306

D
Dairy Farmers of Canada (DFC), 84
desserts, 351
  Apple Blackberry Crumble Pie,
  368–69
  Apple Fruitcake with Whisky
  Glaze, 364–65
  Beautiful Beetday Cake, 362–63
  cautionary tale, 351
  Cranberry Maple Butter Tarts,
  358
  Double Cranberry Blondies, 378
  Garden Carrot Cake, 360
  Pumpkin Muffin-Top Cookies,

379
  Pumpkin Pie, 372
  Saskatoon Cheesecake Swirl,
  366–67
  see also fruits and berries
Double Bran Muffins, 38
Double Cranberry Blondies, 378
duck see poultry
Duck Pilaf with Kamut and Wild
  Rice, 316–17

E
Easy Family-Friendly Barley Pilaf,
  109
Easy Rutabaga (or Turnip) and
  Sweet Potato Casserole, 172
eggs, 52–56
  Crustless Kohlrabi Quiche, 62
  devilled eggs, 56, 58
  egg whites, 54
  hard-cooked eggs, 56
  Make-Ahead Morning French
  Toast Casserole, 61
  omega-3 eggs, 53
  omelettes, 60
  poaching, 59
  Quiche with Potato Crust, 64
  Quick Eggs Florentine, 65
  scrambled eggs, 58

F
Falafel Patties with Tahini Sauce
  and Pickled Onions, 224–27
farmers' markets, shopping at,
  212, 214–15
farming fish, 292
Festive Fruit and Nut Coleslaw,
  192
fibre, 39

fish and seafood, 266, 275, 277
  aquaculture, 292
  Arctic char, 285
  Asian Style Nova Scotia Scallops
    with Miso Glaze, 297
  Bouillabaisse, 276–77
  Bruschetta Grilled Pickerel,
    278–79
  Canadian Canned Salmon Cakes
    with Tartar Sauce, 284–85
  cod, 283
  Cod Cakes with Asian-Style
    Coleslaw, 282–83
  Crab Cakes with Garlic Aioli, 267
  Crispy Oven Baked Pickerel
    with Greek Yogurt Tartar Sauce,
    280–81
  dulse, 275
  Fish Tacos with Red Pepper and
    Corn Salsa, 286–87
  Fresh Shrimp Pasta Salad,
    288–89
  Hot Smoked Salmon and
    Seaweed Salad on Asian-Style
    Spoons, 272
  lobster, 296
  Lobster with Pasta and Cherry
    Tomatoes, 295–96
  mussels, 270, 275
  Mussels in Spicy Tomato Sauce,
    268
  perch, 287
  Pickerel on the BBQ, 281
  Salmon Teriyaki, 293
  Salmon with Peach Salsa, 290
  Seafood Chowder, 274–75
  smoked salmon, 273
  spot prawns, 289
  Spring Trout Cakes, 271

  Tandoori Crusted Cod, 294
Fish Tacos with Red Pepper and
  Corn Salsa, 286–87
flaxseed, 37
food poisoning, 258
food safety rules, 258–60
French-Inspired Vegetarian
  Shepherd's Pie, 228–29
Fresh Shrimp Pasta Salad, 288–89
fruits and berries, 350
  Apple and Dried Cherry Bread
    Pudding, 356
  Apple Blackberry Crumble Pie,
    368–69
  Blueberry Pear & Hazelnut Crisp,
    353
  Cranberry Apple Crisp, 354
  Double Cranberry Blondies, 378
  Ginger Rhubarb Crisp, 352
  Grilled Peaches, 374–75
  honeyberries, 367
  Peach Salsa, 290
  Saskatoon Berry Crisp, 355
  Saskatoon Cheesecake Swirl,
    366–67
  Saskatoon Maple Bread Pudding,
    357
  serving size, 161
  Sour Cherry Pie Filling (or
    Topping), 371
  Yogurt Berry Pops, 376

G
Garden Carrot Cake, 360
garlic, 388
Ginger Rhubarb Crisp, 352
Gluten-Free PEI Potato Lasagna,
  338–39
Gluten-Free Toasted Walnut Pear

  Muffins, 40
goat's milk, 97
goose see poultry
Gourmet Poutine, Eh!?, 180–82
grains, Canadian, 10–12, 100
  barley, 106–08
  breads, 42–48
  cereals, 122
  Creamy Herbed Polenta, 104
  flours, 10–12
  Greek Barley Salad, 115
  Grilled Vegetable, Barley and Feta
    Salad, 207
  Jambalaya, 121
  kamut, 317
  muffins, 33–40
  oats, 119–20
  pancakes, 16–20
  scones, 43
  Wheatberry and Lentil Salad, 118
  whole grains, 102–03
  Wild Rice and Vegetable Pilaf,
    116
  see also barley; oats
Great Canadian Cheese Fondue,
  72
Greek Barley Salad, 115
Grilled Cheese Sandwiches, 82
Grilled Corn, 175–76
Grilled Flank Steak on Roasted
  Kale Salad, 334–35
Grilled Jerk Chicken Thighs, 301
Grilled Peaches, 374–75
Grilled Turkey Scallopini Sandwich
  with Pickled Vegetable Mayo,
  314–15
Grilled Vegetable, Barley and Feta
  Salad, 207

H
Harvest Apple and Thyme Roasted
  Chicken, 302–03
hemp hearts, 198–99
Herb Stuffed Pork Loin Roast,
  248–50
herbes de Provence, 255
honeyberries, 367
Hot Smoked Salmon and Seaweed
  Salad on Asian-Style Spoons, 272
Hummus, Canadian Style, 238

I
iodine, 46–47, 390

J
Jambalaya, 121

K
kale, 147
  Grilled Flank Steak on Roasted
    Kale Salad, 334–35
  Kale Tossed Salad with Roasted
    Garlic Dressing, 204
  Red Lentil and Kale Soup, 147
Kale Tossed Salad with Roasted
  Garlic Dressing, 204
"Kick-Ass" Barbecued Burgers,
  328
kohlrabi, 62–63
  Crustless Kohlrabi Quiche, 62

L
lamb, 244, 262
  Curried Lamb Stew with Fall
    Vegetables, 261–62
  Lamb Chops, 263
Lamb Chops, 263
leeks, 63

legumes, 218–23
Canadian Cassoulet, 254–55
Chickpea and Cauliflower Curry, 237
Chickpea Burgers, 232–33
Chipotle Black Bean Chili, 234–36
Falafel Patties with Tahini Sauce and Pickled Onions, 224–27
Hummus, Canadian Style, 238
roasting chickpeas, 233
Slow Cooker Baked Beans, 230–31
see also lentils
Lentil and Roasted Sweet Potato Salad, 200
lentils, 149
Beef Steak and Lentil Salad, 331–32
French-Inspired Vegetarian Shepherd's Pie, 228–29
Lentil and Roasted Sweet Potato Salad, 200
Quebec Style Pea Soup, 146
Red Lentil and Kale Soup, 147
Red Lentil Waffles, 22–23
Spicy Red Lentil Soup, 148
see also legumes
Lettuce Cups, 256–57
Lobster with Pasta and Cherry Tomatoes, 295–96

M

Mac and Cheese, 92–93
Make-Ahead Morning French Toast Casserole, 61
Maple Brussels Sprout Slaw, 194
Maple Parsnip Soup, 145
Maple Pulled Pork, 251

maple syrup, 24, 26, 390
Apple Maple Cheddar Spread, 73
Cranberry Maple Butter Tarts, 358
Fresh Ginger Maple Syrup Dressing, 211
Maple Brussels Sprout Slaw, 194
Maple Parsnip Soup, 145
Maple Pulled Pork, 251
Saskatoon Maple Bread Pudding, 357
Spiced Ambercup Squash Soup with Maple Syrup, 132
menu suggestions, 381–83
muffins, 33–40
Double Bran Muffins, 38
Gluten-Free Toasted Walnut Pear Muffins, 40
Pumpkin Oatmeal Muffins, 32
Zucchini & Carrot Breakfast Muffin, 34
Mushroom and Spinach Cannelloni with Italian Cheese Blend Sauce, 94–95
Mushroom Soup, 140
mushrooms, 95, 141
Beef and Mushroom Stew, 341
Mushroom and Spinach Cannelloni with Italian Cheese Blend Sauce, 94–95
Mushroom Soup, 140
porcini mushrooms, 317
Shepherd's Pie with Beef and Mushrooms, 340
shiitake mushrooms, 257
Mussels in Spicy Tomato Sauce, 268
mustard seed, 289

N

New Potatoes with Shallots and Mint, 183
Not Your Regular Mashed Potatoes, 168
nutritional analysis of recipes, 385–86

O

Oat Barley Cookies, 127
oat flour, 11
Oatmeal Buttermilk Pancake Batter, 19
oats, 119–20
Jambalaya, 121
Oat Barley Cookies, 127
Oatmeal Buttermilk Pancake Batter, 19
Overnight Blueberry Irish Oatmeal for Two, 124
Pumpkin Oatmeal Muffins, 32
Toasted Oatmeal Cookies, 126
Ontario Home Economics Association (OHEA), 385
Overnight Blueberry Irish Oatmeal for Two, 124

P

pancakes, 14
Basic Barley Pancake Batter, 20
Buckwheat Buttermilk Pancake Batter, 18
Cornmeal Pancake Batter, 17
Oatmeal Buttermilk Pancake Batter, 19
Red Lentil Waffles, 22–23
Whole Grain Whole Wheat Batter, 16
pantry makeover, 30–31
parchment paper, 388

Parmesan cheese, 167
peaches, 375
Grilled Peaches, 374–75
Peach Salsa, 290
Pear Sauce, 28
Pearl Barley and Butternut Squash Risotto, 110–11
pears, 29
Blue Cheese and Pear Phyllo Tarts, 76–79
Blueberry Pear & Hazelnut Crisp, 353
Gluten-Free Toasted Walnut Pear Muffins, 40
Pear Sauce, 28
Roasted Red Pepper, Pear, Corn and Carrot Soup, 150–51
PHEc see Professional Home Economist (PHEc)
Pickerel on the BBQ, 281
Pickled Red Onions, 226
pizza, 88
Shaved Asparagus Pizza, 86, 88
Spinach and Goat Cheese Pizza, 90–91
porcini mushrooms, 317
pork, 244
Canadian Cassoulet, 254–55
cooking pork, 245–46
Herb Stuffed Pork Loin Roast, 248–50
Lettuce Cups, 256–57
Maple Pulled Pork, 251
Pork Tenderloin with Wild Rice Stuffing, 252–53
Pork Tenderloin with Wild Rice Stuffing, 252–53
potatoes, 169
French-Inspired Vegetarian

Shepherd's Pie, 228–29
Gluten-Free PEI Potato Lasagna, 338–39
Lentil and Roasted Sweet Potato Salad, 200
New Potatoes with Shallots and Mint, 183
Not Your Regular Mashed Potatoes, 168
Quiche with Potato Crust, 64
Roasted Sweet Potatoes and Cranberries, 170
Root Vegetable Potage, 135
Shepherd's Pie with Beef and Mushrooms, 340
Sweet and Red Potato Salad, 202
poultry, 300
Braised Goose in Dark Beer, 318–19
Chicken Cacciatore with Hot House Peppers, 310
cooking chart, 305
Duck Pilaf with Kamut and Wild Rice, 316–17
Grilled Jerk Chicken Thighs, 301
Grilled Turkey Scallopini Sandwich with Pickled Vegetable Mayo, 314–15
Harvest Apple and Thyme Roasted Chicken, 302–03
leftover chicken, 303
Stuffed Chicken Burgers, 309
Turkey Tourtiere, 312–13
West Indian–Style Curry Chicken, 306
white vs dark meat, 308
Professional Home Economist (PHEc), 385
Pumpkin Muffin-Top Cookies, 379

Pumpkin Oatmeal Muffins, 32
Pumpkin Pie, 372
pumpkins, 33, 49
   Autumn Pumpkin Seed Bread, 48
Pumpkin Muffin-Top Cookies, 379
Pumpkin Oatmeal Muffins, 32
Pumpkin Pie, 372
pumpkin puree, 390

Q
Quebec Style Pea Soup, 146
Quiche with Potato Crust, 64
Quick Eggs Florentine, 65

R
Ratatouille, 167
Red Fife flour, 10
Red Lentil and Kale Soup, 147
Red Lentil Waffles, 22–23
Red Pepper and Corn Salsa, 286
red peppers, roasting, 151
resistant starch, 193
Roasted Brussels Sprouts with Cranberries, 162
Roasted Garlic Dressing, 204
Roasted Red Pepper, Pear, Corn and Carrot Soup, 150–51
Roasted Sweet Potatoes and Cranberries, 170
roasting red peppers, 151
Root Vegetable Potage, 135

S
safety rules for food, 258–60
salad dressings, 208
   Birch Syrup Salad Dressing, 208
   Fresh Ginger Maple Syrup Dressing, 211
   Honey Mustard Salad Dressing, 211

Ice Syrup Salad Dressing, 210
   Roasted Garlic Dressing, 204
salads, 186
   Apple Hemp Heart Salad, 198
   Asian-Style Coleslaw, 282
   Asian-Style Edamame and Corn Salad, 240
   Beef Steak and Lentil Salad, 331–32
   Beet Apple Coleslaw, 190
   Bohemian Style Cucumber Salad, 196
   Festive Fruit and Nut Coleslaw, 192
   Fresh Shrimp Pasta Salad, 288–89
   Grilled Vegetable, Barley and Feta Salad, 207
   Kale Tossed Salad with Roasted Garlic Dressing, 204
   Lentil and Roasted Sweet Potato Salad, 200
   Maple Brussels Sprout Slaw, 194
salad dressings, 208–11
   Shaved Zucchini and Summer Squash Salad, 201
   Sweet and Red Potato Salad, 202
   Winter Pea Salad, 193
Salmon Teriyaki, 293
Salmon with Peach Salsa, 290
salsa
   Peach Salsa, 290
   Red Pepper and Corn Salsa, 286
salt, 390
Saskatoon Berry Crisp, 355
Saskatoon Cheesecake Swirl, 366–67
Saskatoon Maple Bread Pudding, 357

sauces and syrups
   Greek Yogurt Tartar Sauce, 380
   maple syrup, 24, 26
   Pear Sauce, 28
   Tahini Sauce, 227
   West Coast Blackberry Syrup, 27
   Yogurt Cucumber Sauce, 309
Savoury Cheddar Shortbread Diamonds, 80–81
scones, 43
seafood see fish and seafood
Seafood Chowder, 274–75
serving size, vegetables and fruits, 161
Shamrock Soup, 152–53
Shaved Asparagus Pizza, 86, 88
Shaved Zucchini and Summer Squash Salad, 201
Shepherd's Pie with Beef and Mushrooms, 340
shopping at farmers' markets, 212, 214–15
Silky Summer Corn Bisque, 144
Slow Cooker Baked Beans, 230–31
Slow Cooker Beef and Barley Stew, 336
Slow Cooker Bistro Beef and Beer Simmering Steak, 337
smoked salmon, 273
soups, 130–31
   Borscht, 154–56
   Corn Chowder, 142
   Curried Carrot Soup, 138
   Maple Parsnip Soup, 145
   Mushroom Soup, 140
   Quebec Style Pea Soup, 146
   Red Lentil and Kale Soup, 147
   Roasted Red Pepper, Pear, Corn and Carrot Soup, 150–51

Root Vegetable Potage, 135
Shamrock Soup, 152–53
Silky Summer Corn Bisque, 144
Spiced Ambercup Squash Soup
with Maple Syrup, 132–34
Spicy Red Lentil Soup, 148
Traditional French Onion Soup,
139
Sour Cherry Pie Filling (or
Topping), 371
sources, online, 397–99
soy beverages, 125
spelt flour, 12
Spiced Ambercup Squash Soup
with Maple Syrup, 132–34
Spicy Red Lentil Soup, 148
spinach, 91
Baked Tomato Spinach Spaghetti
Squash, 165
Herb Stuffed Pork Loin Roast,
248–50
Mushroom and Spinach
Cannelloni with Italian Cheese
Blend Sauce, 94–95
Spinach and Goat Cheese Pizza,
90–91
Spinach and Goat Cheese Pizza,
90–91
Spring Trout Cakes, 271
squash, 111
Baked Tomato Spinach Spaghetti
Squash, 165
Barley Stuffed Acorn Squash,
112–14
Pearl Barley and Butternut
Squash Risotto, 110–11
Shaved Zucchini and Summer
Squash Salad, 201
Spiced Ambercup Squash Soup

with Maple Syrup, 132–34
starch, resistant, 193
Stir Fried Baby Bok Choy, 166
storing fresh produce, 188–89
Stuffed Chicken Burgers, 309
sugar beets, 156
sugars, added, 361
Sweet and Red Potato Salad, 202
sweet potatoes and yams, 171
Easy Rutabaga (or Turnip) and
Sweet Potato Casserole, 172
Lentil and Roasted Sweet Potato
Salad, 200
Roasted Sweet Potatoes and
Cranberries, 170
Root Vegetable Potage, 135
Sweet and Red Potato Salad, 202

T
Tahini Sauce, 227
Tandoori Crusted Cod, 294
Toasted Oatmeal Cookies, 126
Traditional French Onion Soup, 139
turkey see poultry
Turkey Farmers of Canada, 313
Turkey Tourtiere, 312–13

V
vegetables, 160
Asian eggplant, 179
Asian Style Eggplant, 178
asparagus, 137
Baked Tomato Spinach Spaghetti
Squash, 165
bean sprouts, 257
beets, 191
corn, 176
Easy Rutabaga (or Turnip) and
Sweet Potato Casserole, 172

Gourmet Poutine, Eh!?, 180–82
Grilled Corn, 175–76
kale, 147
kohlrabi, 62–63
New Potatoes with Shallots and
Mint, 183
Not Your Regular Mashed
Potatoes, 168
potatoes, 169
Ratatouille, 167
Red Pepper and Corn Salsa, 286
Roasted Brussels Sprouts with
Cranberries, 162
Roasted Sweet Potatoes and
Cranberries, 170
serving size, 161
Stir Fried Baby Bok Choy, 166
sweet potatoes and yams, 171
turnips and rutabagas, 174
zucchini, 206
see also salads; soups
vinegars
apple cider, 238–39, 387
balsamic, 250
Vineland Research and Innovation
Centre, 179
vitamin K, 206
VQA wines, 71

W
waffles, 22–23
walnuts, 41
West Coast Blackberry Syrup, 27
West Indian–Style Curry Chicken,
306
Wheatberry and Lentil Salad, 118
whisky, Crown Royal, 365
Whole Grain Whole Wheat Batter
(pancakes), 16

whole wheat flour, 10
Whole Wheat Seed Bread, 44, 46
Wild Rice and Vegetable Pilaf, 116
wines, VQA, 71
Winter Pea Salad, 193

Y
yogurt, 197
Yogurt Berry Pops, 376
Yogurt Cucumber Sauce, 309
Yorkshire Pudding, 345

Z
zinc, 326
zucchini, 206
Shaved Zucchini and Summer
Squash Salad, 201
Zucchini & Carrot Breakfast
Muffin, 34
Zucchini & Carrot Breakfast
Muffin, 34

All images are from Mike McColl with the exception of the following:

Page XIV, 49, 158 - June Matthews

Page 6, 21, 98, 99, 108, 103 – Barley Council of Canada

Page 13 – Alberta Barley

Page 29 – Corinna Wyles-Plumley

Page 33 – Maria Nicholls

Page 36 – Saskatchewan Flax Development Commission

Page 50, 55 – Egg Farmers of Canada

Pages 66, 69, 85 – Dairy Farmers of Canada

Page 67, 75, 264, 265 – Nancy Greiter

Page 85 – Stephanie Barbeau

Page 128, 143, 348, 358 – practicalmarketing.com

Page 137, 141, 191, 236 – Mairlyn Smith

Page 157, 298, 391 – Jennifer Rennie

Page 158 – bistrofreshpotatoes.com

Page 171, 242, 380 – dollarphotos.com

Page 184, 206 – Astrid Mushall

Page 203 – Natalie Bolichowski

Page 216 – Manitoba Canola

Page 216-217 – Saskatchewan Pulse Growers

Page 242, 322 – Rachel Brown

Page 247, 396 – Brian Gould Photography

Page 298, 299, 304 – Chicken Farmers of Canada

Page 321 – Craft Beer, Whitecap

Page 322, 323, 333 – Courtesy of Canada Beef

Page 348, 349 – Red Prince Apples

Page 384 – Ontario Apples

The following recipes have been previously published and used with permission:
Gluten-Free Toasted Walnut Pear Muffins (page 40) was previously published in the Complete Gluten-Free Cookbook, by Donna Washburn and Heather Butt, Robert Rose, 2007.

Autumn Pumpkin Seed Bread (for a Bread Machine) (page 48) was previously published in 300 Best Canadian Bread Machine Recipes, by Donna Washburn and Heather Butt, Robert Rose, 2010.

Jambalaya (page 121), Overnight Blueberry Irish Oatmeal for Two (page 124), Spicy Red Lentil Soup (page 148) and Winter Pea Salad (page 193) were previously published in Healthy Starts Here, by Mairlyn Smith, Whitecap Books, 2011.

Slow Cooker Bistro Beef and Beer Simmering Steak (page 337) was adapted from The Best Family Slow Cooker Recipes, by Donna-Marie Pye, Robert Rose, 2003.

Apple Maple Cheddar Spread (page 73), Blue Cheese and Pear Phyllo Tarts (page 76), Savoury Cheddar Shortbread Diamonds (page 80), Shamrock Soup (page 152), Stuffed Chicken Burgers (page 309) are used with permission from the Dairy Farmers of Canada.

Mushroom and Spinach Cannelloni with Italian Cheese Blend Sauce (page 94) are used with permission from Mushrooms Canada.

Grilled Turkey Scallopini Sandwich with Pickled Vegetable Mayo (page 314) are used with permission from the Turkey Farmers of Ontario.

"Kick-Ass" Barbecued Burgers (page 328), Beef Steak and Lentil Salad (page 331), and Cracked Pepper and Horseradish–Crusted Oven Roast with Easy Pan Gravy (page 342) are used with permission from Canada Beef.